Migration and Border-Making

Annual of European and Global Studies

An annual collection of the best research on European and global themes, the *Annual of European and Global Studies* publishes issues with a specific focus, each addressing critical developments and controversies in the field.

Published volumes:
Religion and Politics: European and Global Perspectives
Edited by Johann P. Arnason & Ireneusz Paweł Karolewski

African, American and European Trajectories of Modernity: Past Oppression, Future Justice?
Edited by Peter Wagner

Social Transformations and Revolutions: Reflections and Analyses,
Edited by Johann P. Arnason & Marek Hrubec

The Moral Mappings of the South and North
Edited by Peter Wagner

European Integration: Historical Trajectories, Geopolitical Contexts,
Edited by Johann P. Arnason

Migration and Border-Making: Reshaping Policies and Identities
Edited by Robert Sata, Jochen Roose and Ireneusz Pawel Karolewski

The Politics of Debt and Europe's Relations with the 'South'
Edited by Stefan Nygård

https://edinburghuniversitypress.com/series-annual-of-european-and-global-studies.html

Annual of European and Global Studies

Migration and Border-Making

Reshaping Policies and Identities

Edited by Robert Sata, Jochen Roose
and Ireneusz Pawel Karolewski

EDINBURGH
University Press

Edinburgh University Press is one of the leading university presses in the UK. We publish academic books and journals in our selected subject areas across the humanities and social sciences, combining cutting-edge scholarship with high editorial and production values to produce academic works of lasting importance. For more information visit our website: edinburghuniversitypress.com

Edinburgh University Press Ltd
The Tun – Holyrood Road, 12 (2f) Jackson's Entry, Edinburgh EH8 8PJ

First published in hardback by Edinburgh University Press 2020

Typeset in 11.5/13.5 Minion Pro by
IDSUK (DataConnection) Ltd
A CIP record for this book is available from the British Library

ISBN 978 1 4744 5348 6 (hardback)
ISBN 978 1 4744 5349 3 (paperback)
ISBN 978 1 4744 5350 9 (webready PDF)
ISBN 978 1 4744 5351 6 (epub)

Contents

Contents

Contributors

Maria Apanovich is a Lecturer in the Department of Demography and Migration Policy of Moscow State Institute for International Relations (MGIMO University). She obtained her MA in Berlin (Consortium of Universities, Free University of Berlin, Potsdam University, and Humboldt University) and her PhD in Political Science from MGIMO University, where she worked as a lecturer in the Department of Political Theory from 2013 to 2017 before working as a lecturer in the Department of Demography and Migration Policy. Her main areas of research are migration and integration policies, especially highly qualified migration and student migration.

Leonardo Cavalcanti is Adjunct Professor of Latin American Studies at the University of Brasília and Director of the International Migration Observatory of Brazil (OBMigra). He obtained his PhD in Sociology from the University of Salamanca. He was Professor from 2008 to 2013 in the Department of Sociology of the Universidad Autónoma de Barcelona (UAB). He conducted postdoctoral studies at Columbia University (Institute for Social and Economic Research and Policy) and the University of Oxford (Centre on Migration, Policy and Society). His main areas of research are comparative studies on Latin American migration, with an emphasis on transnational perspectives on migration and the labour market. His more recent book publications include *Dicionário Crítico de Migrações Internacionais* (with Tuila Botega, Tânia Tonhati and Dina Araujo; Editora da Universidade de Brasília, 2017).

Karel Černý holds a doctoral degree in Sociology. He focuses on historical sociology and the Middle East. He is also conducting research on Muslim immigrants in the Czech Republic, Europe and the United States in comparative perspective. He was a Fulbright fellow at the University of California in Santa Barbara and is currently a Researcher and Lecturer at Charles University in Prague, Faculty of Humanities. He was responsible for a research grant dealing with the structural roots of the Arab uprisings (2013–15) and is now in charge of a research project theorising the Arab Spring from the perspective of sociological theories of revolution. He continues his empirical and field research on Iraqi Yazidis and their shifting diaspora in Iraq, Europe and the United States. His recent publications include *Instability in the Middle East: Structural Roots and Uneven Modernisation 1950–2015* (Charles University Press, 2017) and *Yazidis: A Community on the Run* (Nakladatelství Lidové Noviny, 2017).

Ireneusz Pawel Karolewski is Professor of Political Theory and Democracy Research at the University of Leipzig. He was Professor of Political Science at the University of Wrocław and Adjunct Professor of Political Science at the University of Potsdam. Since 2008, he has been Visiting Professor and Visiting Scholar at Harvard University (2014, 2015), the Hebrew University of Jerusalem (2014), the Université de Montréal (2013), New York University (2012), Pondicherry University (2011), the University of California, Santa Barbara (2010, 2011, 2013) and the Institut des Sciences Politiques in Lille (2007, 2008). His main areas of research are collective identity and nationalism in Europe. His publications include *European Identity Revisited* (Routledge, 2016), *New Approaches to EU Foreign Policy* (Routledge, 2014), *Civic Resources and the Future of the European Union* (Routledge, 2012), *The Nation and Nationalism in Europe* (Edinburgh University Press, 2011) and *Citizenship and Collective Identity in Europe* (Routledge, 2010).

Ayhan Kaya is Professor of Politics and Jean Monnet Chair of European Politics of Interculturalism at the Department of International Relations, Istanbul Bilgi University; Director of the Jean Monnet Centre of Excellence; and a member of the Science Academy, Turkey. He is currently an ERC Advanced Grant holder, and working on youth radicalisation in Europe. He received his PhD and MA degrees at the University of Warwick. Kaya was previously a Jean Monnet Fellow at the European University Institute, Robert Schuman Centre for Advanced Studies, Florence, and Adjunct Lecturer at New York University, Florence, in 2016–17. He previously worked and taught at the European University Viadrina as Aziz Nesin Chair in 2013, and at Malmö University as the Willy Brandt Chair in 2011. Some of his books are *Populism and Heritage in Europe: Lost in Unity and Diversity* (Routledge, 2019), *Populism* *in European Memory* (co-edited with Chiara de Cesari; Routledge, 2019); *Turkish Origin Migrants and Their Descendants: Hyphenated Identities in Transnational Space* (Palgrave, 2018), *Europeanization and Tolerance in Turkey* (Palgrave, 2013) and *Islam, Migration and Integration: The Age of Securitization* (Palgrave, 2012). Kaya is conducting ERC Advanced Grant research on radicalisation among native youth and Muslim-origin youth in Europe between 2019 and 2024.

Aleksandra Koluvija is a PhD student at the Institute for German Studies (IGS) at the University of Birmingham. She has a legal background and an MA in Political Science. Since 2009, she has worked for the United Nations University (UNU-EHS), the German Federal Employment Agency (BA), the German Federal Office for Migration and Refugees (BAMF) and civil society organisations, focusing on integration, inclusion, anti-discrimination, migration and refugees. She began her PhD at the University of Birmingham in 2017 with a focus on the human rights-based approach to refugee integration and the work of civil society organisations in refugee integration in Germany. Her main areas of research are human rights, inclusion, anti-discrimination, migration, refugee integration, the migrant and refugee perspective, and the work of civil society actors.

Anna Kurpiel is Assistant Professor of Social Sciences at the Willy Brandt Center for German and European Studies, University of Wrocław. She graduated in Ethnology and Cultural Anthropology from the Jagiellonian University. She obtained her PhD from the University of Wrocław in 2013. Her PhD thesis was published as *Macedonian War Refugees in Lower Silesia: Adaptation, Migration, Remembrance* (Wydawnictwo Nauka I Innowacje, 2015). Her research interests include migrations, national and ethnic minorities, cultural heritage and borderlands.

Jochen Roose is Coordinator for Surveys and Party Research at the Konrad Adenauer Foundation in Berlin. He is also Adjunct Senior Researcher at the Free University Berlin. Previously, he worked at the Social Science Research Center Berlin, the University of Leipzig, the Free University Berlin and the Willy Brandt Centre for German and European Studies, University of Wrocław. He holds a doctoral degree and a habilitation from the Free University Berlin. He has been a Visiting Researcher at Georgetown University, Washington, DC; the University of Kent at Canterbury Dresden University of Technology; and the University of

Hamburg. His research interests are focused on Europeanisation, participation and methods of social research. In these fields, he has published a wide range of articles and book chapters and edited multiple volumes. Among his book publications are *Fans* (ed. with M. S. Schäfer and T. Schmidt-Lux; Springer, 2017), *Social Movements and Social Theory* (ed. with H. Dietz; Springer, 2016), *Empirische Sozialforschung* (with H. Kromrey and J. Strübing; UVK, 2016, 2017), *Advances in European Borderlands Studies* (ed. with E. Opilowska and Z. Kurcz; Nomos, 2017) and *Vergesellschaftung an Europas Binnengrenzen* (VS, 2010).

Robert Sata is Associate Research Fellow at the Political Science Department, Central European University (CEU). His research focuses on ethnic relations, minority rights and the politics of identity. He also works on issues of populism, political discourse and public spheres, gender politics and discrimination. He has taught courses in Political Science on CEU's MA programmes, at McDaniel College, Budapest, and Babeş-Bolyai University, Cluj-Napoca. His recent publications are 'Caesarean politics in Hungary and Poland', *East European Politics* (2019); 'Saviour of Europe, foe of the EU: illiberal populist discourse in Hungary' in Dagmar Kusa and James Griffith (eds), *Demos vs. Polis? Responsible Citizenship in Post-transitional Societies* (Kritika & Kontext, 2019); 'Agonistic politics of the European Parliament: party and party group alignments and voting behavior' in Hakan G. Sicakkan (ed.), *Integration, Diversity and the Making of a European Public Sphere* (Edward Elgar, 2016); and 'Citizenship and identity: being Hungarian in Slovakia and Romanian in Serbia and Ukraine', *Minority Studies* (2016).

Tânia Tonhati is a Lecturer at the Catholic University of Brasília. She obtained her PhD in Sociology from Goldsmiths, University of London. Since 2014 she has been working as a Researcher in the Brazilian International Migration Observatory, University of Brasília. She has taken part in many research projects about migration in Brazil and the UK. She worked at the University of Oxford as a researcher in the Brazilian research team on the 'Theorizing the Evolution of European Migration Systems' project. She participated in several surveys held by the Brazilian Research Group in the UK, which mapped Brazilian migrant profiles, difficulties and labour trajectories. In Brazil, she participated in research projects about Haitians in Brazil, funded by the International Organization for Migration and the Brazilian Labour Ministry, and about Cuban doctors in Brazil, funded by the

Pan American Health Organization. Her main areas of research are Brazilian migration, transnational families, care and migration policies. Her more recent publications include two books: *Dicionário Crítico de Migrações Internacionais* (with Leonardo Cavalcanti, Tuila Botega and Dina Araujo; Editora da Universidade de Brasília, 2017) and *Transnational Families, Migration and Brazilian Family Practices* (CRV, 2019).

Introduction: Patterns and Implications of Migration and Rebordering

Jochen Roose, Ireneusz Pawel Karolewski
and Robert Sata

A world on the move

MIGRATION IS CURRENTLY changing the world, in particular social interactions and political processes across nationally bounded societies. Certainly, in all periods, people have been on the move and this has changed societies constantly, even though to a varying degree. Sometimes people would come as refugees, workers, merchants or guests, at other times as enemies, invaders or destroyers. Frequently, these encounters between strangers led to change generating innovation; sometimes the encounter was to their mutual benefit, but at other times conflict was born, the latter probably more often than not. With the establishment of modern statehood came political attempts to regulate migration and to control borders, and more recently, to discourage people from coming. Seen from a historical perspective, the current trends of migration and attempts at migration control are nothing new. However, migration has had its own constellations, its pressures and its trends, evolved over the years together with the different migration regimes enabling and restricting migration to varying degrees. This is why migration patterns at any time deserve particular attention and a sound analysis, since they have various socio-political implications. In this sense, exploring constellations of migration and a variety of migration regulation regimes can inform us not only about ongoing changes that can be expected in societies, but also about how far the current migration situation is imprinted by the past.

Currently, migration has become a central focus of European societies, as the 'refugee crisis' has been dominating the continental political agenda since 2015. While people from Syria, Iraq, Afghanistan and various places in Africa keep arriving in the southern member states of the EU, the EU itself has been deeply conflicted about how to deal with mass migration from the Global South. Despite the current focus on European mass migrations, refugee flows and new boundaries have not been an exclusively European phenomenon, as for instance Africa and South America have been subject to regional migration flows as well, often to an even higher degree than Europe. In the USA, Donald Trump won the 2016 presidential election probably largely due to the promise of building a wall against migrants from the South. During his presidency, he has often criticised US migration policy hitherto and complained about migration from 'shithole countries' like Haiti, thus embracing a new global populism centring on migration. Still, the problem of mass migration has existed for decades without much public debate either by the EU or by the international community, with the UN as the only actor to consequently select the topic as a central theme of global development.

Right-wing populist parties in various countries mobilise against migrants and the threat of cultural change they allegedly bring. While Australia has been fundamentally reconfiguring its immigration policy towards more restrictions for years now, Brazil and Argentina are witnessing increasing immigration and discussing or initiating revisions of their migration policy hitherto. The 2016 decision in the United Kingdom to leave the European Union was also strongly influenced by the public discussion about too many migrants having entered the country, even though this migration wave was mainly of EU citizens from Central and Eastern Europe. These highlights illustrate that migration systems are in flux worldwide, leading to more restrictive measures, attempts at control and an increase in anti-migration populism. This coincides with the largest ever number of people on the move. People leave their country to find better places to live, to leave war, poverty or environmental threats behind them, and we can only expect more and more people to consider the question of migration in the future.

This volume deals with the ongoing processes of migration and boundary-making and -remaking in Europe and other parts of the world. The reasons for migration and the constellations in which they occur are manifold. Individual countries and world regions marked by different constellations of migration waves might have different migration causes and migration policies. This volume takes stock of recent and hitherto unpublished research on the refugee crisis in Europe, the migration dynamics in the Middle East and migration flows in Latin

America. We are interested in particular in how migration is framed politically, socially and culturally in the countries in question. We are obviously unable to adequately cover all world regions, but the contributors to the volume offer insights from a wide range of countries: Brazil, Germany, Hungary, Iraq, Turkey and Russia. We purposefully maximise the variety of the cases: not only do all these countries represent different regions, but also the group shows a high degree of diversity with regard to socio-economic development, political stability, political polarisation and violence. As such, we are interested in the global variety of experiences with migration and in the parallels visible among the different parts of the world.

Against this backdrop, this volume aims at discussing both new patterns of migration across the globe and socio-political implications of the current migration flows for societies and polities in Europe and other parts of the world. Alongside the refugee and migrant crisis in Europe – one of the most divisive political issues in recent European history – we can observe new patters of boundary-making across Europe, the Middle East, Latin America and Eurasia as well as beyond these regions. We are in particular interested in how migration changes political discourses and mobilises identities, often claiming 'to protect the homeland'. In the process, we want to understand specifics of these processes and identify mechanisms producing new boundary-making as a response to migration, as well as to capture various cultural settings in which this boundary-making occurs.

In the following, let us sketch out some general lines of the global migration situation. This picture can be only quite rough, as it provides a general background for the more detailed studies in the chapters to follow. We look at migration flows quantitatively to grasp the scale and the scope of migration today. We then briefly discuss some theories of migration and examine the pull and the push factors responsible for putting people on the move. We next take a quick look at migration policies and border management, just to introduce the context of migration and problematise the discussion in political theory on the 'right to exclude' migrants. We discuss some of the economic advantages as well as disadvantages of international migration before introducing how migration is perceived and discussed by home societies – the immobile part of the population. Far from aspiring to fully cover all these ongoing controversies with regard to migration and boundary-making, we rather want to raise some central issues and provide some fundamental information (although as will become

3

visible, scholarship does not always have clear-cut data at its disposal) that help contextualise the chapters that follow.

The scale and scope of migration worldwide

The number of migrants, people who leave their home country and cross a national border to live permanently in another country, is higher today than ever before. Especially, the last three decades have been marked by a sharp increase in the number of transnational migrants. The actual number of people living outside of their country of birth is unknown. Worldwide information is dependent mostly on national data collection, which is done based on inconsistent definitions. While the UN's intention is to collect data on foreign-born people, some countries base their statistics on citizenship. Accordingly, the data provided by the UN is an informed estimate rather than exact information.

The number of migrants has increased continuously since the 1960s (Figure 0.1). While the increase slowed down a bit between 1990 and 2000, it has continued again at a higher rate in the following decades. The number of people who live in a country other than their country of birth is 3.5 times higher in 2019 than it was in 1960.

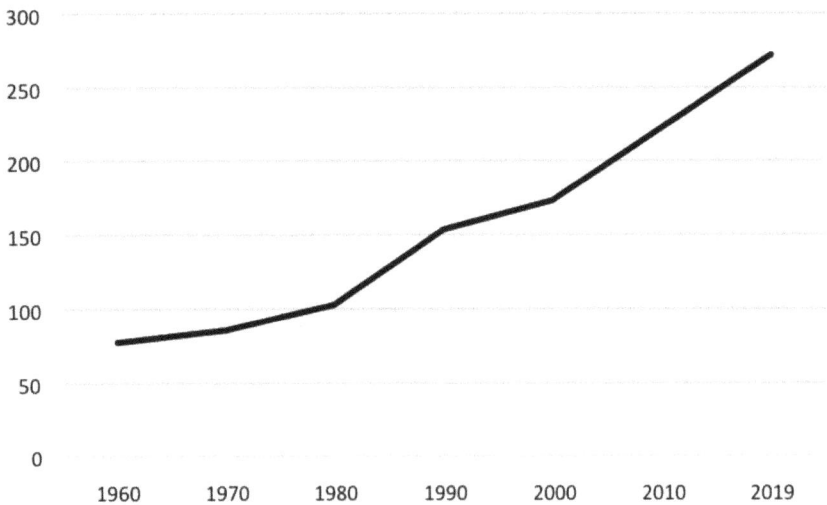

Figure 0.1 Migrants worldwide, 1960–2019 (millions)

Source: United Nations, www.un.org/en/development/desa/population/migration/data/estimates2/estimates19.shtml

While this increase looks quite remarkable, we need to take the development of the world population into account. First, we see that migrants are a small minority as compared to the overall world population (Figure 0.2). A bit more than 3 per cent of the world population lives outside of their country of birth, implying that the majority of around 97 per cent of the people live in their country of birth.

Against this backdrop, the increase in migration is rather moderate relative to the world population over the years. Yet, comparing 1960 and 2019, the migrants' share of the world population rose by 35 per cent. This is still a significant increase even for a period of nearly sixty years, but it is still much lower than the 35 per cent increase in absolute numbers. It is noteworthy that more men than women migrate and this trend is stable over the observed period. In 1960, 2.7 per cent of the male population were migrants as compared to 2.4 per cent of the female population. In 2019, 3.5 per cent of the male population lived outside of their country of birth, while the share among women was 3.4 per cent. However, today, more female migrants are moving independently for work, education and as heads of households than was the case fifty years ago, when it was often assumed that men migrate usually for employment or education, while women move for marriage or family reunification.

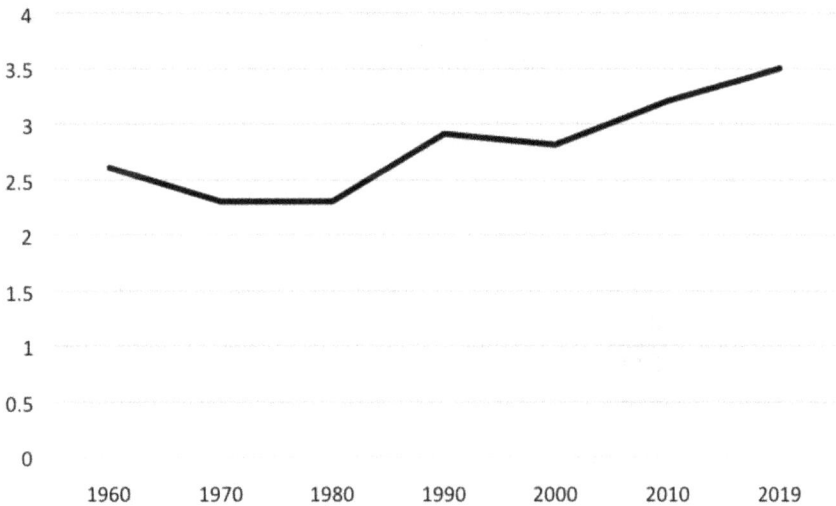

Figure 0.2 Migrants worldwide relative to population, 1960–2019 (percentage)

Source: United Nations, www.un.org/en/development/desa/population/migration/data/estimates2/estimates19.shtml

The largest share of all migrants can be identified in Europe and Asia, each accounting for nearly a third of the world's migrant population. Countries with the largest absolute number of migrants are (in this order) the USA, Germany, the Russian Federation and Saudi Arabia. In order to understand why people migrate to some specific countries rather than others, the best approach would be to ask them. Obviously, social sciences are unable to survey all or even a representative share of migrants worldwide. While in some regions this would be possible at least for legal migrants, and it has actually been done occasionally, it is difficult in other parts of the world. Also, the answers may only be partly reliable as the real reasons for migration may be untold or mis-represented: in most countries these reasons are relevant for the legal status of refugees/migrants, being decisive for the granting of legal status in the host country. Hence, on a world scale we have to approach the issue somewhat more indirectly.

One reason to become a migrant is unrelated (or only marginally related) to the migrants themselves. This is the change of countries' borders. Some people become migrants without ever migrating, sim-ply because, in the course of changing borders and declarations of independence, the place they live happens to become part of a country different from their country of birth. Such changes have happened in the course of history time and again. A large number of migrants in the Russian Federation came into being mainly as a result of the dis-solution of the Soviet Union. In 1980, the Soviet Union (SU) hosted 3.3 million migrants, which equalled 1.2 per cent of its population. As in 1991 the Soviet Union ceased to exist, the Russian Federation, the largest successor of the SU, hosted 11.5 million foreign-born people, which equalled 7.8 per cent of its population (Pohl 1999). This sudden statistical increase is due to the fact that people born, for instance, in Ukraine, Belarus and other parts of the ex-SU became foreign-born people without changing the place they lived. Simi-lar phenomena apply to other countries whose borders have been redrawn such as the Czech Republic, Germany, Yemen, East Timor and South Sudan.

The phenomenon of immobile migrants, who became migrants without migrating, should not be set aside as a statistical artefact. Obvi-ously, these people constitute a special category and do not correspond to the traditional idea of a migrant as a mobile person, arriving in a new social and political environment. However, the immobile migrants also face serious consequences in respect of issues such as fundamental citizen rights and perceptions as members of the local or national community, which are all influenced by these redrawn borders.

A more frequent case of migration refers to people moving from one country to another. The reasons for this are manifold and often hard to discern. However, migration theories provide some clues as to why people decide to move. Lee's (1966) push-and-pull model provides a simple but helpful framework to identify likely explanations for migration flows at the macro level. The framework identifies push factors as disadvantages at the place of origin, while pull factors are advantages at the place of destination. These factors in combination initiate and guide migration flows. However, Lee added another important factor often neglected in other accounts: the intervening obstacles. These are factors increasing difficulties for migrants on their way to their host countries. On the one hand, the success of this model is based on its generality, allowing for a wide range of factors. Yet, on the other hand, it suffers from underspecification, as it provides only limited clues as to what the more relevant factors are. For that reason, it represents rather a way to organise plausible assumptions than a fully fledged theory. The only substantial indications for relevant push-and-pull factors that Lee gives all refer to economy and the degree of modernity, or as Lee calls it, the 'state of progress' (1966: 53–4), which actually describes the economic prosperity of a country or region, including the availability of public services.

In fact, international migration flows indicate the relevance of exactly these factors. The large and affluent countries are those with the highest number of migrants. Among the four countries with the highest number of migrants, this clearly applies to three of them (USA, Germany and Saudi Arabia). The pattern becomes even clearer if we look at the countries with high numbers of migrants in relative terms rather than the absolute numbers. According to UN data, the highest relative number of migrants is found in the Arab countries such as the United Arab Emirates, Qatar and Kuwait, with shares of non-citizens of over 70 per cent (Table 0.1). In Europe, Liechtenstein and Luxembourg rank highest with 67.0 per cent and 47.4 per cent of foreign-born population respectively. In this regard, Australia is similar to Switzerland with 30 percent of foreign-born population, while China has the lowest number of non-citizens residing in the country with only 0.07 percent. We should also note that after 2015, Turkey and Lebanon are the countries with the highest numbers of Syrian refugees (in both absolute and relative terms – 3.6 million in Turkey and 0.93 million in Lebanon) mainly due to their geographical proximity.

Table 0.1 Share of migrants in selected countries (percentages)

Country	Share of migrants	Notes	Country	Share of migrants	Notes
United Arab Emirates	87.9	C R	Italy	10.4	B
Qatar	78.7	C	Portugal	8.7	B
Kuwait	72.1	C R	Russian Federation	8.0	B
Liechtenstein	67.0	B	Turkey	7.0	B R
Luxembourg	47.4	B	Hungary	5.3	B R
Oman	46.0	C	Chile	5.0	B
Singapore	37.1	B	Argentina	4.9	B
Lebanon	34.1	B R	Czech Republic	4.8	C
Jordan	33.1	C R	Namibia	4.3	B
Australia	30.0	B	Rwanda	4.3	B R
Switzerland	29.9	B	Burkina Faso	3.5	B R
Israel	23.0	B R	Togo	3.5	C R
New Zealand	22.3	B	Benin	3.3	C B R
Canada	21.3	B	Chad	3.2	B R
Sweden	20.0	B	Burundi	2.8	B R
Austria	19.9	B	Zimbabwe	2.8	B R
Belgium	17.2	C	Uruguay	2.4	B
Ireland	17.1	B	Mali	2.4	B R
Norway	16.1	B	Romania	2.4	B
Cyprus	16.0	B	Republic of Korea	2.3	C
Germany	15.7	B	Kenya	2.0	B R
Iceland	15.5	B	Cameroon	2.0	B
USA	15.4	B	Japan	2.0	C
Estonia	14.4	B	Central African Rep.	1.9	C
United Kingdom	14.1	B	Poland	1.7	B
Netherlands	13.4	B	Ghana	1.5	B
Spain	13.1	B	Mozambique	1.1	B R
France	12.8	B	Zambia	1.0	B R
Croatia	12.5	B R	Mexico	0.8	B R
Denmark	12.5	B	India	0.4	B R
Latvia	12.4	B	Brazil	0.4	B
Slovenia	12.2	B	Haiti	0.2	B
Libya	12.1	C	Philippines	0.2	C R
Greece	11.6	B	Vietnam	0.1	C R
Belarus	11.3	B	China	0.1	C

Source: UN, <www.un.org/en/development/desa/population/migration/data/estimates2/countryprofiles. asp> (last accessed 14 January 2020).

Notes: B = foreign-born population. C = non-citizens. R = refugees in country added.

The overall pattern is best understood through a combination of factors that relate to Lee's ideas: obviously, the rich and especially the very rich countries rank high. This is most apparent for the Arab countries but is also true within Europe for Liechtenstein, Luxembourg and Switzerland. The Scandinavian countries tend to attract migrants not only due to their economic prosperity but also because of the relatively generous welfare state there.

While the economic prosperity in the country of residence is clearly a pull factor, push factors are also visible in the rank order of countries. Lebanon and Jordan are not overwhelmingly rich but they neighbour Syria, which has been suffering from an extensive and brutal civil war for more than eight years now. Refugees tend to stay relatively nearby, mostly in neighbouring countries – hoping to be able to return home. In Turkey too the number of migrants has risen sharply as a result of the civil war in Syria. Turkey reported 1.37 million foreign-born residents in 2010 and 5.88 million in 2019, including 3.79 million refugees.

The intervening obstacles are also visible from the number of migrants per country. On the one hand, Jordan and Lebanon are the destination of refugees because the border is relatively easy to cross, while Turkey at some point invested considerable effort in controlling the influx of refugees (see also Kaya in this volume). On the other hand, the traditional migration countries, such as the United States, Canada and Australia, host a comparatively high number of migrants due to a tradition of allowing people to enter the country. Even though restrictions have continuously increased and the political discourse on immigration (in particular in the US after the Trump election of 2016) has become more populist, the legacy of immigration in these countries is still visible in the table.

Still, the idea of push-and-pull factors is a simplified skeleton of a migration theory. Migration research has pointed out the relevance of chain or network migration (Schrover 2015), of institutions in general (Bertocchi and Strozzi 2008) and of migration systems more specifically (e.g. Beichelt and Barnickel 2013). Migration research has produced a wide range of more specific arguments and theories (for overviews see e.g. Gold and Nawyn 2019; Massey et al. 1993; White and Poston 2016).

For instance, Stephen Castles, Hein de Haas and Mark J. Miller (2014) point out in their seminal work on migration that the rationalist and voluntarist understanding of migration can only present a limited approach. They argue that the push-and-pull model of migration lists factors of migration in an arbitrary manner without explaining their mutual interactions and can therefore be quite misleading (Castles et al. 2014: 28). Also, the simplistic push-and-pull models tend to be deterministic, as they lean towards demographic, environmental and economic factors as catalysts of migration. However, migration 'pressures' such as population growth or environmental degradation might generate innovation, rather than migration, while scarcity can inhibit long-distance migration, as individuals cannot afford its costs. On the other hand, better education and easily accessible information on better-off countries can produce the sentiments of relative deprivation and higher aspirations without much change in the local conditions (Castles et al. 2014: 29).

Push-and-pull models view migration as a function of geographical differences in the supply and demand for labour and the quality of living conditions, as if there existed 'international migration markets' based on individual cost–benefit calculations. As a consequence, these models define migration as an investment decision, expecting future 'returns'. These 'hyper-rational' migrants are supposed to have perfect knowledge of wages, employment opportunities and migration policies in the region, which allows them to make cross-country comparisons. In this view, human agency is decisive in explaining the international migration market and hence migration dynamics. In contrast, structure-orientated approaches focus on limited financial resources, colonial legacies, power asymmetries and cultural capital (such as family and community ties) that heavily affect migrants' decisions. For instance, Heaven Crawley and Jessica Hagen-Zanker (2019: 13) show, in their research based on qualitative interviews with migrants to Europe, that it is (often incomplete and inaccurate) perceptions of 'a good country' of emigration that are decisive in deciding on the destination country, rather than a careful calculation of economic and political factors.

Furthermore, Marxism-inspired approaches focus on migration as a consequence of capitalism, in particular the exploitation of the Global South by the wealthy North, solidified by the unequal terms of trade between advanced capitalist countries and the underdeveloped ones. In this view, migration from the Global South does not follow free and rational choice; instead, migrants are forced to move to wealthier countries, in which they become part of an urban proletariat subject to economic, sexual and psychological exploitation. The structural result of such a development is the reinforcement of the inequalities between the

Global South and the rich North, as migration drives up the profits of the already wealthy people in the North, while depriving the poor South of the badly needed workforce and subjecting the migrants to exploitation in their countries of arrival (Castles et al. 2014: 32).

While the push-and-pull models view migration as conducive to the personal well-being of migrants, Marxist models highlight the exploitation of migrant labour by states and corporations as the key aspect of capitalism. While there are certainly differences between high-skilled and low-skilled labour migration, governments, corporations and employment agencies are prone to put pressure on the migrant labour force in order to create a vulnerable workforce. In this view, public xenophobia, racism and restrictive migration policies have the function of increasing the legitimisation of migrants' exploitation, rather than only serving the political mobilisation of voters through anti-migration sentiments (Castles et al. 2014: 36). While the push-and-pull models clearly overestimate individual agency, Marxist approaches tend to focus overly on structural factors and depict migrants as completely deprived of decisional capacity. This methodological victimisation of migrants often goes hand in hand with a romantic view of harmonious rural communities uprooted by capitalism, which often underestimates dire and exploitative life conditions of traditional societies in the Global South.

In sum, there is a complexity involved in migration where a variety of motives and multifaceted consequences are involved (Massey and Taylor 2004). Social motives seem to play a great role in migration, in particular the existence of ethnic networks in the country of destination, common language (due to the colonial past of the target country) or family ties. This has been highlighted in the research on migration networks, that is, on interpersonal ties connecting the migrants and social capital linked with that (Castles et al. 2014: 39). Existing diasporas can be attractive to further migration, as they offer social capital in addition to economic incentives in the country of destination (Koser 2003, 2007). In addition, migration can be understood as a system, in which initial migration generates a feedback that increases migration even further. For instance, through remittances from the initial migrants, new migration can be promoted, as poorer individuals in their country of origin can also afford to migrate (Massey 1990). Migration over larger distances is carried out by relatively better-off individuals, while the poorest usually migrate only over short distance to escape conflicts or disasters. In contrast, the extremely poor lack a migration capability. Hatton and Williamson (1998) have shown in their study that development in poorer countries initially boots further migration, rather than limits it.

Drawing and controlling borders

By definition, international migration, the long-term movement of people from one country into another, is dependent on the existence of separate countries, divided by borders. While in pre-modern times, people also migrated on a large scale, they were not international migrants because there were no nation-states with fixed borders to move in between. Borders are fundamental for the self-understanding of modern states, since they specify the territory as a crucial framework of reference. One of the state's core tasks is to govern all affairs within this territory and avoid negative influence from beyond the borders. It is only with the introduction of national borders that people could cross these borders to migrate internationally.

Borders, including state borders, can be understood as mechanisms to reduce complexity as they declare everything beyond these borders as irrelevant (or at least less relevant) for the country in question (Schimank 2005). This concept, fictitious (or ideal-typical, to use the terminology of Max Weber) as it is, requires the control of borders. Sheller and Urry claim that the main function of borders is to 'limit, channel, and regulate movement or anticipated movement' (2006: 211). Hence, border control has been identified as a central obligation of modern states, which goes hand in hand with the very concept of state power, that is, the capability to maintain a monopoly of legitimate violence on a given state territory. In this sense, modern states are 'sorting machines' of people with access privileges and those without them (Mau 2006). However, borders have varying degrees of efficiency. For instance, some borders can be more easily crossed than others, as exemplified with the US–Mexico border or the Southern borders of the EU. Despite some claims (Ohmae 1990), globalisation has not rendered this border control irrelevant (Mau 2006; Paasi 2009). Quite to the contrary, border control remained highly relevant and a highly contested policy field at the same time, even more so after 9/11 (Brunet-Jailly 2012). Since then, states have employed an even wider array of measures to control border crossings (Basaran 2011; Carrera and Hernanz 2015) and thereby regulate who is allowed to enter the state territory and who is refused access. While strict border controls have for a long time been a concern for the Global North only, during the last decade, border control restrictions have also extended to the

Global South (Bakewell 2009; Donzelli 2013: 20), though partly in reaction to pressures from the Global North (Adepoju et al. 2010).

The actual imposition of border governance with respect to people rests on two pillars: control of border passing and issuing of visas. The control of land or sea borders has always been difficult, in particular with long coastal borders, which is why increasing technological efforts and investments are focused on this task (Antal 2010; Bossong and Carrapiço 2016). In parallel, border controls tend to be extended beyond the traditional borderlines (Chalfin 2012; Faure-Atger 2008; Rosas 2006; see also Tonhati and Cavalcanti in this volume), as they are carried out, for instance, at traffic nodes far away from the territorial border (Adey 2004).

In general, border control serves two purposes. First, it aims to efficiently avoid illegal and unwanted border crossings. Second, it is of highly symbolic importance, signalling the sovereignty of the state, its capability to control and its territorial power. Since borders are of the utmost symbolic importance, so are the closing and the opening of borders. The European Union with its project of abolishing internal border controls pays tribute to this symbolic dimension of borders time and again (Scott 2012). This applies even more to the symbolic closure of borders, as public debates often refer to the idea of guaranteeing the security of the citizenry by closing borders (see Sata in this volume). The most prominent example is the 2016 electoral campaign of Donald Trump in the USA, when he promised to build a wall at the border to Mexico to allegedly reduce criminality and bring back law and order. At that time, in most parts of the US–Mexico border there was already an elevated fence (or wall), which, however, has proven to be incapable of blocking illegal migration from Mexico to the USA. Nevertheless, the symbolism of building a 'proper' wall and thereby protecting the in-group from the out-group was so present in large parts of the US public discourse that factual arguments had become irrelevant.

While the rhetoric of closed borders is most prominent, borders are intended to be open for specified categories of people. Business and tourism are classical reasons to let people into a country. In order to achieve this utilitarian selectivity, countries establish visa regulations (Salter 2006; Whyte 2008). By codifying the need for visas, states define criteria of legal access. The most important first criterion in the worldwide visa regime is the 'quality' of citizenship. People with Danish, Finish or US citizenship enjoy the easiest access worldwide, as they may enter 130 other countries without a visa, while, for instance, citizens of Afghanistan can only enter twelve other countries without a visa (Whyte 2008). The visa requirement can imply very different burdens and costs. Some visas are hard to acquire while others are more or less a formality, granted on the spot.

The privilege of visa-free access is granted primarily to 'wealthy, democratic and open countries', concludes Whyte (Whyte 2008: 143) from his analysis of visa-free travel. Mau and Brabandt (2011) argue, on the basis of their detailed analysis of the visa policies of Austria, the USA and Finland, that the right to visa-free entry is granted only with increasing selectivity. Visa regulations are getting more similar among OECD countries, while the asymmetry with respect to the poorer non-OECD countries persists. While visas are intended only for a limited time, mostly ninety days, they are also relevant for long-term migration because, according to estimates, a large share of illegal immigrants enter the country legally using tourist visas (Mau and Brabandt 2011: 5).

Besides legal entry with a visa, people may also enter a country if they require protection. People threatened because of 'race, religion, nationality, membership of a particular social group or political opinion' are protected as refugees by the 1951 Refugee Convention (Article 1.2). A considerable migration share into wealthy countries is of refugees asking for asylum or similar forms of temporary or permanent protection. For instance, in 2013, a quarter of the immigrants coming into the European Union applied for asylum.[1] The actual interpretation and handling of this right vary considerably (Brown 1999). However, while the right to asylum is often not granted, people are often not deported to their country of origin for various reasons. Effectively, in spite of a rejected application, people may stay in the country of destination permanently. On the other hand, the practice of asylum policy is aimed at preventing refugees reaching the territory of the host country where they could claim civil rights. This is the case not only with the US and Australia but also with the EU, where the Schengen Convention of 1985, which supplements the Schengen Agreement, later to be replaced by the Dublin Convention in 1990, targets 'remote control' of migration through, for instance, extraterritorial refugee camps.

The right to exclude migrants?

Migration had been marginalised as subject matter in political science for a long time. For decades, both legal and political theory focused mainly on the issue of asylum and human rights connected to it, rather than the geopolitical reality of mass migration, since large-scale migration played a minor role in these considerations (but see Kneebone 2009; Gatrell 2013). One of the reasons was probably that the post-World War II order and the Cold War put the issue of migration on the political and academic backburner. As forced displacement of people was integral to the Soviet politics of ethnic governance of the Eastern Bloc (Pohl 1999), compulsory mass migration was practised within the Soviet Union (but also in other countries of the Eastern Bloc) alongside the redrawing of borders and occupation of entire countries by Soviet troops as legitimate means of politics until 1991 (Martin 1998). The countries of the Eastern Bloc rejected participation in the 1951 Refugee Convention (the Geneva Convention) and its 1967 Protocol (the New York Protocol), as they were defined in Moscow as the instruments of 'Western imperialism' (Kowalski 2016).

Migration was largely ignored in the West in the context of the Cold War bipolar world order and the logic of zones of influence. Only since 1991 have former Communist countries started joining the UN refugee conventions. The interest in forced migration was politically reignited in the 1990s, mainly due to the genocides in former Yugoslavia, Rwanda and Burundi and the necessity for Western democracies to adapt their asylum systems to new waves of refugees from the Balkans and Africa (see Steiner 2000; Gibney 2004; Woolley 2014; Haddad 2008). Nonetheless, broader aspects of mass migration became central to political analysis in the West only with the 'hypermigration' (for the term see Bauböck 2011) that has reached Europe since 2011 (Betts and Loescher 2011; Jacques 2012; Fiddian-Qasmiyeh et al. 2014).

Contemporary Western political theory, heavily influenced by John Rawls, defines political justice mainly within a nation-state and ignores mass migration as a political issue. One of the most famous statements by Rawls is that societies are nationally closed and by their very nature provide a 'more or less complete and self-sufficient scheme of cooperation, making room within itself for all the necessary activities of life, from birth to death' (Rawls 1993: 18). That is why political theory has been struggling with the issue of mass migration to Europe and other parts of the world, the major challenge being how liberal democracies can combine two competing political principles: the moral universalism of treating every person equally and the exclusive character of democracies organised in nation-states (Abraham 2010; Akakpo and Lenard 2014). While political theory can cope relatively well with standard migration (asylum seekers and guest workers in moderate numbers), it is quite helpless with non-standard migration involving large numbers of mixed-motives migrants arriving in a short period of time (Carens 2014; 2015; Hidalgo 2014; Miller 2016a; 2016b).

Recently, the debate on the political ethics of immigration has focused on the right of nation-states to exclude others (Blake 2014). While a group of Kantian authors (e.g. Carens 1987; 2014; Pogge 2002) argue in favour of open borders and are committed to moral universalism, others (Miller 2016a; Walzer 1983; Simmons 2001; see also Stilz 2009) highlight the exclusionary nature of nation-states and the right of their citizens to determine the extent of migration, which has a potential to stimulate cultural and socio-economic change. The key argument is presented by David Miller, who stresses that the citizens of the receiving country need to have a meaningful say in determining how their own society will develop in the future: 'Unless the newcomers are simply replicas of the natives, the society will be transformed over time. People who are already citizens of that society are entitled to take a view about this transformation' (Miller 2016b: 42). In this regard, Miller favours 'weak cosmopolitanism', in which states' responsibilities are limited to human rights (defined as the opportunity to meet one's basic needs), as opposed to the 'strong cosmopolitanism' of the 'no limits to asylum' approach. According to Miller, safe countries have the moral obligation to provide necessary protection. However, this does not equal a transnational right to migration. In addition, receiving countries differ in their capacities to help refugees and to integrate them 'depending not only on factors like GDP and existing population density, but also on whether they have well-established policies for integrating refugees socially' (Miller 2016b: 44).

In contrast, critics of Miller point out that the borders of the nation-states are indefensible as 'filters' of freedom of movement, since they have been erected in an arbitrary manner, based on historically contingent developments (Cole 2000; 2006; 2014). Against this background, the political theory of immigration seems to be split down the middle on the obligations of wealthy countries towards migrants. The radically universalist positions highlight the arbitrary discriminating function of the national border, while others point to nations as principal spheres of justice and democratic organisation (Walzer 1983). In this context, one of the more intriguing positions is represented by Michael Blake (2014), who argues that next to humanitarian responsibilities there is also an obligation for states to avoid imposing unwanted obligations on their citizens, who, as in Miller's argument, should make decisions about mass migration subject to democratic decision-making rather than decisions by political elites.

Economic controversies over mass migration

A great deal of controversy with regard to mass immigration has also been visible in recent economic research. Analyses of the impact of immigration on the economy of the receiving countries have always espoused contradictory positions (e.g. Czaika 2009; Borjas 2014; 2016; Collier 2013). Early studies in immigration economics tend to paint a rather bleak picture. For instance, Friedrich Edding (1951), exploring the impact of the refugees on the post-World War II West German economy, states clearly that 'an influx of penniless masses in such a short time would mean extraordinary difficulties for any land' (Edding 1951: 15). Meanwhile, the economic analysis of immigration has become not only more differentiated but also more ambivalent with regard to the political consequences of mass immigration. While after World War II, countries like Germany encouraged labour immigration, in recent years a number of leading economists have brought attention to the potentially 'dark side' of mass immigration. The most controversial work so far has probably been *Exodus: How Migration is Changing Our World*, by Oxford economist Paul Collier (Collier 2013). According to Collier, mass immigration will have both a number of negative and positive effects. The former will be in particular the downturn pressure on the wages of indigenous workers and increasing prices of affordable housing (crowding-out effects). In addition, Collier criticises the generous welfare systems in Western Europe, the lack of efficient immigration control and the problematic policies of multiculturalism as the main causes of not only the failed integration of immigrants and the acceleration of immigration but also brain-drain effects in the sending countries. Even though Collier claims to offer an economic balance sheet of pros and cons of mass immigration, he focuses on the disadvantages of migration, both in the countries of origin and in the host countries.

Against this backdrop, Collier suggests a number of policy measures such as immigration ceilings, selection of immigrants based on skills, geographical dispersion of immigrants in the receiving country, stronger school integration and strengthening of symbols and ceremonies of common citizenship with regard to the immigrants. One of Collier's core arguments is that the generous welfare systems in advanced countries are a major incentive for people to migrate and at the same time the main hindrance of migrants' social integration. This does not seem to be very surprising, as it has become widely recognised among scholars that 'migrants to Europe integrate too often into welfare, whereas those in North America integrate into work' (Hansen and Randeria 2016). Furthermore, Collier criticises the policies of multiculturalism, which in his view hampers the provision of public goods by decreasing cooperation in a diverse society. This assessment draws partly on Robert Putnam's research (Putnam 2007) suggesting that higher levels of diversity in the US might correlate with lower levels of trust: 'The greater the proportion of immigrants in a community, the lower were mutual levels of trust between immigrants and the indigenous population. In other words, far from proximity leading to greater mutual understanding, it leads to heightened mutual suspicion' (Collier 2013: 74).

In a similar vein, Harvard labour economist George J. Borjas (2016) offers a rather critical assessment of immigration in the US. He argues that immigration has not affected the average American citizen immensely. Still, it has created both winners and losers. While the losers tend to be non-migrant workers, who compete for the same jobs as immigrants, indigenous employers have benefited very much from the pressure on wages, in particular if they employed immigrants. Both Collier and Borjas argue partly sociologically. It is the specific culture of migrants (in both the UK and the US) that is likely to have an impact on their own productivity. Borjas points out that the gap between the wages of migrants and of indigenous workers is larger than a few decades ago and that the migrants need more time than previous migrant generations to catch up. Additionally, to Borjas migrants are more than just workers: they are also people who have lives outside of their workplaces and who may respond differently to the norms of the country to which they immigrated.

This rather negative interpretation of mass immigration has been criticised by various scholars and commentators. For instance, Michael Clemens and Justin Sandefur (2014) sharply reject many of Collier's claims. They argue that a number of Collier's conjectures are based on faulty reasoning and lack empirical data. For instance, Collier's reasoning might be based on doubtful assumptions such as that diversity is problematic per se. Clemens and Sandefur criticise both Collier's interpretation of Putnam's diversity study and the former's ignorance of research showing that immigration can have largely positive effects. In a more technical analysis, Michael Clemens and Lant Prichett (2016) argue that economic arguments in favour of strict migration rules are based on problematic assumptions, such as that (1) migrants bring large fractions of their economic productivity with them and cannot improve it due to the limitations of their culture, and (2) the restricting country is near the level at which the aggregate impact of migration would begin reducing overall economic productivity. Both assumptions either remain unsupported by evidence or have yet to be demonstrated for the country or region in question. Clemens and Prichett's analysis points out 'that with empirically plausible rates of "assimilation" [...] there can be a large flow and stock of foreign born without substantially diminishing the global efficiency gains from reduced migration barriers' (2016: 44). Borjas's analysis of migration has also been subject to criticism. For instance, David Card and Giovanni Peri argue that Borjas tends to present a one-sided view of immigration without much attention to newer research offering a more nuanced picture of the labour market aspects of immigration (Card and Peri 2016; see also Card 2012).

The varying positions on mass immigration in political theory and economics also have implications for how the wider public perceives migration and what political responses are envisaged to cope with the challenge. This is largely reflected in public attitudes towards migration.

Attitudes towards migration

Our final perspective on the phenomenon of mass migration shifts away from the migrants towards the non-migrating majoritarian population. Acceptance and non-acceptance of migrants by the host country population is a major factor driving migration policy. Even if society is ageing and accordingly the economy is in need of new labour via immigration, policies may still remain restrictive, responding to reservations in the public. The 2016 referendum vote in the United Kingdom to leave the EU has been argued to be caused, at least partially, by the controversial immigration debate during the Brexit campaign (e.g. Gietel-Basten 2016).

An increase in the immigration level is rejected nearly universally worldwide. The International Social Survey Programme (ISSP) gathers data from a wide range of countries around the world for a comparative assessment of attitudes. In 2013, people were asked whether the number of immigrants to their country should be increased a lot, increased a little, stay the same, reduced a little, or reduced a lot. A preference for increased immigration is remarkably rare. In India and South Africa, a sizeable minority of the population wants to increase immigration a lot. A small increase is also favoured by a sizeable minority in Lithuania, Japan, Finland and the Philippines. In all other countries surveyed, less than 15 per cent of the population could accept an increase in immigration. The overwhelming opposition to more immigrants is shown in Figure 0.3.

In half of the countries surveyed, a majority preferred a reduction in immigration. It is likely not to be by chance that two European English-speaking countries rank first in the call for less immigration: the UK

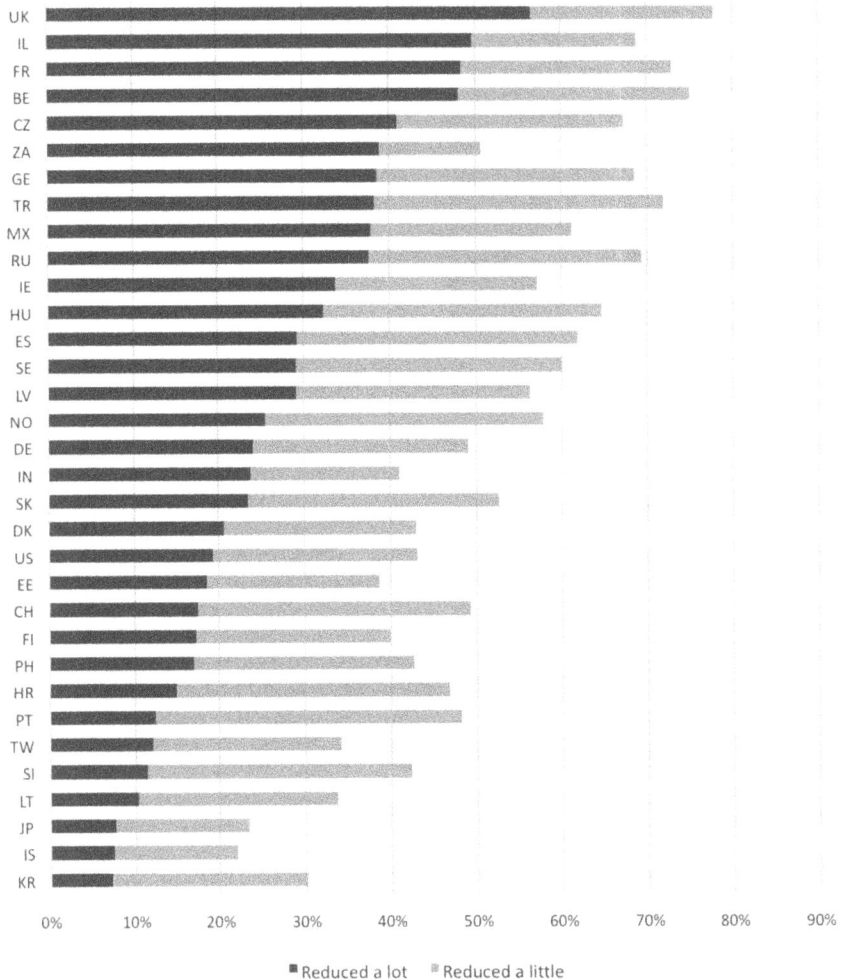

■ Reduced a lot ▨ Reduced a little

Figure 0.3 Preferred change in number of new immigrants to own country

Source: ISSP 2013 data; own calculation; weighted data.

Note: Abbreviations follow ISO-3166 (ALPHA-2), <https://www.iso.org/iso-3166-country-codes.html> (last accessed 14 January 2020).

and Ireland. On the other side we see the Asian countries: South Korea and Japan are comparatively positive towards a similar level or more immigration. The same applies to Iceland.

Explanations for favouring or rejecting immigration point in two directions. One prominent line of argument refers to economic conditions. It is not only the more affluent countries where people reject immigrants. The individuals' professional skills compared to the skills of the potential immigrants are also relevant for attitudes towards immigration. If the immigrants with their professional skills are serious competitors, immigration is rejected. In cases where the immigrants are considerably less qualified, acceptance of immigration is more likely (e.g. Mayda 2006).

A second line of argument refers to the perceived cultural threat. According to this reasoning it is not the economic situation which is decisive but rather the perception that too many immigrants might threaten domestic culture. In a broad review of the literature, Hainmueller and Hopkins conclude that the perceived cultural impact of immigration on the nearer personal environment is significant, while they call the aforementioned idea of labour market competition a 'zombie theory' due to the lack of empirical evidence (Hainmueller and Hopkins 2014: 41). Additionally, they point to the importance of elite and media discourse that can heavily influence how the public perceives immigration.

Overall, immigrants find themselves most often in a comparatively hostile environment. The welcoming of immigrants is the rare exception rather than the rule in societies around the world. This fact may also contribute to explaining why migration is less frequent than the global economic disparities would lead us to expect, thus presenting an intervening factor.

Migration and borders: what has changed?

At first glance, the grand picture of migration looks as it always has. Many people have been on the move, while others have been afraid of migrants for various reasons. Fences have been built but also surmounted. Apparently, nothing much has changed.

Even though this impression is not completely wrong, it is not entirely correct either. The basic pattern of migration remains globally the same. Directions of migration, the main reasons for migration, the basic attitudes towards migrants and the symbolic as well as manifest measures to close borders and strengthen border controls – all these aspects have been seen before. However, we can also see gradual changes which may accumulate to a qualitative shift. First, the size of migration has been increasing. This applies mainly to Europe and more precisely to the EU. The so called 'refugee crisis' represents in fact a long-term increase of immigration into the EU from Sub-Saharan Africa and Arabic-speaking countries. Even though this can be attributed to some extent to the war in Syria and war refugees, this does not suffice as a reliable explanation. Rather, the influx of people from the Southern countries into the North has already been going on for much longer than the Syrian war, and even an end to this war might not end the flow of migrants approaching European borders hoping for a better life.

The global inequality is too enormous and the attraction of the EU too high for an end to immigration to be expected in the near future. In addition, the reduction of travel costs allows a larger share of the world's population to migrate to Europe or at least to approach its borders. The same applies, even though currently to a lower degree, to a number of other countries and continents. Additionally, global communication networks allow fast spreading of the know-how of how to get to 'the promised land', wherever that might be. However, social media spread not only true information but also rumours, exaggerations and simple lies. Hence, decisions to migrate are based not always on sound and correct information but often on diffuse and biased bits and pieces of information, drawing a rough and often misleading picture of the situation on the way or in the countries of destination. As a result of these information-distorting factors, the global flow of people has increased and will probably increase further.

The second shift concerns public discourse. Attitudes rejecting migration and xenophobic world views have always been present in public discourses of immigration. Accordingly, the current tones forcefully rejecting further immigration are not exceptional. However, global terrorism gave the debate about migration a new turn. It is not based so much on a substantial argument, since the probability of becoming a victim of a terrorist attack is still negligible and states could invest resources more effectively in combatting terrorism rather than avoiding migration. Arguments about the fending off of potential immigrants acquired a moralist twist and became strengthened in global public discourse in the course of rising populism worldwide. As a consequence, political positions against immigration gained an additional moral ground, as they became equated with the survival of Western societies, rather than being about labour market competition or cultural change. Prominent politicians keep offensively proclaiming the closing of borders in the name of security. Most prominently, US president Donald Trump has proposed radical measures against immigration to the USA. However, his speeches and actions are not a singular phenomenon but rather part of a broader shift in global public discourse. In the past, the protection of refugees used to be, at least in public discourse, a morally powerful position which was hard to attack. Even though political actions were mostly different from this discourse, centring on strict measures against the entry of migrants, the discourse demanded openness for those who needed and therefore deserved protection. With the ubiquitous reference to the risk of terrorist attacks, a moral argument has been put forward against fundamental openness towards migration.

This discursive shift has serious implications for both migration policy and the situation of migrants after their arrival. The migration policy of most countries is likely to become even stricter, as the moral justification for it comes easier. Xenophobic attitudes and possibly also xenophobic behaviour will receive growing support from this discourse and are likely to expand in various countries. As a result, what can be observed is not only a shift in support for one position at the expense of the other but rather the further *polarisation* of a debate which has already been polarised before. Thus, constructive discussions about the handling of migration are becoming even less likely, even though the challenges at hand are getting more severe. This might not be a very optimistic outlook, but this volume intends to pinpoint various in-depth issues in the context of growing political polarisation on migration, the local realities of migration and various experiences with migration on different continents.

Outline of the book

The underlying assumption of this book is that the configuration of migration as well as the political response to migration are changing. These changes are not confined to single countries or even world regions. However, not everything we observe is new and not every dimension of migration stands at a crossroads. Our intention is to make similar developments more visible but also to show some differences, since at the same time, developments vary considerably and cannot be covered by a simple, unifying analytical scheme. The intention of this volume is to bring together case studies focusing on different regions and highlighting different aspects of migration.

The chapter by Jochen Roose, 'Do Migrants Think Differently about Migration? An *Experimentum Crucis* for Explaining Attitudes on Migration', will explore how the migrants themselves think about migration. The chapter focuses on attitudes towards migration as a major force shaping the global migration system. The acceptance or rejection of further migration can form a strong political force with considerable impact on migrants' chances to enter a country. So far, the attitudes of resident migrants have received little attention in migration research, even though resident migrants are the most direct competitors to future migrants in socio-economic terms. The chapter posits that the expectations of resident migrants with regard to further migration might be different from the attitudes of the autochthonous population. While direct labour competition might lead to higher rejection of further migration by migrants, a cultural threat from further migration is less plausible for resident migrants. Moreover, positive contact with migrants is more likely for migrants themselves, which might result in more migration-friendly attitudes, according to the contact hypothesis. The chapter uses data from the European Social Survey showing that resident migrants tend to support further migration more than the autochthonous population. This applies to most countries for most forms of migration (qualified/unqualified and culturally similar/different). Only in countries with comparatively high support for further migration among the autochthonous population (Sweden and Germany) do the migrants seem to be more sceptical.

The chapter by Robert Sata entitled 'Fencing in the Boundaries of the Community: Migration, Nationalism and Populism in Hungary' argues that the financial and migration crisis in Europe not only provided grounds for the nationalist populist politics of the Hungarian government since 2010 but also presented an opportunity to reconceptualise Hungarian community. Using a systematic content analysis of the official speeches of Hungary's prime minister since 2010, the chapter traces back the creation of this new nationalist populist narrative to show how national identity conceptions are intertwined with anti-establishment, anti-migrant, anti-Muslim and anti-EU discourses. This new conception of national identity mobilises against the collapse of traditional national values as well as against the liberal rationalism embodied by EU institutions, and puts Hungarian nationals above all others. In this setting, the discursive construction and use of 'otherness' in public discourse stand for the representations of migrants as a deviant group of people, enemies of the Hungarian nation, with a threatening ideology that must be opposed. Moreover, the EU and its governance system, secular organisation, religious tolerance and liberal foundation only exacerbate this threat, making the EU 'the other', against which the national identity must be protected.

Aleksandra Koluvija's chapter, 'Rethinking Refugee Integration: The Importance of Core Values for Cultural Debate in Germany', explores the impact of the European refugee crisis on the so-called culture debate in Germany. The chapter posits that even though high numbers of asylum seekers have entered Germany since 2015, the debate on approaches to integration has experienced a kind of 'softening'. The chapter departs from various approaches to social integration in order to investigate the current political debate on German identity surrounding the concept of refugee integration. As the number of asylum seekers in Germany made the political debate on the issue of integration inevitable, much of the debate was propelled by the concern to preserve the German identity in a process of changing cultural circumstances. The process implies a confrontation between the identification of German core values and a discussion on a 'guiding culture' (*Leitkultur*) on the one hand and a 'welcoming culture' (*Willkommenskultur*) on the other. Given that in Germany the integration debate is focusing on finding durable solutions where both parties – the host society and the refugee – can profit, the chapter identifies and analyses core parts of the discussion. Against this background, it is suggested that the definition of 'integration' is highly dynamic and will further develop within a German core value and culture debate. The predominant factor regarding successful integration is the refugees' willingness to internalise German identity, learn the language and seek employment. The chapter argues, however, that a more up-to-date view on integration is needed.

The war in Syria has made Turkey in 2014 the country hosting the largest number of refugees in the world (United Nations 2016: 1). In the chapter 'The Unfolding of the Syrian Refugee Crisis in Turkey: From Temporariness to Permanency', Ayhan Kaya describes how the policy and the discourse in respect of refugees developed in Turkey. While at first refugees were welcomed for a short-term stay, it became evident after some time that the situation would continue for a longer period. The Turkish state had to adapt to this situation but the state, the Turkish population and the refugees are still facing considerable difficulties. The acceptance of such a large number of refugees is supported by the idea of Muslim fraternity but the socio-political situation is more complex. The main premise of this chapter is that there is a parallel between the state of temporariness granted to the Syrian refugees by the Turkish government on the one hand, and the Islamic set of discourses and policies generated by the government in the second half of the 2000s leading to the de-Europeanisation of Turkey on the other. The break-up of Turkey's European perspective has partly contributed to the destabilisation of the Middle East and the emergence of the Syrian crisis. This has resulted in the favouring of Sunni Muslim Syrian refugees on the part of the central and local administrations run by the Justice and Development Party (JDP) government, at the expense of Kurdish, Alevi, Christian, Circassian and Yazidi groups originating from Syria. Interestingly, it seems to be partly similar to the ways in which some EU member states, such as Hungary, favoured Christian refugees rather than Muslim-origin refugees.

The chapter by Karel Černý, 'The Middle Eastern Refugee Crisis and the Islamic State: Motivations of Iraqi Yazidis for Migrating to Europe', focuses on refugees representing the Yazidi minority in Iraq. The chapter is based on field research conducted on the territory of the Kurdish regional government in northern Iraq. The research included more than thirty in-depth semi-structured interviews with refugees (internally displaced people, IDPs), both inside and outside refugee camps. The chapter discusses the many and complex motivations that the refugees take into consideration when making decisions about their past migration inside Iraq and especially about possible future migration to Europe. The case study presents the perspective of the Yazidi refugees themselves, which is in some respects unique to this religious minority, but findings from this field research also contribute to the more general discussion about the many motivations of refugees from the war zones in the contemporary Middle East. The chapter argues that there is not just one but multiple causes explaining Yazidi migration. The main motives are essential, but alone insufficient, to explain the emigration decision. The chapter argues that, for instance, majority society's radicalisation would not in itself generate a sense that there exists a direct mortal threat if the state institutions were capable of physically protecting minorities against the majority and extremist organisations. Similarly, the collapse of state institutions alone would not have led to a direct sense of immediate danger if the collapse had occurred in a tolerant and open society, and if the minorities were not systematically being threatened. Finally, Yazidi refugees would probably not be emigrating abroad if the functions of the failing state institutions had been successfully taken up by the Yazidi elites and a self-organised Yazidi society in order to defend the Yazidis against the radicalising majority.

Maria Apanovich's chapter, 'Current Migration Trends in Russia: The Role of the CIS Region Twenty Years after the Collapse of the Soviet

Union', provides an overview of the migration trends in the Russian Federation from the 1990s to the 2010s in the context of the drastic changes in the political, economic and social structure in Russia. This chapter focuses mainly on labour migration to Russia and explores the Russian Federation's current Migration Policy Concept, adopted in 2012 as a political action plan up until 2025, as well as criticism of it. The chapter analyses the Concept and its application in the field of labour policy in order to determine the difficulties faced in the implementation process as well as its potential for improvement. In the context of international globalisation there has been an increase in the importance of several factors in Russia's immigration policy: (1) the mutual recognition of qualifications, diplomas and equivalent documents confirming education; (2) the creation of conditions for the admission of highly qualified foreign professionals in accordance with the requirements of the country's economy; (3) the availability of information about the key reasons for the stay; (4) new developments in the field of education for the training of specialists with foreign citizenship. On the basis of the findings, the chapter formulates several political recommendations, including the necessary simplification of information flows between public administration and the education sector in Russia, and an improved feedback loop between the expansion of technological potential and the availability of qualified labour.

Natural disasters have struck Haiti severely. As a consequence, many people have left the country and headed, among other destinations, to Brazil. Tânia Tonhati and Leonardo Cavalcanti describe how Brazil has become an immigration society, a situation which was new to the country. Besides the practical problems of hosting a large number of people in need, the state had to develop a policy which is able to handle the Haitian immigrants and provide them with a legal status fitting their situation. The chapter 'The North Amazon Border: Haitian Flow to Brazil and New Policies' suggests that to understand contemporary borders, there is a need to go beyond the geographical and physical 'fences', checkpoints and office counters. Based on a case study of the recent migration flow of Haitians to Brazil, from 2010 to 2015, the chapter explores how the North Amazon border, long forgotten by the Brazilian government, has become a place of negotiation, resilience and political attention. Haitians moved from being a few dozen immigrants to Brazil in 2010 to become the main immigrant group in the formal labour market in the country in 2013, overtaking the classic migration flows to Brazil, such as the Portuguese. The unexpected presence of this migratory flow in the country through the North Amazon border has caught the attention of the Brazilian government, resulting in a search for new policies and strategies to 'control' and 'regulate' this flow and the border. Against this backdrop, this chapter reflects on Brazilian migration policy, in particular in terms of managing migratory flows and the negotiation of borders.

Anna Kurpiel's chapter, 'Macedonian Refugees from the Greek Civil War: From Separation to a Transnational Community', deals with Macedonians who went to Poland as a result of the Greek Civil War in 1947–8, which is a highly interesting case of transnational and transcultural migration. Even though the general pattern of migration as well as the institutional care provided by Poland at that time were similar with regard to all groups of migrants from Greece, the chapter argues that Macedonian migration to Poland was a different phenomenon. First, the Slavic Macedonians in Poland as opposed to ethnic Greeks were a 'minority within the minority', and this condition influenced their life trajectories as a separate group considerably. Second, Macedonian migration to Poland was deeply rooted in the political situation of post-World War II Europe, which had an impact on the actual opportunities and resources of Macedonians (i.e. connected to repatriation or war compensation) as well as the politics of remembrance, which remained in a close relationship with their cultural identity. The chapter explores characteristics of Macedonian migration on the one hand; on the other hand, it proceeds on the basis of a chronological pattern ranging from 'separation' via 'assimilation' to 'new space of identification'. In addition, the chapter discusses further *problématiques* such as Macedonian identity, the question of Macedonian homeland(s), integration within the refugees' group and with Poles, and the politics of remembrance among Macedonians in Poland. The analysis is based on biographical interviews with Macedonian refugees, which were conducted in Poland, Macedonia and Canada, as well as selected documents from Polish and Macedonian archives.

Note

1. In 2013, 1.38 million people with citizenships of none of the twenty-eight EU member states migrated into EU countries, but only 0.43 million of them applied for asylum. In 2015, half of the immigrants applied for asylum. In the same year, 2.36 million people with citizenships of none of the twenty-eight EU member states entered the EU, out of which 1.32 million people asked for asylum in the EU. Even though the actual application process may be registered with some delay, leading to somewhat imprecise data, the general ratio seems to be valid. See Eurostat, online data code migr_imm1ctz and migr_asyappctza (last accessed 13 January 2020).

References

Abraham, David (2010) 'Doing justice on two fronts: the liberal dilemma in immigration.' *Ethnic and Racial Studies* 33(6): 968–85.

Adepoju, Aderanti, Femke van Noorloos and Annelies Zoomers (2010) 'Europe's migration agreements with migrant-sending countries in the Global South: a critical review.' *International Migration* 48(3): 42–75.

Adey, Peter (2004) 'Surveillance at the airport: surveilling mobility/mobilising surveillance.' *Environment and Planning A* 36(8):1365–80.

Akakpo, Crispino E.G., and Patti T. Lenard (2014) 'New challenges in immigration theory: an overview.' *Critical Review of International Social and Political Philosophy* 17(5): 493–502.

Antal, John (2010) 'Border battles: the future of border security technology along the US–Mexican border.' *Military Technology* 34(11): 53–62.

Bakewell, Oliver (2009) *South–South Migration and Human Development: Reflection on African Experiences.* Human Development Research Paper 7. New York: United Nations Development Programme.

Basaran, Tugba (2011) *Security, Law and Borders: At the Limits of Liberties.* Abingdon: Routledge.

Bauböck, Rainer (2011) 'Temporary migrants, partial citizenship and hypermigration.' *Critical Review of International Social and Political Philosophy* 14 (5): 665–93.

Beichelt, Timm, and C. Barnickel (2013) 'Patterns and reactions: migration policy in the new EU member states.' *East European Politics and Societies* 27(3): 466–92.

Bertocchi, Graziella, and Chiara Strozzi (2008) 'International migration and the role of institutions.' *Public Choice* 137(1): 81–102.

Betts, Alexander, and Gil Loescher (eds) (2010) *Refugees in International Relations.* Oxford: Oxford University Press.

Blake, Michael (2014) 'The right to exclude.' *Critical Review of International Social and Political Philosophy* 17(5): 521–37.

Borjas, George J. (2014) *Immigration Economics.* Cambridge, MA: Harvard University Press.

Borjas, George J. (2016) *We Wanted Workers: Unraveling the Immigration Narrative.* New York: W.W. Norton.

Bossong, Raphael, and Helena Carrapiço (eds) (2016) *EU Borders and Shifting Internal Security: Technology, Externalization and Accountability.* Cham: Springer.

Brown, Adèle (ed.) (1999) *Asylum Practice and Procedure: Country by Country Handbook.* London: Trenton.

Brunet-Jailly, Emmanuel (2012) 'Securing borders in Europe and North America.' Pp. 100–18 in *A Companion to Border Studies,* edited by Thomas M. Wilson and Hastings Donnan. Maldon, MA: Wiley-Blackwell.

Card, David (2012) 'Comment: the elusive search for negative wage impacts of immigration.' *Journal of the European Economic Association* 10(1): 211–15.

Card, David, and Giovanni Peri (2016) '*Immigration Economics* by George J. Borjas: a review essay.' *Journal of Economic Literature* 54(4): 1333–49.

Carens, Joseph H. (1987) 'Aliens and citizens: the case for open borders.' *The Review of Politics* 49: 251–273.

Carens, Joseph H. (2014) 'An overview of the ethics of immigration.' *Critical Review of International Social and Political Philosophy* 17(5): 538–59.

Carens, Joseph H. (2015) *The Ethics of Immigration*. Oxford: Oxford University Press.

Carrera, Sergio, and Nicholas Hernanz (2015) 'Re-framing mobility and identity controls: the next generation of the EU migration management toolkit.' *Journal of Borderlands Studies* 30(1): 69–84.

Castles, Stephen, Hein de Haas and Mark J. Miller (2014) *The Age of Migration: International Population Movements in the Modern World*, 5th edn. Basingstoke: Palgrave Macmillan.

Chalfin, Brenda (2012) 'Border security as late-capitalist "fix".' Pp. 283–300 in *A Companion to Border Studies*, edited by Thomas M, Wilson and Hastings Donnan. Maldon, MA: Wiley-Blackwell.

Clemens, Michael A., and Lant Pritchett (2016) *The New Economic Case for Migration Restrictions: An Assessment*. IZA DP No. 9730, <http://ftp.iza.org/dp9730.pdf> (last accessed 6 December 2019).

Clemens, Michael, and Justin Sandefur (2014) 'Let the people go: the problem with strict migration limits.' *Foreign Affairs*, January/February Issue, <https://www.foreignaffairs.com/reviews/review-essay/2013-12-16/let-people-go?nocache=1> (last accessed 6 December 2019).

Cole, Phillip (2000) *Philosophies of Exclusion: Liberal Political Theory and Immigration*. Edinburgh: Edinburgh University Press.

Cole, Phillip (2006) 'Towards a symmetrical world: migration and international law.' *Ethics and Economics* 4: 1–7.

Cole, Phillip (2014) 'Beyond reason: the philosophy and politics of immigration.' *Critical Review of International Social and Political Philosophy* 17(5): 503–20.

Collier, Paul (2013) *Exodus: How Migration is Changing Our World*. Oxford: Oxford University Press.

Crawley, Heaven, and Jessica Hagen-Zanker (2019) 'Deciding where to go: policies, people and perceptions shaping destination preferences.' *International Migration* 57(1): 20–35.

Czaika, Mathias (2009) *The Political Economy of Refugee Migration and Foreign Aid*. Basingstoke: Palgrave Macmillan.

Donzelli, Stefania (2013) *Border Studies. Theoretical Approaches, Themes of Inquiry, and Suggestions for Future Work*. Working Paper 571. The Hague: International Institute of Social Studies.

Edding, Friedrich (1951) *The Refugees as a Burden, a Stimulus, and a Challenge to the West German Economy*. Dordrecht: Martinus Nijhoff.

Faure-Atger, Anais (2008) *The Abolition of Internal Border Checks in an Enlarged Schengen Area: Freedom of Movement or a Web of Scattered Security Checks?* Brussels: Centre for European Policy Studies.

Fiddian-Qasmiyeh, Elena, Gil Loescher, Katy Long and Nando Sigona (eds) (2014) *The Oxford Handbook of Refugee and Forced Migration Studies*. Oxford: Oxford University Press.

Gatrell, Peter (2013) *The Making of the Modern Refugee*. Oxford: Oxford University Press.

Gibney, Matthew J. (2004) *The Ethics and Politics of Asylum: Liberal Democracy and the Response to Refugees*. Cambridge: Cambridge University Press.

Gietel-Basten, Stuart (2016) 'Why Brexit? The toxic mix of immigration and austerity.' *Population and Development Review* 42(4): 673–80.

Gold, Steven J., and Stephanie J. Nawyn (eds) (2019) *Routledge International Handbook of Migration Studies*, 2nd edn. Abingdon: Routledge.

Haddad, Emma (2008) *The Refugee in International Society: Between Sovereigns*. Cambridge: Cambridge University Press.

Hainmueller, Jens, and Daniel Hopkins (2014) 'Public attitudes toward immigration.' *Annual Review of Political Science* 17(1): 225–49.

Hansen, Randall, and Shalini Randeria (2016) 'Tensions of refugee politics in Europe: electoral, welfare-state, and demographic politics are obstacles to refugees.' *Science* 353(6303): 994–5, <http://science.sciencemag.org/content/353/6303/994> (last accessed 6 December 2019).

Hatton, Timothy J., and Jeffrey G. Williamson (1998) *The Age of Mass Migration: Causes and Economic Impact*. Oxford: Oxford University Press.

Hidalgo, Javier S. (2014) 'Freedom, immigration, and adequate options.' *Critical Review of International Social and Political Philosophy* 17(2): 212–34.

Jacques, Mélanie (2012) *Armed Conflict and Displacement: The Protection of Refugees and Displaced Persons under International Humanitarian Law*. Cambridge: Cambridge University Press.

Kneebone, Susan (2009) *Refugees, Asylum Seekers and the Rule of Law: Comparative Perspectives*. Cambridge: Cambridge University Press.

Koser, Khalid (ed.) (2003) *New African Diasporas*. London: Routledge.

Koser, Khalid (2007) *International Migration: A Very Short Introduction*. Oxford: Oxford University Press.

Kowalski, Michal (2016) 'From a different angle: Poland and the Mediterranean refugee crisis.' *German Law Journal* 17(6): 967–80.

Lee, Everett S. (1966) 'A theory of migration.' *Demography* 3(1): 47–57.

Martin, Terry (1998) 'The origins of Soviet ethnic cleansing.' *The Journal of Modern History* 70(4): 813–61.

Massey, Douglas S. (1990) 'Social structure, household strategies, and the cumulative causation of migration.' *Population Index* 56(1): 3–26.

Massey, Douglas S., and J. Edward Taylor (eds) (2004) *International Migration: Prospects and Policies in a Global Market*. Oxford: Oxford University Press.

Massey, Douglas S., Joaquín Arango, Graeme Hugo, Ali Kouaouci, Adela Pellegrino and J. Edward Taylor (1993) 'Theories of international migration: a review and appraisal.' *Population and Development Review* 19(3):431–66.

Mau, Steffen (2006) 'Die Politik der Grenze: Grenzziehung und politische Systembildung in der Europäischen Union.' *Berliner Journal für Soziologie* 16(1): 115–32.

Mau, Steffen, and Heike Brabandt (2011) 'Visumpolitik und die Regulierung globaler Mobilität: Ein Vergleich dreier OECD-Länder.' *Zeitschrift für Soziologie* 40(1): 3–23.

Mayda, Anna Mari (2006) 'Who is against immigration? A cross-country investigation of individual attitudes toward immigrants.' *Review of Economics and Statistics* 88(3): 510–30.

Miller, David (2016a) *Strangers in Our Midst: The Political Philosophy of Immigration.* Cambridge, MA: Harvard University Press.

Miller, David (2016b) 'How to think about immigration: control, protection, discretion and democracy.' *Juncture* 23(1): 41–6.

Ohmae, Kenichi (1990) *The Borderless World: Power and Strategy in the Interlinked Economy.* New York: Harper Business.

Paasi, Anssi (2009) 'Bounded spaces in a "borderless world"? Border studies, power, and the anatomy of the territory.' *Journal of Power* 2(2): 213–34.

Pogge, Thomas (2002) 'Cosmopolitanism: a defence.' *Critical Review of International Social and Political Philosophy* 5(3): 86–91.

Pohl, J. Otto (1999) *Ethnic Cleansing in the USSR, 1937–1949.* Westport: Greenwood Press.

Putnam, Robert (2007) 'E pluribus unum: diversity and community in the twenty-first century: the 2006 Johan Skytte Prize Lecture.' *Scandinavian Political Studies* 30(2): 137–74.

Rawls, John (1993) *Political Liberalism.* New York: Columbia University Press.

Rosas, Gilberto (2006) 'The thickening borderlands: diffused exceptionality and "immigrant" social struggles during the "war on terror".' *Cultural Dynamics* 18(3): 335–49.

Salter, Mark B. (2006) 'The global visa regime and the political technologies of the international self: borders, bodies, biopolitics.' *Alternatives: Global, Local, Political* 31(2): 167–89.

Schimank, Uwe (2005) 'Weltgesellschaft und Nationalgesellschaften: Funktionen von Staatsgrenzen.' Pp. 394–414 in *Weltgesellschaft: Theoretische Zugänge und empirische Problemlagen*, edited by Bettina Heintz, Richard Münch and Hartmann Tyrell. Stuttgart: Lucius & Lucius.

Scott, James Wesley (2012) 'European politics of borders, border symbolism and cross-border cooperation.' Pp. 83–99 in *A Companion to Border Studies*, edited by Thomas M. Wilson and Hastings Donnan. Maldon, MA: Wiley-Blackwell.

Schrover, Marlou (2015) 'Chain migration (network migration).', in *The Wiley Blackwell Encyclopedia of Race, Ethnicity, and Nationalism*, edited by John Stone, Dennis M. Rutledge, Anthony D. Smith, Polly Rizova and Xiaoshuo Hou. Oxford: Wiley-Blackwell, <https://doi.org/10.1002/9781118663202.wberen592> (last accessed 6 December 2019).

Sheller, Mimi, and John Urry (2006) 'The new mobilities paradigm.' *Environment and Planning A* 38: 207–26.

Simmons, A. John (2001) 'On the territorial rights of states.' *Noûs* 35: 300–26.

Steiner, Niklaus (2000) *Arguing About Asylum: The Complexity of Refugee Debates in Europe.* New York: St. Martin's Press.

Stilz, Anna (2009) 'Why do states have territorial rights?' *International Theory* 1(2): 185–213.

United Nations (2016) *International Migration Report 2015.* New York: United Nations.

Vidor, Jacob L. (2013) *Measuring Immigrant Assimilation in Post-Recession America*. Civic Report No. 76. March, <https://www.manhattan-institute.org/pdf/cr_76.pdf> (last accessed 6 December 2019)

Walzer, Michael (1983) *Spheres of Justice: A Defense of Pluralism and Equality*. New York: Basic Books.

White, Michael J., and Dudley L Poston (eds) (2016) *International Handbook of Migration and Population Distribution*. Dordrecht: Springer.

Whyte, Brendan (2008) 'Visa-free travel privileges: an exploratory geographical analysis.' *Tourism Geographies* 10(2): 127–49.

Woolley, Agnes (2014) *Contemporary Asylum Narratives: Representing Refugees in the Twenty-First Century*. Basingstoke: Palgrave Macmillan.

1

Do Migrants Think Differently about Migration? An Experimentum Crucis for Explaining Attitudes on Migration

Jochen Roose

Introduction

IN THE LAST DECADES and particularly in the last few years we have seen migrants in large numbers across Europe. The opening of the Western European labour markets to the accession countries in Central Eastern Europe motivated many to migrate to the more affluent countries. The United Kingdom was the destination of many, not least because it opened its labour market earlier than others. During the following years, other countries also saw the influx of a considerable number of immigrants. The Great Recession in Europe after 2007 became another driver of inter-EU migration, in this case from South to North (Lafleur and Stanek 2017). Finally, and intensively discussed, the war in Syria jointly with violent conflicts in other world regions contributed to the global migration flows of which a considerable share is directed towards Europe (Elitok and Fröhlich 2019; see also the introduction to this volume for an overview).

Migration and, even more so, increasing migration – to some degree irrespective of the starting level – has a strong impact on societies. Immigrants are not always welcomed. A normative literature discusses intensively to what extent the nation-state has the right, possibly even the duty, to regulate and reduce migration, or whether people have a right to migrate irrespective of or depending on their motives (see the discussion in the introduction to this volume). Empirically, the same question arises. People hold opinions on migration, often strong opinions. More often than not a majority reacts with rejection and favours a reduction of immigration, if not a complete block on it. The rise of right-wing parties that respond to these sentiments and shifts in the political arena can be a secondary effect of migration streams. In the recent past, Europe has seen these secondary effects with the rise of right populist, xenophobic parties (Thorleifsson 2019; Vetter 2017; Wodak et al. 2013). Brexit has been attributed to the migration issue as well (Gietel-Basten 2016). Probably the attitudes on migration with their impact on political sentiments change the face of European societies more than the migrants ever could.

It comes as no surprise that attitudes on migration are of major interest for social sciences. Various explanations for the rejection of immigration are on offer, some of them partly contradictory or with mixed empirical support. Surveys cover attitudes on migration time and again, making it possible to deal with complex models on the relation of nationalism, identities, xenophobia and so on (for example, Ceobanu and Escandell 2008; Rippl et al. 2005). There are persistent findings on the relation between educational degree and labour market position on the one hand and attitudes on immigration on the other hand (Hainmueller and Hopkins 2014). Also, we find stable cross-country differences (see the introduction to this volume for an overview). The differences seem to be linked to religious denomination, historical development and the number of migrants already in the country. The mobilisation of attitudes favouring national closure by political entrepreneurs contributes to the spread of these attitudes and makes them politically relevant (Hutter 2014; Kriesi et al. 2012).

What have received much less attention are migrants' attitudes to further immigration. At first sight, this neglect may come as no surprise. Besides the methodological problems of general surveys, in which migrants appear only in limited numbers, the main reason is the political irrelevance of migrants. They are comparatively small in numbers and as long as they have not acquired citizenship they are not entitled to vote. Accordingly, shifts in the political realm are not to be expected from migrants. However, from a conceptual point of view migrants are highly interesting. Some of the influences discussed as being influential for maintaining attitudes rejecting immigration are fulfilled nearly ideal-typically by migrants while other factors are basically non-existent. Migrants are a very special but at the same time highly illuminating case in respect of attitudes on migration.

This chapter compares the attitudes on immigration held by migrants and by non-migrants. Theoretical considerations lead to different expectations. Depending on the theoretical arguments we refer to, migrants should reject further immigration more or less than non-migrants. The comparison of migrant and non-migrant population comes close to being an *experimentum crucis*, a quasi-experimental setting that allows a decision between alternative explanations.

Explaining attitudes towards immigration

In the research on attitudes on immigration, four theories or more confined hypotheses have been proposed (Ceobanu and Escandell 2010; Hainmueller and Hopkins 2014; McLaren 2003; Ward and Masgoret 2006; Weber 2017; Yakushko 2018): the economic group conflict theory, the cultural group conflict theory, the in-group favouritism hypothesis and the contact hypothesis.

The economic group conflict theory assumes that people tend to reject other groups if they compete with them. The rejection is based on a real competition about scarce tangible resources. Feelings of dislike arise to avoid cognitive dissonance (Festinger 1957; Wicklund and Brehm 1976). The evidence for this approach is based on the observation that people with lower qualification tend to reject immigration more than people with higher education. As immigrants usually enter the labour market for the low qualified, it is in this section of the labour market where competition increases and accordingly hostile attitudes arise (Esses et al. 1998; Hainmueller et al. 2015; Stephana et al. 2005). The economic group conflict theory is supported in some comparative studies, as Mayda (2006) can show that support for immigration is higher in a country if the native population is more highly educated than the immigrants (see also Facchini and Mayda 2012). However, Billiet, Meulemann and de Witte (2014) find only very limited support for the hypothesis in their country comparison.

While these studies concentrate on material gains or threats, the cultural group conflict theory focuses on cultural differences. Recent political debates and mobilisations have focused on the rejection of a cultural change brought by immigrants. This is mirrored in survey results (Schneider 2008). Card et al. (2012) show on the basis of the European Social Survey (ESS) of 2012 that concerns about the immigrants' compatibility with the domestic culture are much more important for the support of migration than economic concerns.

Both the economic group conflict theory and the cultural group conflict theory come in two versions. One version is based on the idea that a factual conflict due to a competitive constellation and manifest or predicted manifest influences is decisive. The realistic group conflict theory has a long tradition dating back to the 1950s (Jackson 1993; Sherif 1951). The research group around Tajfel suggested a second version which argues that the classification of different groups already triggers mutual rejection (Tajfel et al. 1971; Tajfel and Turner 1979). Tajfel exposed in experiments the impact of minimal groups that are formed on no other basis than the assignment to different groups. The pure assignment to an obviously arbitrarily formed group triggered in-group favouritism and a degradation of the other group. According to this approach, a realistic conflict is not even necessary for rejecting the out-group and favouring the in-group. The in-group favouritism hypothesis assumes support and positive attitudes towards the in-group on the sole ground of being assigned to this group.

A fourth approach focuses on the personal instead of the group level. Allport (1954) suggested with his contact hypothesis that prejudices against a group can be reduced by experience, by direct contact with members of this group. However, Allport never suggested that all kinds of contact were suitable to reject prejudices. Rather, a number of conditions have to be met, like experiences which do not reinforce existing prejudices or the contact being voluntary. Research has substantiated these assumptions to a considerable degree, further specifying the conditions (Pettigrew 1986).[1] Following these assumptions, contact with immigrants should bring about more positive attitudes towards immigrants and less rejection of immigration as immigration loses its threatening potential (Ariely 2017; Hjerm 2009; Semyonov and Glikman 2009; Wagner et al. 2006).

Empirical tests of these four theories – that is, the economic group conflict theory, the cultural group conflict theory, the in-group favouritism hypothesis and the contact hypothesis – mostly focus on how parts of the population are differently exposed to immigrants, for example in respect of economic competition, cultural confrontation in one's personal environment or by contact. Widely neglected in its empirical potential is a comparison of the population segments which differ most clearly in these aspects from each other: migrant and non-migrant populations. On the grounds of the theoretical arguments, we can specify expectations for this comparison, building on migrants' specific situation and experiences.

Starting from the economic group conflict hypothesis, the most direct competitors on the labour market for immigrants are further immigrants. By and large the position on the labour market will be similar. Hence, we should expect more rejection of further immigration among migrants than among non-migrants.

The cultural group conflict theory results in a different assumption. Experience of cultural difference is commonplace for immigrants. Regardless of how large differences actually are, the experience of a cultural shock is awaiting all immigrants. Being constantly confronted with cultural difference, further cultural difference will not trigger the same amount of threat and rejection. Following the cultural group conflict theory, compared to the non-migrants, migrants will reject immigration less.

The contact hypothesis reinforces the previous hypothesis. Migrants will have more contact with other migrants. This is most likely for migrants from the same country of origin, as usually communities form among ex-patriates. However, contact with migrants from other origins is also somewhat more likely due to segregation and links among people with a similar life situation and similar problems. Accordingly, the contact hypothesis would also suggest that immigrants will reject further immigration less than non-migrants.

The community building among immigrants and their similar situation suggest another mechanism, which relates back to the in-group favouritism hypothesis. The group of immigrants as such could be sufficient to trigger group solidarity. If migrants identify with the group of immigrants they should also favour further immigration. In this case they would reject immigration less than the non-migrants.

The application of the theoretical ideas on migrants result, in three of the four cases, in identical predictions. The cultural group conflict theory, the contact hypothesis and the in-group favouritism hypothesis are empirically not separable. However, this group of theories can be empirically distinguished from the economic group conflict theory, which points in a different direction:

- H1: Migrants reject further immigration *more* than non-migrants (economic group conflict theory).
- H2: Migrants reject further immigration *less* than non-migrants (cultural group conflict theory, contact hypothesis, in-group favouritism hypothesis).

Data and method

The empirical analysis uses the 2016 wave of the ESS. The ESS is a comparative study conducted in a wide range of European countries. The 2016 wave provides data for twenty-two countries (Jowell et al. 2007), and is particularly suitable for this research question because it covers attitudes on immigration and has migrants in the sample. However, as migrants are only covered to the extent that they appear in the random sample, their number is not overly large.

The definition of 'migrant' in this analysis was unconventionally strict. The aim was to identify particularly clear cases of people who migrated as adults. The idea was to come up with a group of migrants who self-consciously look back on their own migration history and have a life memory of the experience of being an immigrant. To ensure this, only people who came to the country of residence at the age of 18 or above were considered as migrants.[2] As well, to guarantee that respondents did not return to the home country of their parents, both parents of those included in the sample were required to be born outside of the country.

This analysis is confined to countries that have in their respective sample a minimum of 50 unweighted cases which qualify for the given definition of migrants. This leaves 15 countries out of 22 in the analysis. Obviously, the threshold of 50 is an arbitrary choice. A threshold of 100 would have excluded three more countries (Finland with 56 migrants in the sample, Denmark with 73 and the Netherlands with 92). Slovenia is close to the threshold, with 43 migrants in the sample, while Portugal (34 migrants) and Lithuania (31 migrants) have considerably fewer. The countries included in the study can be found in the consecutive figures (next section).

The non-migrants need a concise definition as well. For this group too, the aim was to isolate the clearest cases. Therefore, only respondents who were themselves born in the country and whose parents were also born in the country fulfil the definition as non-migrants. People who regarded themselves as part of an ethnic minority were also excluded. In two cases, this selection reduced the number of respondents considerably. In Israel, only one fifth of the respondents were non-migrants according to these criteria. In Switzerland, somewhat over a third qualified as non-migrants in this sense. In all other countries, only a relatively small share of respondents was excluded.

The acceptance of further immigration is not measured in the ESS in a direct, encompassing question because such acceptance depends on the kind of people immigrating. Rich people of the same cultural background receive higher acceptance than unskilled labour from poor, culturally different countries. Therefore the kind of immigration is specified in the questions and we have a set of four questions on immigration by specified groups, which we will discuss in turn.

Attitudes on immigration: migrants and non-migrants compared

As noted above, a set of four questions in the ESS ask about acceptance of immigration. They vary in respect of the geographical origin of the immigrants, distinguishing Europe from other parts of the world, and in respect of the racial/ethnic background, which may be the same as or different from the host country's culture.

We turn first to the cultural difference, starting with immigrants with the same cultural and ethnic background as the hosting country. In Figure 1.1 we compare to what extent respondents want to allow many or no immigrants of the same race/ethnic group as most people in the respective country.[3]

The general acceptance of immigrants from the same racial/ethnic background as the majority in the respective country is quite high. The average across respondents is in no country above 2.5 (1 for allowing many immigrants and 4 for allowing none) and mostly considerably below 2. Immigrants who are described as ethnically similar are widely accepted.

The main interest concerns the difference between migrants and non-migrants. In only five countries is there a significant difference between the two groups (in addition, in Spain the difference is weakly significant,

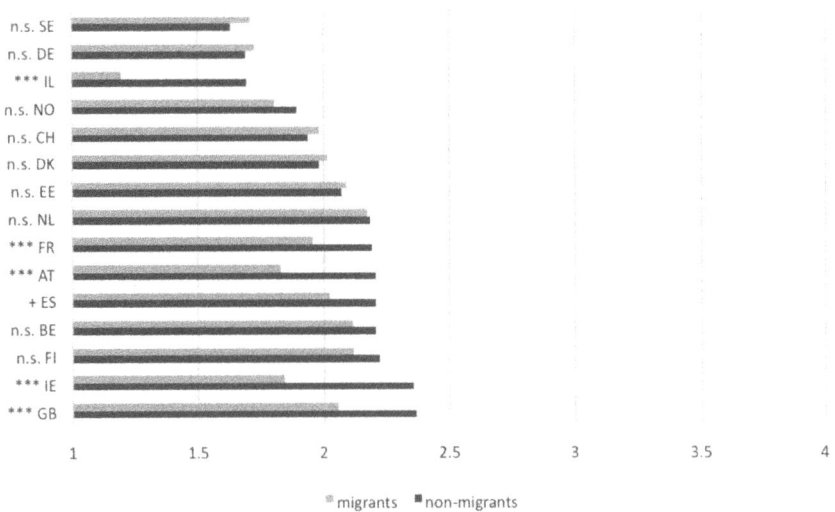

Figure 1.1 Allow many/few immigrants of same race/ethnic group as majority

Source: European Social Survey 2016.

Notes: 1 – 'Allow many to come and live here'; 2 – 'Allow some'; 3 – 'Allow a few'; 4 – 'Allow none'. Significance levels: + 10%, * 5%, ** 1%, ***0.1%. Own calculation.

Abbreviations follow ISO-3166 (ALPHA-2), <https://www.iso.org/iso-3166-country-codes.html> (last accessed 14 January 2020).

at the 10 per cent level). In all other countries the difference is insignificant. This similarity between migrants' and non-migrants' attitudes is primarily found among those countries where the rejection of ethnically similar immigration is lower. In countries such as Sweden, Germany, Norway, Switzerland, Denmark, Estonia and the Netherlands, the acceptance of ethnically similar immigrants is higher among non-migrants than in the other countries and the migrants share this view. However, in countries where the non-migrants reject ethnically similar immigration somewhat more, like the United Kingdom, Ireland, Austria and France, the migrants are significantly more open to further immigration of this kind. The first exception to this rule is Israel. Here, migrants are much more in favour of ethnically similar immigration than migrants or non-migrants in all other countries. In Finland and Belgium, on the other hand, non-migrants reject ethnically similar immigration somewhat more, and the respective migrant population is similar in its rejection.

In respect of the hypotheses, most important is the direction of the difference between migrants' and non-migrants' attitudes. In all countries where we find a significant difference, the migrants accept ethnically similar immigration more than the non-migrants. These comparisons support the cultural group conflict theory, the contact hypothesis and the in-group favouritism hypothesis. Vice versa, the findings contradict the economic group conflict theory. There is not a single country where migrants reject further immigration by ethnically similar people more than non-migrants as the economic group conflict theory suggests.

Second, we turn to ethnically different immigrants (Figure 1.2).[4] First of all, there is still a tendency towards accepting further immigrants. However, acceptance is lower than in the case of immigrants with a similar ethnic background.

Out of the fifteen countries, four show no difference in the attitude between migrants and non-migrants. Out of the remaining eleven countries, in four of them the migrants reject further immigrants more than the non-migrants do. These are Sweden and Germany, in which the acceptance of ethnically different immigrants is most widespread. Here, the migrants do not follow the high acceptance by the non-migrant population but remain somewhat more hesitant. In Estonia too, the rejection of ethnically different immigrants is significantly higher among migrants than among non-migrants. These countries are in line with the economic group conflict theory.

Israel is a special case again. Here the rejection of ethnically different immigrants is the highest among migrants and non-migrants for this

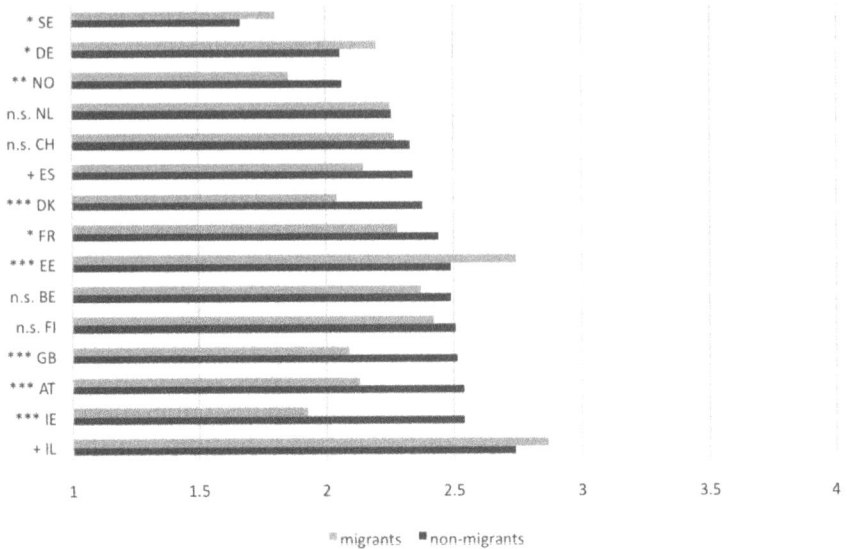

Figure 1.2 Allow many/few immigrants of different race/ethnic group from majority

Source: European Social Survey 2016.

Notes: 1 – 'Allow many to come and live here'; 2 – 'Allow some'; 3 – 'Allow a few'; 4 – 'Allow none'. Significance levels: + 10%, * 5%, ** 1%, ***0.1%. Own calculation.

Abbreviations follow ISO-3166 (ALPHA-2), <https://www.iso.org/iso-3166-country-codes.html> (last accessed 14 January 2020).

entire comparative study. 'Ethnically different' seems to translate into 'non-Jewish', and this is rejected by a large part of the population. The migrants in Israel reject it a bit more than the non-migrant population, but both groups stand out in the comparison between countries, and the difference between them is only weakly significant. The inter-Israeli difference also supports the economic group conflict theory.

Contrary to these four, in the remaining seven countries migrants want to allow more ethnically different immigrants to enter the country than the non-migrants. This majority of countries with a significant result supports the contact hypothesis, the in-group favouritism hypothesis and the cultural group conflict theory. The last especially receives support as ethnic difference in society coincides with cultural difference in the national ideology (Hutchinson and Smith 1994). It is likely that respondents associate ethnic difference with cultural difference in their assessment. However, only half of the countries support this interpretation, while another quarter either does not show any difference or show the difference going in the other direction. Therefore, we find only weak support for the cultural group conflict theory, the contact hypothesis and the in-group favouritism hypothesis, though the competing economic group conflict theory receives considerably less support.

Most immigrants come from poorer countries to improve their economic situation. Though obviously decisions to migrate are more complex, economic motives are of major importance. Ravenstein had already noted in his laws of migration that economic motivations are most important:

> Bad or oppressive laws, heavy taxation, an unattractive climate, uncongenial social surroundings, and even compulsion (slave trade, transportation), all have produced and are still producing currents of migration, but none of these currents can compare in volume with that which arises from the desire inherent in most men to 'better' themselves in material respects. (quoted after Lee 1966: 48, Ravenstein 1889)

The question concept in the ESS takes this dominance of economic reasons into account. Respondents were asked whether they would allow many or no immigrants from poorer countries. This question is asked for European countries and countries beyond Europe.

Immigrants from poorer European countries receive a little less support than the racially or ethnically different immigrants, though this difference is small (Figure 1.3).[5] Still, by and large people want to allow some though not many further immigrants. Again, Israel stands out, as the acceptance of further immigration from poorer European countries is lower among migrants and non-migrants than in any other of the countries compared. However, we have to keep in mind that Israel is not part of Europe, so in contrast to the other respondents even a continental identification among Israeli interviewees would not include people from other European countries.

Concerning the difference between migrants and non-migrants, the overall pattern is very similar to the acceptance of racially or ethnically different immigrants. In five countries there is no difference between the non-migrant and the migrant population concerning their attitudes on further immigration. The countries without a significant difference between migrants and non-migrants are again Finland, Belgium, Switzerland and the Netherlands, this time accompanied by Denmark. In the same four countries as previously, migrants reject further immigration from poorer European countries more than the non-migrant population. These are Sweden and

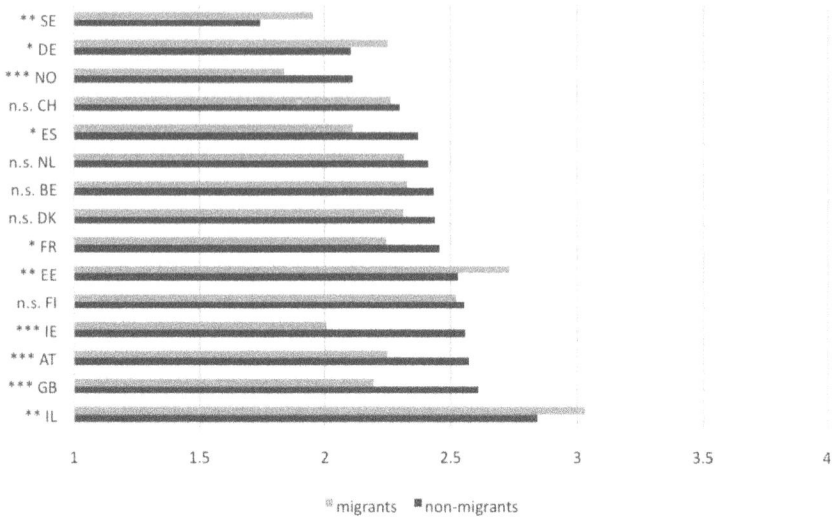

Figure 1.3 Allow many/few immigrants from poorer countries in Europe

Source: European Social Survey 2016.

Notes: 1 – 'Allow many to come and live here'; 2 – 'Allow some'; 3 – 'Allow a few'; 4 – 'Allow none'. Significance levels: + 10%, * 5%, ** 1%, ***0.1%. Own calculation.

Abbreviations follow ISO-3166 (ALPHA-2), <https://www.iso.org/iso-3166-country-codes.html> (last accessed 14 January 2020).

Germany, where support for further immigration is highest among the non-migrant population, and Estonia and, as mentioned, Israel, where migrants reject immigration from poorer European countries more than the non-migrant population. In the remaining six countries, migrants support further migration from poorer European countries more than the non-migrant population.

Again, we have weak support for the cultural group conflict theory, the contact hypothesis and the in-group favouritism hypothesis. This support is not overly strong because we find the expected significant difference between migrants' and non-migrants' attitudes in less than half of the countries.

Immigration from poorer countries outside of Europe receives less approval again (Figure 1.4).[6] The averages are between 'allow some' and 'allow few'. Israel again stands out with the highest disapproval of further immigration. This applies to both migrants and non-migrants in Israel.

In four countries the difference in non-migrants' and migrants' attitudes is insignificant. These are again the usual suspects – Finland, the Netherlands and Switzerland – but this time Spain too does not show

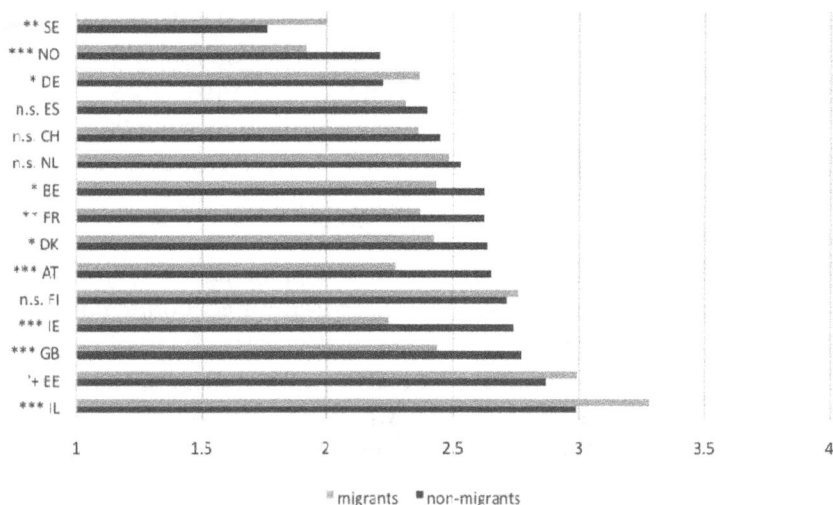

Figure 1.4 Allow many/few immigrants from poorer countries outside Europe

Source: European Social Survey 2016.

Notes: 1 – 'Allow many to come and live here'; 2 – 'Allow some'; 3 – 'Allow a few'; 4 – 'Allow none'. Significance levels: + 10%, * 5%, ** 1%, ***0.1%. Own calculation.

Abbreviations follow ISO-3166 (ALPHA-2), <https://www.iso.org/iso-3166-country-codes.html> (last accessed 14 January 2020).

a significant difference. In four countries, migrants reject immigration from poorer countries outside of Europe more than the non-migrant population. These countries are again Sweden, Germany, Estonia and, as mentioned, Israel. In the remaining seven countries, migrants are significantly more in favour of immigration from poorer countries beyond Europe than non-migrants. Thus, nearly half of the countries support the cultural group conflict theory, the contact hypothesis and the in-group favouritism hypothesis, while they contradict the economic group conflict theory. However, the result is not straightforward as still more than half of the countries either have a non-significant result or even clearly contradict the pattern.

Conclusion

In the explanation of attitudes to migration we find a range of theories. These theories primarily focus on rejection of immigrants, as prejudices and discrimination are major problems in countries that aim at equal rights and general fairness. Though these phenomena are without any doubt widespread and highly problematic, it seems important to realise the relatively high acceptance of further immigration found in Europe, on the basis of the results of the ESS conducted in 2016.

The main aim of this chapter, however, is theory testing in a design that resembles a quasi-experiment. Theories explaining attitudes to immigration build on social psychology and particularly group psychology, which are particularly well suited to be tested in an experimental design. We tested these prominent explanations for rejection of immigration: the group conflict theory, based on economic competition or cultural difference; the contact hypothesis, which takes rejection of immigrants for granted and focuses on a process to reduce this rejection; and in-group favouritism, which has shown support for the in-group at the expense of an out-group even without any substantial competition or conflictual situation.

Empirical studies of migration attitudes traditionally focus on non-migrants or the general population, who by and large have not migrated themselves. Instead, we focus on the attitudes of migrants, an issue that has not been systematically discussed. However, people who experienced migration themselves and live in a country other than their birth country have a very specific relation to migration in general and can be expected to differ in their attitudes from others. Furthermore, applying theoretical assumptions to the comparison of migrants and non-migrants enables us to test the theories from a different angle.

According to the economic group conflict theory, migrants should reject immigration more than the non-migrant population because economic competition is strongest among migrants themselves. On the contrary, the cultural group conflict theory may explain rejection of immigration by non-migrants, but for migrants the assumption of a cultural threat does not hold. Contact with migrants will differ for the non-migrant population depending on the living environment and other factors, but it is universal among migrants. Both cultural group conflict theory and the contact hypothesis may explain the rejection of further immigration or the lack of reduced prejudices and reduced rejection of immigration for non-migrants, but for migrants these mechanisms are unlikely. Finally, in-group favouritism leads to contrary assumptions for migrants and non-migrants.

In effect, not only do the theories predict a difference between migrants and non-migrants but the direction of the difference even helps us to identify the more valid theory. In the case of economic group conflict, migrants should reject further immigration even more than the

Table 1.1 Summary of findings

	Same race/ ethnic group	Different race/ ethnic group	European countries	Non-European countries
Economic group conflict theory		DE, EE, IL, SE	DE, EE, IL, SE	DE, EE, IL, SE
Cultural group conflict, contact, ingroup favoritism	AT, ES, FR, GB, IE, IL	AT, DK, ES, FR, GB, IE, NO	AT, ES, FR, GB, IE, NO	AT, BE, DK, FR, GB, IE, NO
Inconclusive (no difference)	BE, CH, DE, DK, EE, FI, NL, NO, SE	BE, CH, FI, NL	BE, CH, DK, FI, NL	CH, ES, FI, NL

Note: Abbreviations follow ISO-3166 (ALPHA-2), <https://www.iso.org/iso-3166-country-codes.html> (last accessed 14 January 2020).

non-migrant population. On the contrary, rejection of further immigration among migrants should be less than among non-migrants according to the cultural group conflict theory, the contact hypothesis and the in-group favouritism hypothesis. Accordingly, we can separate the economic group conflict hypothesis from the other explanations by looking specifically at the comparison between migrants and non-migrants.

The results are less conclusive than hoped for but still particularly helpful for the discussion. For the set of fifteen countries, we find different results depending on which country we look at. Table 1.1 summarises the findings for the four indicators.

Interestingly, across the four indicators the results are remarkably stable for the countries. For all four indicators, in some countries there is no significant difference between non-migrants and migrants, in some countries the results point towards the economic group conflict theory, while in others the cultural group conflict theory, the contact hypothesis and the in-group favouritism hypothesis are supported.

Sweden, Germany, Estonia and Israel support three out of four indicators of the economic group conflict theory. On the other hand, Austria, France, the United Kingdom and Ireland reject the economic group conflict theory and rather support the cultural group conflict theory, the contact hypothesis and the in-group favouritism hypothesis for all four indicators. Support additionally comes from Spain and Norway for three and Denmark for two indicators. For all or nearly all indicators, the difference between non-migrants' and migrants' attitudes remains insignificant in Belgium, Switzerland, Finland and the Netherlands. Thus overall, support for the economic group conflict theory is weaker than for the cultural group conflict theory, the contact hypothesis and the in-group favouritism hypothesis.

However, as some countries in the comparison support one side of the theory across multiple indicators, while others support the other side, it would be premature to simply discard the economic group conflict theory on these grounds. Rather, the question arises of which factors can explain this pattern. The special situation of Israel was mentioned before, but the remaining three countries remain a puzzle. It is striking that migrants tend to be relatively more sceptical concerning further immigration in countries where support for immigration by the migrant population is highest: Sweden and Germany. There might be a threshold of support among migrants. However, Estonia does not comply with this pattern and nor does Norway, although support for immigration among the non-migrant population there is on a similar level to that in Germany. Further factors come to mind, such as the composition of the migrants, the composition of likely future immigrants, the migration history, prevailing debates on immigration and many more factors. Introducing all these considerations, we would end up with very singular stories for each country, which is contrary to the idea of a quasi-experiment focusing on a specific group difference.

Overall, the quasi-experiment rather rejects the economic group conflict theory and rather supports the cultural group conflict theory, the contact hypothesis and the in-group favouritism hypothesis. For immigration societies, these findings have nevertheless important implications. We see that economic redistribution is an inadequate response to xenophobia because that is not primarily triggered by economic threat. Of course there are good reasons for an appropriate welfare state, but it would be unwise to delegate the handling of xenophobia to social welfare provisions. Rather, immigration seems to challenge societies in cultural terms. This challenge has implications for society as a whole. It opens up the question of a cultural core and cultural borders. It reshapes the cleavage structure and generates new political actors. Globalisation and, as an important part of it, migration reshape societies, and the attitudes towards migration with its driving factors is a major aspect of this reconfiguration.

Notes

1. However, empirical support is unequivocal. Weber (2017) shows that a high share of immigrants in the immediate neighbourhood is linked to lower support

for further immigration. Instead, more immigrants in the larger region come together with more support for further integration. There seems to be a threshold for the acceptance-supporting effect of contact.

2. Also, migrants had to be born outside of the country of residence.
3. The wording in the source questionnaire which is used for the translation is: 'Now, using this card, to what extent do you think [country] should allow people of the same race or ethnic group as most [country] people to come and live here?' '[country]' stands for the respective country in which the respondent is asked. The answer categories are: 1 – 'Allow many to come and live here'; 2 – 'Allow some'; 3 – 'Allow a few'; 4 – 'Allow none'.
4. The wording of the question in the source questionnaire is: 'How about people of a different race or ethnic group from most [country] people? Still use this card.' The response options are identical to the previous question (see note 3).
5. The wording of the question in the source questionnaire is: 'And how about people from the poorer countries in Europe? Still use this card.' The response options are identical to the previous questions (see note 3).
6. The wording of the question in the source questionnaire is: 'How about people from the poorer countries outside Europe? Use the same card.' The response options are identical to the previous questions (see note 3).

References

Allport, Gordon W. (1954) *The Nature of Prejudice*. Cambridge: Cambridge University Press.

Ariely, Gal (2017) 'Global identification, xenophobia and globalisation: A cross-national exploration.' *International Journal of Psychology* 52: 87–96.

Billiet, Jaak, Bart Meuleman and Hans de Witte (2014) 'The relationship between ethnic threat and economic insecurity in times of economic crisis: analysis of European Social Survey data.' *Migration Studies* 2(2): 135–61.

Card, David, Christian Dustmann and Ian Preston (2012) 'Immigration, wages, and compositional amenities.' *Journal of the European Economic Association* 10(1): 78–119.

Ceobanu, Alin M., and Xavier Escandell (2008) 'East is West? National feelings and anti-immigrant sentiment in Europe.' *Social Science Research* 37(4): 1147–70.

Ceobanu, Alin M., and Xavier Escandell (2010) 'Comparative analyses of public attitudes toward immigrants and immigration using multinational survey data: a review of theories and research.' *Annual Review of Sociology* 36(1): 309–26.

Elitok, Seçil Paçacı, and Christiane Fröhlich (2019) 'Displacement, refugees, and forced migration in the MENA region: the case of Syria.' Pp. 107–18 in *Routledge International Handbook of Migration Studies*, 2nd edn, edited by Steven J. Gold and Stephanie J. Nawyn. Abingdon: Routledge.

Esses, Victoria M., Lynne M. Jackson and Tamara L. Armstrong (1998) 'Immigrants and immigration: an instrumental model of group conflict.' *Journal of Social Issues* 54(4): 699–724.

Facchini, Giovanni, and Anna Maria Mayda (2012) 'Individual attitudes towards skilled migration: an empirical analysis across countries.' *The World Economy* 35(2): 183–96.

Festinger, Leon (1957) *A Theory of Cognitive Dissonance*. Stanford: Stanford University Press.

Gietel-Basten, Stuart (2016) 'Why Brexit? The toxic mix of immigration and austerity.' *Population and Development Review* 42(4): 673–80.

Hainmueller, Jens, and Daniel Hopkins (2014) 'Public attitudes toward immigration.' *Annual Review of Political Science* 17(1): 225–49.

Hainmueller, Jens, Michael J. Hiscox and Yotam Margalit (2015) 'Do concerns about labour market competition shape attitudes toward immigration? New evidence.' *Journal of International Economics* 97(1): 193–207.

Hjerm, Mikael (2009) 'Anti-immigrant attitudes and cross-municipal variation in the proportion of immigrants.' *Acta Sociologica* 52(1): 47–62.

Hutchinson, John, and Anthony D. Smith (eds) (1994) *Nationalism*. Oxford: Oxford University Press.

Hutter, Swen (2014) *Protesting Culture and Economics in Western Europe: New Cleavages in Left and Right Politics*. Minneapolis: University of Minnesota Press.

Jackson, Jay W. (1993) 'Realistic group conflict theory: a review and evaluation of the theoretical and empirical literature.' *Psychological Record* 43(3): 395–415.

Jowell, Roger, Max Kaase, Rory Fitzgerald and Gillian Eva (2007) 'The European Social Survey as a measurement model.' Pp. 1–31 in *Measuring Attitudes Cross-Nationally: Lessons from the European Social Survey*, edited by Roger Jowell, Caroline Roberts, Amy Fitzgerald and Gillian Eva. London: Sage.

Kriesi, Hanspeter, Edgar Grande, Martin Dolezal, Marc Helbling, Dominic Höglinger, Swen Hutter and Bruno Wüest (2012) *Political Conflict in Western Europe*. Cambridge: Cambridge University Press.

Lafleur, Jean-Michel, and Mikolaj Stanek (eds) (2017) *South–North Migration of EU Citizens in Times of Crisis*. Wiesbaden: Springer.

Lee, Everett S. (1966) 'A theory of migration.' *Demography* 3(1): 47–57.

McLaren, Lauren M. (2003) 'Anti-immigrant prejudice in Europe: contact, threat perception, and preferences for the exclusion of migrants.' *Social Forces* 81(3): 909–36.

Mayda, Anna Mari (2006) 'Who is against immigration? A cross-country investigation of individual attitudes toward immigrants.' *Review of Economics and Statistics* 88(3): 510–30.

Pettigrew, Thomas F. (1986) 'The intergroup contact hypothesis reconsidered.' Pp. 169–85 in *Contact and Conflict in Intergroup Encounter*, edited by Miles Hewstone and R Brown. Oxford: Blackwell.

Ravenstein, Ernest George (1889) 'The laws of migration.' *Journal of the Royal Statistical Society* 52(1): 241–301.

Rippl, Susanne, Dirk Baier, Angela Kindervater and Klaus Boehnke (2005) 'Die EU-Osterweiterung als Mobilisierungsschub für ethnozentrische Einstellungen? Die Rolle von Bedrohungsgefühlen im Kontext situativer und dispositioneller Faktoren.' *Zeitschrift für Soziologie* 34(4): 288–310.

Schneider, Silke L. (2008) 'Anti-immigrant attitudes in Europe: outgroup size and perceived ethnic threat.' *European Sociological Review* 24(1): 53–67.

Semyonov, Moshe, and Anya Glikman (2009) 'Ethnic residential segregation, social contacts, and anti-minority attitudes in European societies.' *European Sociological Review* 25(6): 693–708.

Sherif, Muzafer (1951) 'A preliminary experimental study of inter-group relations.' Pp. 388–424 in *Social Psychology at the Crossroads*, edited by John H. Rohrer and Muzafer Sherif. New York: Harper.

Stephana, Walter G., C. Lausanne Renfrob, Victoria M. Essesc, Cookie White Stephand and Tim Martine (2005) 'The effects of feeling threatened on attitudes toward immigrants.' *International Journal of Intercultural Relations* 29(1): 1–19.

Tajfel, Henri, and Jonathan H. Turner (1979) 'An integrative theory of intergroup conflict.' Pp. 33–47 in *The Social Psychology of Intergroup Relations*, edited by William G. Austin, and Stephen Worchel. Chicago: Nelson-Hall.

Tajfel, Henri, Michael G. Billig, R. Bundy and C. Flament (1971) 'Social categorization and intergroup behaviour.' *European Journal of Social Psychology* 1(1): 149–77.

Thorleifsson, Cathrine (2019) *Nationalist Responses to the Crises in Europe: Old and New Hatreds*. Abingdon: Routledge.

Vetter, Reinhold (2017) *Nationalismus im Osten Europas: Was Kaczyński und Orbán mit Le Pen und Wilders verbindet*. Berlin: Christoph Links.

Wagner, Ulrich, Oliver Christ, Thomas F. Pettigrew, Jost Stellmacher and Carina Wolf (2006) 'Prejudice and minority proportion: contact instead of threat effects.' *Social Psychology Quarterly* 69(4): 380–90.

Ward, Colleen, and Anne-Marie Masgoret (2006) 'An integrative model of attitudes toward immigrants.' *International Journal of Intercultural Relations* 30(6): 671–82.

Weber, Hannes (2017) 'Mehr Zuwanderer, mehr Fremdenangst? Ein Überblick über den Forschungsstand und ein Erklärungsversuch aktueller Entwicklungen in Deutschland.' *Berliner Journal für Soziologie* 25(4): 397–428.

Wicklund, Robert A., and Jack W. Brehm (1976) *Perspectives on Cognitive Dissonance*. New York: Halsted Press.

Wodak, Ruth, Majid KhosraviNik and Brigitte Mral (eds) (2013) *Right-Wing Populism in Europe: Politics and Discourse*. London: Bloomsbury.

Yakushko, Oksana (2018) *Modern-Day Xenophobia: Critical Historical and Theoretical Perspectives on the Roots of Anti-Immigrant Prejudice*. Cham: Palgrave Macmillan.

2

Fencing in the Boundaries of the Community: Migration, Nationalism and Populism in Hungary

Robert Sata

HUNGARY HAS BECOME one of the most vocal critics of international migration despite the fact that the country is not a traditional target but rather a sending or transit country of migration. Ever since prime minister Viktor Orbán declared that he wants to build an 'illiberal state' (for full speech see Tóth 2014), the country has been in the headlines, commentators trying to understand Orbán's radical, nationalist and illiberal shift.[1] The country has been leading the wave of anti-democratic and anti-European developments in the European Union in recent years. Many have been puzzled by how fast and spectacularly the dismantling of democratic institutions took place in a country that used to be a poster-child of post-Communist democratisation and, according to scholars, has had the most institutionalised party system in Eastern Europe (Enyedi 2016). Yet, since 2010, when Orbán returned to power, the priority seems to be to redefine the country, to redraw the boundaries of the national community and the political regime on the basis of a populist nationalist discourse that focuses on reinterpreting political as well as socio-cultural belonging in exclusionary nationalist and illiberal terms.

Some might even think that this shift away from mainstream politics in Hungary might be due to the strengthening of the radical right in recent years. After all, Jobbik (The Movement for Better Hungary – the name in Hungarian implies both 'better' and 'more to the right') has been one of the most successful of such formations across Europe. Jobbik had become the second most popular political party in the country by 2014, being better positioned to mount a challenge to Orbán's Fidesz (Fidesz – Hungarian Civic Union) than the fragmented opposition on the left. Yet, this chapter argues this simple explanation of Orbán turning illiberal to win the hearts of far right voters cannot explain the radicalisation of Hungarian politics. First of all, Jobbik has considerably toned down its radical rhetoric since 2010 to widen its electoral appeal,[2] and, as the chapter argues, Orbán has himself radicalised his electorate with his anti-establishment, anti-Western, anti-Europe and anti-liberal discourse. Orbán has adopted this strategy of mainstreaming the radical or radicalising the mainstream in order to consolidate his illiberal system. Similarly, while Hungary was at the centre of the 2015 European refugee crisis with more than 300,000 people entering the country, none of these migrants stayed to pose any difficulty for Hungary. Instead, the chapter argues that identity fears sparked by migration were mobilised by Orbán to rally support for his illiberal policies that cement his authoritarian rule.

This chapter proceeds as follows: the first section argues that looking at political discourse can help our understanding of political strategies. The chapter examines Orbán's discourse to show how nationalist narratives and populist accounts of crisis (or crises) are used to create a Manichaean view of the world, where the national community is facing existential threats. In this discourse, the discursive definition of the 'self' and the 'others' – the processes of othering – plays a key role, drawing up the borderlines between the 'good people' and its enemies. The chapter argues that, while in 2010–14, Orbán's discourse can be characterised as a prime example of populism based on economic grievance, aimed at fighting foreign capital, from 2015 on we see a major shift to a nationalist populist discourse, aimed against migration. This translates into both the 'self' and 'others' being defined mainly in economic terms for 2010–14, but from 2015 onwards the discourse focuses on drawing up both the tangible and intangible borders of the Hungarian community to fight mass migration. The use of 'otherness' in this exclusionist public discourse stands for the representations of migrants as deviant groups of people, enemies of the Hungarian nation, of a threatening ideology/religion that must be opposed. The chapter concludes that the processes of othering in Orbán's discourse create the narrative of illiberal nationalist populism that is not only anti-migrant and anti-Muslim but also anti-EU and anti-democratic to the extent that, though in the centre of Europe, the Hungarian community is fenced off from the rest of Europe.

Discursive othering: 'us' vs 'them'

The analysis focuses on political discourse because public discourse plays an important role in developing new political strategies that in turn determine new policies. All policies develop and are (re)produced in a constant struggle between competing notions or understandings of identity, issues and society overall (Dryzek 2005). Moreover, political discourses are never independent of the context; they are both influenced by and influence the context, the social and political structures and practices, and at the same time, they reflect a particular representation of this context. Political actors and their political discourses interact in public debates and public spaces and (together with other actors) shape common understandings in a process that can be characterised as intersubjective construction of meaning (Christiansen et al. 1999). In this way, political discourse is a means of discursive construction of reality (Lazar 2005), that is, a means to provide meaningful understandings of the world to the community (Weiss and Wodak 2005; Wodak 1997).

Nationalism, an ideology that values membership in the nation (an imagined community) above all other groups (Anderson 1991) and claims that national and political borders should coincide (Gellner 1983), at its core is about making and maintaining boundaries. Belonging to the national community is constructed using the discursive forms of inclusion and exclusion, 'us' vs 'them' throughout several categories, and it is of particular interest how symbolic boundaries and borders of what constitutes the 'self' and the 'other' are employed in this process. This process of discursive othering is especially important because political discourse is about both ideational aspects and material characteristics (Bacchi 1999; Lazar 2000), where ideational interpretations are often more important than empirical facts. Processes of othering thus create the meaning of both 'us' and 'others'. The nominal strategies employed in deciding who belongs and who does not can be different or can centre on different nominal categories, and this also affects the predicative elements present in the discourse; that is, the 'self' is portrayed more positively than the 'other' in different ways, given that the topoi of justification are different. In this way intangible borders can be more important than physical ones: borders are fundamental not only for modern states but also for delineating the community against 'the others'.

Let us define identity, escaping the 'uneasy amalgam of constructivist language and essentialist argumentation' (Brubaker and Cooper 2000: 6), as being neither primordial nor instrumental but contingent and contextual. Contingency is used to refer to a particular type of group self-identification along multiple axes of identification, salient in group interaction. The particular expression of identity is a function of the conjunction and constellation of different factors; that is, it is contextual. In this sense, while identity is historically constructed, it is always relational and multiple: a particular self-identification is chosen because of a particular context (Bush and Keyman 1997).

The meaning of collective identity is formed by its content and its relational features, denoting that the creation of the in-group identity will produce competitive behaviour with out-groups, a process of social contestation not only within the group, but also between the groups (Abdelal and Herrera 2001). Political discourse can drive this contestation, where borders and boundaries become the key points of interaction between the groups, each seeking recognition from the others for its identity. This becomes even more relevant for mass migration as this phenomenon will challenge traditional community boundaries, bringing new, often culturally very distant groups into contact with each other, thus exacerbating discourses over identity (and the need to protect that identity) at the centre of political contestation.

Public discourse is set in terms of agendas and public frames. These agendas and frames focus public interest on particular subjects in particular ways because 'both the selection of objects for attention and the selection of frames for thinking about these objects are powerful agenda-setting roles' (McCombs and Shaw 1993: 62). Discursive framing is a tool capable of shifting people's attitudes by making aspects of certain issues more salient through different modes of presentation (McCombs 2004). It is frames that give meaning to particular events and construct reality for the general public. Frames shape identities, values and perceptions of both the 'self' and the 'others', since boundaries of the 'self' are often constructed with reference to the 'other' to mark the differences between insiders and outsiders. In political discourse this often translates into the 'self' being positively, the 'other' negatively portrayed. The discursive forms of 'us' vs 'them', the issues of inclusion and exclusion or the making of boundaries and borders between communities are central to identity formation. In this sense, discursive othering is a process of bordering, the way 'we' is defined that excludes 'them,' the particularity of the community being marked by language, tradition or cultural attributes – be they real or imagined – that are shared among the members of the community (Wodak 2007a; 2007b; Yuval-Davis 1997). Using processes of othering in discursive practices often serves to justify the legitimacy of political action and strategy and consequently conditions the identity formation for both 'us' and 'them' (Jensen 2011). Similarly, if 'the other' is portrayed as posing threats to society/national interest, this will result in clear blame attribution to those allegedly responsible for this problem (Meeusen and Jacobs 2017).

Quantitative content analysis and qualitative framing analysis show how the public discourse is set in terms of agendas and public frames. This chapter examines the speeches, declarations, interviews or press statements delivered by Orbán between 2010 and 2018. This choice is warranted by the absolute power Orbán enjoys over his highly centralised party, Fidesz. This control grants Orbán an ultimate say in any policy matter, making him the primary author of current Hungarian public political discourse as well as political strategy. All the speeches have been made available in both Hungarian and English on the government website; I use the English texts for the purposes of this analysis. While the texts contain all types of speeches, from public talks to press statements to notes on opening factories, all speeches are treated the same for the purposes of analysis. All the speeches have been chronologically numbered starting with the 2010 election victory speech.

The Hungarian context

Nationalism and identity politics have been important for Eastern and Central European developments ever since post-Communist regime change. Hungary is a peculiar case since one of the top priorities of democratic Hungarian governments has been the protection of Hungarians abroad (the country having lost two-thirds of its territory and a third of its people to its neighbours after World War I), thought to be best achieved by providing an exemplary system of minority accommodation and extensive self-governance for minority communities living in Hungary (Bárdi 2013). Although Hungarian minority accommodation has been inclusive and liberal, this is nevertheless not to suggest that Hungarian society has ever been this accommodative. Public opinion polls have shown that chauvinism and xenophobia have been common among ordinary Hungarians (e.g. Simonovits and Bernát 2016: 41). The same can be said about the political arena: ever since regime change, the radical right has enjoyed popular support due to nationalism, anti-Semitism and anti-Roma sentiments common in society (Karácsony and Róna 2011). In fact, Jobbik's rise to success was due to the extensive media coverage of the party's paramilitary wing, the Hungarian Guard Movement (Biró Nagy et al. 2013), founded to fight 'gypsy crime' (Karácsony and Róna 2011) and to protect Hungarians.

The radical right's pan-Hungarian agenda, open racism and anti-Semitism might have contributed to the continued shift to the right of the mainstream governing party, Orbán's Fidesz (Minkenberg 2013). It is commonly accepted in the literature that radical right parties can exercise influence on mainstream parties largely through their interaction with each other. Studies of party manifesto data show that there is a 'contagion effect' in policies towards immigrants (Norris 2005; Alonso and da Fonseca 2012); or, as Schain (2006) has argued, mainstream centre right parties readjust their policy preferences – even if radicals are not part of the governing coalition or the legislative parliament – to respond to the eventual success of radical parties in order to pre-empt the erosion of their electoral support (Bustikova and Kitschelt 2009), following the logic of the spatial model of party competition (Downs 1957). Yet, even if one does not deny the effect of the far right, changes might be less direct or timely than one could expect, since any policy effect could be moderated by interaction on multiple levels: among the parties, parliamentary presence and executive actions (Minkenberg 2001). Although we cannot tell what would have been if Jobbik had not been present, one should also keep in mind that Fidesz has been in a super-majority in parliament for most of the time since 2010, and thus has no strategic need to adapt to far right (or any other) demands. In fact, there has been almost no interaction either in parliament or in executive action between Fidesz and Jobbik, although Fidesz has adopted and implemented numerous Jobbik proposals in its policies since 2010.

Based on the above, Hungarian societal attitudes as well as party preferences provide solid ground for identity-based politics. State-building processes in Central and Eastern Europe are 'shaped by elite and popular visions of the state [. . .] as well as by perceived threats to its integrity and welfare' (Culic 2009: 9). Well aware of this, Orbán has been using identity fears to rally support for his illiberal politics. The centrality of identity is shown by the fact that there is no programmatic appeal to the voter: Fidesz has no party programme, the party winning national and European elections since 2010 without producing a manifesto. To see how Orbán employs different conceptions of identity to legitimise his rule, let us proceed and examine how processes of discursive othering or boundary-making are conceptualised in Orbán's discourse both for defining the Hungarian 'self' and for delimiting 'the others,' and how different populist elements are employed in the discourse to rally the people's support for these conceptions.

Although some define populism as a specific organisation type (Taggart 2004), or a specific rhetoric employed by politicians (Betz 2002), or a political style (Moffitt and Tormey 2014), I treat populism as a

> thin-centered ideology that considers society to be ultimately separated into two homogeneous and antagonistic groups, 'the pure people' and 'the corrupt elite', and which argues that politics should be an expression of the *volonté general* (general will) of the people. (Mudde 2004: 543)

As such, anti-elitist rhetoric is not necessarily populist; instead, 'the pure people, the corrupt elite, and the general will' together make up populist ideology (Mudde and Kaltewasser 2013: 151). Populism could thus be both inclusive and exclusive, depending on how it views the borders between the 'people' and the 'elite', and who is or what groups are excluded discursively from the category of 'the people'. Radical right populist discourse also relies on radical frames, the core element of which is often a romantic myth of a homogeneous nation (Minkenberg 2013; see also Ignazi 2003; Mudde 2007). Other traditional themes and frames associated with populist discourse are the reference to crisis, breakdown or threat; an appeal to the people; its anti-establishment, anti-elite character; and the bad manners that have entered public talk (Moffitt and Tormey 2014). Let us focus on how the boundaries between 'us' and the 'other' are constructed and how these change over time, and what populist themes and frames are present and how these interact with processes of othering.

Orbán's discourse 2010–14:
economic nationalism to fight against foreign capital

A quick overview of the keyword-based quantitative analysis of Orbán's speeches for the time of his second government, 2010–14 (Orbán and Fidesz had been in power in 1998–2002), reveals that his primary theme has been the financial/economic crisis (see Table 2.1), which hit Hungary particularly hard. The keyword 'crisis' appears almost 400 times in the speech transcripts, making it the sole most important topic; no other issue has been mentioned this frequently. The Hungarian economy is mentioned 160 times and markets 137 times, clearly marking that the discourse is primarily economy focused. Orbán also speaks about the need to 'protect' (134 mentions)

Table 2.1 Keyword frequency scores of Orbán's speeches, 2010–14 and 2014–18

Sample keywords/phrases	2010–14	2014–18
Against Hungary	10	38
Alien	1	18
Asylum/asylum seeker	0	105
Banker	10	8
Banks	96	60
Border(s)	90	1281
Boundary	0	42
Breakdown	0	2
Christianity	175	529
Citizenship	5	24
Civil	3	70
Constitution	118	467
Crisis	398	416
Debt crisis /sovereign debt	5	24
Diaspora	4	47
Disintegration	15	26
Economic crisis	73	39
Elite	13	127
Ethnic	3	54
EU	71	567
European countries	40	188
European crisis	17	0
European Union	319	1320
Eurozone crisis	1	1
Faith	60	126
Fence	0	219
Financial crisis	10	47
Foreigners	9	65
Fundamental Law	25	65
Gate	14	53
George Soros	0	163
God	61	163
Hungarian citizen	7	50
Hungarian culture/traditions	3	69
Hungarian Diaspora Council	0	6
Hungarian economy	160	121
Hungarian family	39	60

(continued)

Sample keywords/phrases	2010–14	2014–18
Hungarian identity	0	3
Hungarian nation	50	122
Hungarian Standing Conference	1	12
Hungarians	427	1390
Hungarians in	4	55
Immigration /immigrant	2	767
Islam	4	55
Islamic State	0	13
Language	73	79
Market	137	268
Migration /migrant	13	1616
Migration/refugee crisis	0	87
Multinationals	30	23
Muslim	0	86
National identity	5	42
National unity	3	16
NGO	3	71
Our	1870	6359
Our lives	38	94
People of Hungary	74	27
Pray	9	13
Protect	134	909
Protection of national interest	2	21
Refugee	3	266
Religion	34	100
Security	48	462
Socialist	37	111
Soli Deo Gloria	9	9
Soros	0	308
Sovereignty	15	149
Stand on its own	5	12
Terrorism	10	335
Threat	29	288
Trust	96	116
Unity	36	327
Us	648	3043
Speeches numbered	*1–142*	*143–565*

Hungary and Hungarians (mentioned almost 600 times in different configurations). It is interesting to note that all the speeches focus solely on the national group: foreigners, aliens, migration or immigration are barely mentioned at all, making the discourse entirely inward-looking.

At the same time, Orbán's discourse relies heavily on the perception of crisis, breakdown, threat or lack of security – one of the key elements of populist discourse. The financial crisis is evoked in order to justify decisive and immediate action (meaning unorthodox economic policy) to protect against the threats Hungary is facing. Hungarian identity is portrayed solely in economic terms and the financial crisis is a threat to this economic 'self'. It is little wonder that the 'others' are also constructed in financial terms: banks and bankers (106 mentions) and multinationals (30 mentions) stand for multinational capital that is portrayed positioned against the Hungarian economy. On the same note, the discourse also blames the former elite, the previous left-socialist governments, for their incompetence that supposedly led to the crisis. Once again, the economic-financial crisis is portrayed as an existential threat: 'the serious economic crisis [. . .] threatened to push Hungary into bankruptcy' (Speech 36), and in Orbán's discourse, those threatening Hungary are the multinationals, banks, international financial institutions and EU bureaucrats. Orbán is ready to fight these 'others', claiming 'we do not wince with respect to anybody; not from the raised voices of multinational companies, nor from the threats of the bankers, nor from the negative forecasts of financial circles, nor from the raised fingers of Brussels bureaucrats' (Speech 100).

Contrary to what one could expect, cultural dimensions of Hungarian identity are not mentioned at all by Orbán. Hungarian culture or traditions appear only 3 times in the entire period, which in turn only underlines the fact that the focus is on the Hungarian 'self' in economic crisis. The most often used cultural marker of Hungarian identity is language (73 mentions), which for Orbán is the source of Hungarian uniqueness: 'our language is a very unique one, a very ancient one, and is closer to logic and mathematics than to the other languages' (Speech 68). Language thus becomes the main identifier for ethnicity, since Hungarian is a language that no one else speaks in the world and one can 'only remain Hungarian if it is possible to live in the land of one's birth while preserving its language' (Speech 81). In this setting, language becomes an important marker of belonging, 'a secret code for Hungarians that generates the feeling that we belong to the same family' (Speech 68). Yet at the same time, language also becomes a barrier, a division line that defines both the 'self' and the 'other' since, as Orbán himself notes, it is the peculiar language that 'excludes us from the world and encloses us within our own' (Speech 69), excluding all 'others'.

Moreover, Christianity and Christian roots (175 mentions) also become cultural markers of Hungarian identity. This is well illustrated by the fact that the reference to Christianity has no religious meaning in Orbán's discourse. The borderline between the 'self' and the 'other' is not constructed in a religious sense, as no reference to other religions is ever made (Islam mentioned only in reference to Arab countries, Muslims never mentioned). In this way, Christianity is portrayed not as a religion but rather as a cultural or civilisational boundary of the 'self', an identity marker for Hungarianness, portrayed as a set of values, standards and behaviour, as well as a source of the traditional family model. Christianity thus becomes a part of national identity and also delineates Hungary against more secular Europe. Orbán even claims Christianity must be protected against a secular pressure that is common in Europe: 'we must face up against those European political and intellectual trends and forces which aim to push back and undermine Christian culture, Christian civilisation and Christian values' (Speech 15). The Christian roots of Hungarian identity in turn are to provide Hungary with a high moral stance against immoral creditors, because 'work, credit, family, nation [. . .] have become dissolved from the moral foundations that Christianity provided' and 'the loans which our countries are suffering from no longer have any relation to any kind of moral principles' (Speech 15). Christianity thus becomes the borderline between capitalist interest and national sovereignty, understood mainly in economic terms.

Orbán barely discusses citizenship (mentioned only 5 times), though this should be one of the most important markers of the Hungarian community, clearly marking the borderlines of both national and political belonging. In contrast, he does mention 'borders' and 'gates' more often (90 and 14 mentions respectively), yet most of this talk is about the Hungarians beyond the borders of Hungary – as already noted, a topic enjoying special status within Hungarian politics. More importantly, this is the only issue where, instead of new delineations or conflict lines being drawn up, we see Orbán calling for dismantling the borders. Hungary adopted a new law of citizenship granting dual citizenship for Hungarians abroad in 2010 and, as Orbán points out, 'the new era of Hungarian national construction arrived: the unification of the nation, irrespective of borders' (Speech 81). As such, dual citizenship is portrayed as a political tool to reunite the Hungarian nation, irrespective of state borders. In this way, state borders that keep the Hungarian nation apart disappear, since 'those who live in the Carpathian Basin and expatriates who live further afield, must be regarded as full members of the Hungarian nation' (Speech 96). Last but not least, even the unification of the nation is presented as part of Hungary's struggle for economic sovereignty:

> We fought for our own Constitution, for the reunification of our nation and for our economic and financial autonomy. We fought for the families who had found themselves in difficulties because of foreign currency based loans, for our central bank, for the reinforcement of our state and for our tax system that rewards work instead of punishing it. (Speech 92)

While Orbán is ready to propagate a new paradigm, in which state borders become porous for the purposes of uniting the Hungarian nation, and the term 'Hungarians beyond the borders' (a term used for ethnic kin living in neighbouring countries) loses meaning (Speech 74), this does not mean he welcomes a borderless world. Instead, he wants to strengthen national sovereignty and state borders to resist European integration and globalisation that Orbán blames for the economic downturn. Part of the blame for the financial crisis is put on foreign investors who have taken the profits outside of Hungary's borders, and Orbán claims he is 'building a country in which people don't work for the profit of foreigners' (Speech 26). The sanctity of borders is also necessary for securing Hungary's economic interest against unrestricted global capital, so profits that 'slipped out of the country and went to these big, international companies, will from now on not slip across the border, they will remain in Hungary' (Speech 114) and even 'fraud that went beyond our borders' (Speech 90) can be curbed.

The discourse of economic insecurity is filled with other populist discursive strategies. Orbán often speaks as one of the people, identifying with the 'true people', the true Hungarians: 'Because I am familiar with our kind, I also know that Hungarians dislike "spoon-fed talk"' (Speech 26). This is best seen in the frequency of his reference to 'us' and 'our', by far the most frequent keywords in the transcripts of the speeches. Orbán's discourse is also loaded with anti-elite and anti-establishment claims: he challenges the established financial institutions or EU institutions, while the past elite are to be blamed for present-day economic difficulties: 'leaders who, professing a philosophy of "let us eat and drink, for tomorrow we die", or at least tomorrow we will not be in government, were capable of casting whole countries into debt' (Speech 15). An important boundary is drawn between the former elite and the people, since 'the essence of socialist and communist politics [is] to build a political construct based on the bad in people' (Speech 39). This anti-elite or anti-establishment attitude grants Orbán the possibility of distancing himself from his predecessors and claiming that in a sense he is not part of the political elite but speaks in the name of the people and the common will of the people: 'We felt that we had been cheated, that the Hungarian people were being cheated, and through them the Hungarian Government, and then we said, let's start using a different tone of voice' (Speech 129).

All these suggest that using economic fears, Orbán has successfully reconceptualised the Hungarian 'self' solely in economic terms. At the same time, discursive processes of othering have made the IMF, the EU and foreign capital become 'the other' that must be opposed. There is no room for cultural markers in such conceptions of the 'self' or the 'other' besides the reference to Christianity that is hijacked as an identity marker: on the one hand, Hungary stands for traditional values and lifestyles, while on the other hand, all 'others' stand for the modern, globalised world and economy. Using the same processes, former elites or critics of Hungarian economic reforms or political changes are also excluded from the category of 'us' and are declared enemies of national interests. This means a reconceptualisation of the (right) people, of the nation, which is not only uniquely Hungarian but at the same time is not the collective of all people any longer, but it is more selective – the political opposition or critics of Orbán are excluded.

Orbán's discourse 2014–18: exclusivist national populism to fight against migration

Turning to the speeches of the third Orbán government (2014–18), we see a major turn in the political discourse that results in a complete redrawing of the boundaries of Hungarian identity. The change occurs in the beginning of 2015, when Orbán first speaks against mass migration, well before Hungary becomes the centre of the 2015 European refugee crisis. In his State of the Nation Address (27 February 2015, Budapest), he states liberal multiculturalism is a dead option because migration brings 'people, many of whom are unwilling to accept European culture, or who come here with the intent of destroying European culture'. This anti-migrant discourse only further radicalises over time, Orbán soon declaring 'immigration brings crime and terrorism to our countries' (15 March 2016, National Day speech, Budapest). While issues of migration, refugees, asylum seekers or immigration never made it onto the public agenda until 2015, now these become the main topic – approximately half of Orbán's speeches of this period address these issues.

The same radical anti-migrant discourse can be read from the keyword frequency analysis (see Table 2.1), the most striking change being that while mentions of 'crisis' remain at the same level for 2014–18 as they were for 2010–14, mentions of the terms 'migration', 'refugees' and 'asylum' rocket, showing a hundred-fold increase. No other search term shows such extraordinary change for the two time periods examined, which again only underlines that issues of migration have become the sole most important topic for 2014–18. There is also a visible imbalance between the different terms Orbán uses in his discourse with reference to the refugee crisis: the terms 'migrants' and 'immigrant' are used five times more often than the term 'refugee' or 'asylum seeker'. This is not by chance but a clear indication of Orbán's stance: he considers these people not as refugees but rather as migrants, who come to Europe mainly for economic reasons. This is important because conceptualising 'the other' not as somebody in need of help or support, but rather as one seeking economic benefit, in turn means no obligation (or an exemption from offering relief or assistance) for Hungary or the Hungarians.

Economic issues and the financial crisis lose their importance in Orbán's discourse after 2014, well testified by the keyword scores, which are by magnitudes lower than migration scores. More importantly, the 'self' is being discursively reconceptualised together with the redrawing of the 'other', now portrayed either in the image of 'the migrant' or as the EU and its common refugee policy system that would impose refugee quotas on Hungary. While at the time of the financial crisis, international financial organisations and the EU with its institutions were blamed for economic mismanagement, now the EU and its institutions and collective mechanisms, as well as the more liberal European countries, are blamed for bringing migration to Hungary. This reconfigured process of 'othering' is also noticeable in the descriptive statistics of the keyword analysis. There is an abundance of negative references to the EU in the discourse; moreover, there is a significant, four-fold increase in the number of occurrences of 'EU' and 'European Union', suggesting even more blame for the EU and its institutions for Hungary's troubles with the refugee crisis. In this conceptualisation of the EU as the 'other', although Hungary remains within the borders of European civilisation, it is sharply distinguished – in fact opposed to – the EU and its liberal core. Once again, Orbán is not shy of battling this liberal 'other' to ensure that traditional Hungarian identity is preserved: 'Then we will have a battle with the European Union. [...] because the EU wants to implement the mandatory relocation quota and force us to accept it' (Speech 372).

While in 2010–14 Orbán was preoccupied with protecting Hungarian interest and security, conceived mainly in financial terms, from 2015 he similarly only talks about the multiple threats Hungary must face due to migration. Threats have become even more central to understanding of the Hungarian 'self', as illustrated by references to the need for protection or security, which have increased more than five times in his speeches (from just above 200 to more than 1,500 mentions of 'threat', 'protect' and 'security'). According to Orbán, migration is not only a cultural threat to Hungary alone, but a 'clash of civilisations' between Christian Europe and Muslim migrants: 'this change facing Europe – or which, in my opinion, is threatening Europe – can also have an effect at deeper, civilisational layers. The identity of civilisation in Europe could change' (Speech 251). In this way the alien 'other' is understood as not only culturally but also civilisationally different, further distancing the in-group from the out-group, now portrayed as civilisations apart.

This new focus on reinforcing cultural or civilisational borders in Orbán's discourse can also be noticed by examining his reference to Hungary and the Hungarians. First of all, the number of these references has more than doubled as compared to the 2010–14 period. More interestingly, while in the first period, Orbán referred to the Hungarian nation and Hungarians in general terms without much reference to culture, and also quite often used the term 'people of Hungary,' now his discourse barely talks about 'people of Hungary' (only 27 mentions compared to 74 previously) and includes many more references to Hungarian culture and traditions (up from 3 to 69 mentions). This signals that the meaning of 'us' has changed as well: there is no more space for abstract citizens; Hungarian identity has become more interwoven with ethnicity, culture and tradition, a unique civilisation:

Being a Hungarian is a mission, a task, a job of work: to maintain, strengthen and carry forward a great, lonely, thousand-year-old civilisation, built on the Hungarian language and on the foundations of the Hungarian mentality, and surrounded by dissimilar nations. (Speech 398)

This stands for an essentialist, if not a primordialist understanding of identity, in the name of which all other cultures or identities are to be excluded from the national community, as stated in the National Avowal, a prelude to the constitution: 'We commit to promoting and safeguarding our heritage, our unique language, Hungarian culture'. Orbán states that 'the Hungarian government is not in a position to support mass movements of population which would result in a situation conflicting with [this] passage'. (Speech 335).

Surrounded by threatening 'others,' the protection of Hungary's borders becomes paramount for the survival of the nation because 'each nation is defined by its borders' (Speech 257). According to Orbán, 'a country with no borders is not a country at all . . . if there is a country, and if they want it to remain, then it must be able to defend its borders' (Speech 265). This is also the reason why the usage of the term 'border(s)' shows an outstanding twelve-fold increase (from 90 to 1,281 mentions). Orbán also talks specifically about the physical border, the 'fence' that his government built on the southern border (more than 200 mentions), which was erected to stop migrants. In this way, the once invisible borderline of the country materialises in concrete form as the 'fence on the border, which lets everyone know where the Hungarian border is; crossing it or even attempting to cross it at a point other than the designated crossings qualifies as a crime' (Speech 264). Protecting Hungary's borders means protecting Europe, because stopping illegal migration diminishes the threats to 'Europe's essence [that] lies in its spiritual and cultural identity' (Speech 283). Orbán claims that building fences on the external borders will also protect the internally borderless Europe, since 'if we cannot protect our external borders, Schengen will be in danger' (Speech 260). Accordingly, Hungary's borders are to become impenetrable and be protected with 'police officers, soldiers and weapons' (Speech 344), since border protection cannot be done with 'flowers and cuddly toys' (Speech 340).

The reinforcement and rearmament of the borders also draw a line between Orbán and the globalised world, since he claims 'sovereignty, and the organisation of the lives of communities, must be taken care of within the limits of state borders' (Speech 354). Similarly to what we have seen for the speeches of the first period, a borderless world is only available to the Hungarian kin living beyond Hungary's borders, who are welcome to the national community. This is not only an extension of Hungary's borders to include its kin abroad, but also a conscious nation-building effort as Hungarians abroad are supposed to contribute to the greatness of the country: 'I would like the Hungarian diaspora to form links not only with the mother country, but also with the other communities of the Carpathian Basin. This would be an approach which is worthy of a world nation' (Speech 391).

For Orbán, the rejection of mandatory refugee quotas is as important as securing citizenship for the co-nationals: 'the referendum on dual citizenship, which was a national issue of similar proportions, is on the same level as the current question [of mandatory refugee quotas]' (Speech 356). As such, all those that belong to the nation conceived in ethnic terms have the option of membership in the political community, notwithstanding state borders, while all others – even those who are part of the EU refugee allocation scheme – are to be excluded from both citizenship and the understanding of the national self: 'only those who have permission from our elected parliament, government or some other official state body can enter the territory of Hungary, can settle here and live here with us' (Speech 356). This is why border protection becomes more important than the refugee quota. In fact, Orbán claims 'only when we have protected our borders can we ask questions such as how many people we want to receive, or if there should be quotas' (Speech 260).

Opposition to international migration and globalisation can also be noted in Orbán's transformed use of religious references in his discourse. While until 2015, Orbán talked about Christianity not as a religion but rather as an identity marker or a source of morality, since 2015 this reference to Christianity gains a religious meaning. Religion becomes part of the processes of 'othering' in contrasting Christianity or Christian values with Islam and Muslims, terms that Orbán never mentioned previously. In this way, the religion of the 'other' is linked to migration, and in consequence faith becomes an important barrier between 'us' and 'them': Islam or Muslims are portrayed as foreign or alien to both Hungarians and Christian Europe. Orbán is clearly biased in favour of Christian Hungary, declaring Christianity to be above Islam and Hungarian identity or culture above all others, particularly non-European cultures. This supremacy of the nation and its Christian belief makes his public discourse clearly anti-Islam or anti-Muslim, as Orbán readily admits: 'to be clear and unequivocal, I can say that in Hungary Islamisation is subject to a constitutional ban' (Speech 335).

This very exclusionist understanding of Hungarian and European 'self' identity, culture or religion, with no place for non-European or non-Christian migrants, can also be found in other aspects of Orbán's speeches that all serve the discursive conceptualisation of 'the other' as not only culturally and religiously different but threatening to the 'self.' The constructed image of the threat to security is used not only to create civilisational borders between Europeans and the migrants but also to keep the 'others' away from Europe: 'If we allow a competition to evolve between two civilisations here, in Europe, we Christians will lose' (Speech 264). Moreover, migration is linked to criminality, since 'wherever there are large numbers of immigrants, crime rates increase' (Speech 285), and even to terrorism: 'not all [migrants] have come with good intentions; in the wake of all this, to distribute these people among the countries of Europe is nothing short of distributing the threat of terrorism or terrorists' (Speech 285). The conception of the 'other' as a security threat to the 'self' is best illustrated by Orbán's talk about terrorism: while until 2014, terrorism was not a subject of public talk (10 mentions), since 2014, terrorism and terrorist organisation are mentioned approximately 335 times. Orbán claims it is 'the free flow of people without any controls or checks [that] creates the risk of terrorism' (Speech 471), which again only makes the call for border fences and stringent border protection measures more urgent.

On another note, Orbán's discourse not only is increasingly nationalist but continues to use the very same populist strategies that he has relied upon from 2010 onwards. The only difference is that after 2015, Hungarian interest has been reconfigured from a protection of Hungarian economy to the protection of Hungarian culture and European civilisation from mainly Muslim immigration. Orbán continuously re-creates the image of crisis and threats that is then accompanied by appeals to the people for support. He portrays himself as a national saviour, speaking in the name of the nation, serving national interest or the people's will: 'In the past few years we have achieved far more than we might think. Today once more, deep down a strong Hungarian nation is being forged' (Speech 238).

Not only does Orbán claim to be the representative of ordinary people but his discourse is anti-elite (although his government has been in power since 2010), claiming leaders are disconnected from reality: the European elite 'is sitting in a closed, ideological shell, which means it has hardly any connection to reality' (Speech 299) and the former leftist government was 'closing its eyes and ears to a fundamentally important issue and ploughing ahead regardless of what the people are saying' (Speech 356). Orbán portrays himself and his government as the true voice that speaks in the name of the Hungarian people and community, in the service of the national interest, which is perceived as an ultimate goal, above all other considerations: 'The prevailing political leadership has today attempted to ensure that people's personal work and interests, which must be acknowledged, are closely linked to the life of the community and the nation, and that this relationship is preserved and reinforced' (Speech 219). Once again, only members of the 'true community' matter, and success is a matter of preserving and cherishing the boundaries of this community because 'we shall either be successful together or not at all. Either we all advance together, or we all sink into the mud' (Speech 238).

In the same way, Orbán's anti-EU discourse has only strengthened since 2015. The EU continues to be a threatening 'other' for the exclusionist understanding of the Hungarian 'self'. Hungary, although a member state, is in opposition to the EU, since

> we alone, Hungarians who live here and who claim this country as our own, can decide [. . .] we must reject all EU and Brussels attempts and designs which seek to take from us and assign to someone else the right to decide. (Speech 294)

Once again, borders increase in importance, since they divide those who can have a say from those who cannot, and decision is reserved only for the 'true people' that are represented legitimately by Orbán and his government alone. In this light, rejecting the refugee quota system is not a simple disagreement between the EU and Hungary but an existential fight that pervades every aspect of policy, since Orbán claims that 'the procedures which have been instituted against Hungary in the last few days in a variety of legal forms can be seen as a kind of revenge for the fact that we have dared to confront Brussels' immigration policy' (Speech 294).

Although Orbán claims Hungary is the defender of Europe, situated at the continent's border, being 'the continent's gatehouse and bastion' (Speech 439), the discursively constructed division between Europe and Hungary is irreconcilable. Ever since 2010, Hungary has been positioned against the rest of Europe. The only exceptions to this division within Europe are the Visegrád Four (V4) countries, since Orbán's Central European neighbours have joined Hungary and also support national sovereignty over integration: 'they also have strong identities'

(Speech 472). This signals the increased importance of regional borders – or the creations of new borders within EU borders – to distinguish between different parts of Europe that stand in opposition to each other. Moreover, creating regional borders, Orbán not only re-creates the divide between East and West Europe or old and new members of the EU, but also claims the East can now stand up against the West, correcting the past imbalance: 'I would like to make it clear that Central Europe has entered an era in which it is apparently quite able to stand on its own two feet, and is able to define itself' (Speech 322).

Conclusions and discussion

Ever since Orbán entered office in 2010, his political discourse has been focused on discursively creating the image of existential crisis (or crises) and the enemies of the nation to be blamed for this crisis (or crises). This means that identity politics are at the centre of Orbán's discourse, with a constant discursive reconstruction of both the 'self' and the 'others', where the 'other' is not only different but threatening: foreign capital is to be blamed for Hungary's near bankruptcy, while migration is linked to bringing criminality and terrorism to Hungary. The only important change in this discourse of the crisis happens in 2015, when the previous populist narrative of economic insecurity is replaced by the narrative that Hungary is experiencing an existential threat because of migration pressure on its borders. In this way Orbán's discourse has shifted from a standard populist discourse of economic nationalism to what I call the discourse of populist nationalism, where politics is based on a national identity that is characterised by exclusionary views of 'us' and 'them', where the rights of the nation stand above all others: the political opposition, multinationals, the EU or individual migrants. According to Orbán's discourse of populist nationalism, the world is Manichaean and is posing multiple threats to Hungary: there is a cultural threat of non-European migrants, traditional values are challenged by the pressure of globalisation, and the world order based on liberal democracy challenges sovereignty, which in turn endangers the survival of the national community.

Orbán discursively creates the image of the threatening world to reject liberal democracy in favour of a world of state-sponsored intolerance, where the boundaries defining the community are solely reserved for ethnic Hungarians and all efforts must be made to prevent 'others' from watering down the uniqueness of the national 'self'. Orbán's discourse of populist nationalism thus stands for a discourse of xeno-phobic nationalism that is combined with populist elements: it challenges the establishment and the elite, while it sympathises and identifies with the 'true' people. As the discourse evolves, the people are defined more and more in ethnic terms, excluding all outsiders from the community, in a way that is opposed to the liberal understanding of national membership, which can be chosen or renounced individually (Brubaker 1994). The discourse is clearly not only anti-migrant or anti-Muslim but anti-European, since not only is Orbán sceptical about the merits of the EU but Brussels is often the scapegoat for Hungary's problems. In this way the EU, European elites and liberal democracy are perceived as 'others' even though Hungary claims to belong to the European community and culture and is often portrayed as the protector of Europe and its Christian values and traditions.

It is the processes of othering, bordering or redrawing the boundaries of the community that establish the conflict lines that stand between Hungarian traditional society and immigrants; between Hungary's national sovereignty and EU solidarity and commitment to Europeanisation; between 'illiberal democracy' and Europe with its common governance systems, secular organisation, religious tolerance and liberal foundation – as evidenced in Orbán's own words, taking stock of his regime's achievements:

> Money capitalism replaced by a work-based economy. Fragmentation replaced by citizenship and the unification of the nation. A system of liberal politics replaced by a system of national politics. Reinstating the rights of Christian culture instead of value neutrality. Liberal public morals replaced by the unconditional respect of human dignity. (Speech 201)

Notes

1. 'Hungary's "illiberalism" should not go unchallenged' (*Washington Post*, 16 August 2014); 'Orbán wants to build "illiberal state"' (*EUObserver*, 28 July 2014); 'Orbán the unstoppable' (*Economist*, 27 September 2014).
2. Party leader Gabor Vona told Reuters: 'I honestly want to transform Jobbik into a people's party and to do that I know what is necessary. I know when and where to draw the line', <http://www.euractiv.com/section/europe-s-east/news/hungary-s-far-right-jobbik-party-challenges-for-power> (last accessed 9 December 2019).

References

Abdelal, R., and Y. M. Herrera (2001) 'Treating identity as a variable: measuring the content, intensity, and contestation of identity.' Paper presented at the APSA, San Francisco, 30 August to 2 September.

Alonso, S., and S. C. da Fonseca (2012) 'Immigration, left and right.' *Party Politics* 18(6): 865–84.

Anderson, B. (1991) *Imagined Communities*. London: Verso.

Bacchi, C. L. (1999) *Women, Policy, and Politics*. London: Sage.

Bárdi, N. (2013) 'Magyarország és a kisebbségi magyar közösségek 1989 után.' *Metszetek -Társadalomtudományi folyóirat* 2–3: 40–79.

Betz, H. (2002) 'Conditions favoring the success and failure of radical right-wing populist parties in contemporary democracies.' Pp. 197–213 in *Democracies and the Populist Challenge*, edited by Y. Mény and Y. Surel. Basingstoke: Palgrave Macmillan.

Biró Nagy, A., T. Boros and Z. Vasali (2013) 'More radical than the radicals: the Jobbik party in international comparison.' Pp. 229–53 in *Right Wing Extremism in Europe: Country Analyses, Counter Strategies and Labor Market Oriented Exit Strategies*, edited by R. Melzer and S. Serafin. Berlin: Friedrich Ebert.

Brubaker, R. (1994) *Citizenship and Nationhood in France and Germany*. Cambridge, MA: Harvard University Press.

Brubaker, R., and F. Cooper (2000) 'Beyond identity.' *Theory and Society* 29(1): 1–47.

Bush, K. D., and F. E. Keyman (1997) 'Identity-based conflict: rethinking security in a post-Cold War world.' *Global Governance* 3(3): 311–28.

Bustikova, L., and H. Kitschelt (2009) 'The radical right in post-Communist Europe: comparative perspectives on legacies and party competition.' *Communist and Post-Communist Studies* 42(4): 459–83.

Christiansen, T., K. E. Jørgensen and A. Wiener (eds) (1999) *The Social Construction of Europe*. London: Sage.

Culic, I. (2009) 'Dual citizenship policies in Central and Eastern Europe.' *Working Papers in Romanian Minority Studies* 15: 5–36.

Downs, A. (1957) *An Economic Theory of Democracy*. New York: Harper.

Dryzek, J. S. (2005) *The Politics of the Earth: Environmental Discourses*. Oxford: Oxford University Press.

Enyedi, Z. (2016) 'Populist polarization and party system institutionalization.' *Problems of Post-Communism* 63(4): 210–20, <https://doi.org/10.1080/10758216.2015.1 113883> (last accessed 9 December 2019).

Gellner, E. (1983) *Nations and Nationalism*. Ithaca: Cornell University Press.

Ignazi, P. (2003) *Extreme Right Parties in Western Europe*. Oxford: Oxford University Press.

Jensen, S. Q. (2011) 'Othering, identity formation and agency.' *Qualitative Studies* 2(2): 63–78.

Karácsony, G., and D. Róna (2011) 'The secret of Jobbik: reasons behind the rise of the Hungarian radical right.' *Journal of East European and Asian Studies* 2(1): 61–92.

Lazar, M. M. (2000) 'Gender, discourse and semiotics: the politics of parenthood representations.' *Discourse and Society* 11(3): 373–400.

Lazar, M. M. (ed.) (2005) *Feminist Critical Discourse Analysis: Gender, Power and Ideology in Discourse.* New York: Palgrave Macmillan.

McCombs, M. E. (2004) *Setting the Agenda: The Mass Media and Public Opinion.* Malden, MA: Blackwell.

McCombs, M. E., and D. L. Shaw (1993) 'The evolution of agenda-setting research: twenty five years in the marketplace of ideas.' *Journal of Communication* 43(2): 58–67.

Meeusen, C., and L. Jacobs (2017) 'Television news content of minority groups as an intergroup context indicator of differences between target-specific prejudices.' *Mass Communication and* Society 20(2): 213–40.

Minkenberg, M. (2001) 'The radical right in public office: agenda-setting and policy effects.' *West European Politics* 24(4): 1–21.

Minkenberg, M. (2013) 'From pariah to policy-maker? The radical right in Europe, West and East: between margin and mainstream.' *Journal of Contemporary European Studies* 21(1): 5–24, <http://dx.doi.org/10.1080/14782804.2013.766473> (last accessed 9 December 2019).

Moffitt, B., and S. Tormey (2014) 'Rethinking populism: politics, mediatisation and political style.' *Political Studies* 62: 381–97.

Mudde, C. (2004) 'The populist zeitgeist.' *Government and Opposition* 39(4): 541–63.

Mudde, C. (2007) *Populist Radical Right Parties in Europe.* Cambridge: Cambridge University Press.

Mudde, C., and C. R. Kaltwasser (2013) 'Exclusionary vs. inclusionary populism: comparing contemporary Europe and Latin America.' *Government and Opposition* 48(2): 147–74.

Norris, P. (2005) *Radical Right: Voters and Parties in the Electoral Market.* Cambridge: Cambridge University Press.

Schain, M. A. (2006) 'The extreme-right and immigration policy-making: measuring direct and indirect effects.' *West European Politics* 29(2): 270–89, <https://doi.org/10.1080/01402380500512619> (last accessed 9 December 2019).

Simonovits, B., and A. Bernát (eds) (2016) *The Social Aspects of the 2015 Migration Crisis in Hungary.* Budapest: TÁRKI Social Research Institute. <http://old.tarki.hu/hu/news/2016/kitekint/20160330_refugees.pdf> (last accessed 4 November 2018).

Taggart, P. (2004) 'Populism and representative politics in contemporary Europe.' *Journal of Political Ideologies* 9(3): 269–88.

Tóth, C. (2014) 'Full text of Viktor Orbán's speech at Băile Tuşnad (Tusnádfürdő) of 26 July 2014.' *Budapest Beacon*, <https://budapestbeacon.com/full-text-of-viktor-orbans-speech-at-baile-tusnad-tusnadfurdo-of-26-july-2014> (last accessed 4 November 2018).

Weiss, G., and R. Wodak (2005) 'Analyzing EU discourses: theories and applications'. Pp. 121–36 in *A New Agenda in (Critical) Discourse Analysis*, edited by R. Wodak and P. Chilton. Amsterdam: John Benjamins.

Wodak, R. (ed.) (1997) *Gender and Discourse.* London: Sage.

Wodak, R. (2007a) 'Discourses in European Union organizations: aspects of access, participation and exclusion.' *Text & Talk* 27(5–6): 655–80.

Wodak, R. (2007b) '"Doing Europe": the discursive construction of European identities.' Pp. 70–94 in *Discursive Constructions of Identity in European Politics*, edited by R. C. Mole. London: Palgrave Macmillan.

Yuval-Davis, N. (1997) *Gender & Nation*. London: Sage.

3

Rethinking Refugee Integration: The Importance of Core Values for Cultural Debate in Germany

Aleksandra Koluvija

INTERNATIONALLY, GERMANY IS increasingly perceived as a major actor in integration policy, particularly as it has recently accepted many asylum seekers and had intense debates on their integration. From 2015 to 2017, nearly 1.4 million people applied for asylum in Germany and around 45 per cent of those received a protected status and legitimate right to remain (BAMF 2017: 48–50). The mass arrival of asylum seekers in such a short time span has rekindled an old debate on German cultural identity and approaches to the integration of foreigners into German culture. Much of the debate is sparked by the concern to preserve German identity in a process of acculturation. The process implies a confrontation with the identification of German core values and has rekindled a discussion on a 'guiding culture' (*Leitkultur*) and a 'welcoming culture' (*Willkommenskultur*). Beyond that, the mass arrival of refugees has had various socio-political implications and caused new developments in the German political and cultural setting.

Given that the integration debate in Germany is focusing on finding durable solutions where the host society and the refugee can peacefully coexist, this chapter focuses on the core parts of the integration debate. It proceeds as follows: the first section highlights definitions of the term 'integration' and notes the lack of a unique understanding of the term among different actors. The second section reviews refugee integration in Germany and shows that the predominant factor in various German definitions of integration is the refugees' willingness to internalise German identity, learn the language and seek employment. The third section focuses on the debate about integration and highlights how it is unclear what culture refugees should integrate into. The fourth and last section proposes ways to rethink German integration policies, arguing for applied observational research and a human rights perspective. As such, this chapter identifies the notion of integration as a lasting question with no definite answer, but suggests instead that integration is a learning process, which should continuously be observed through empirical studies and future scenario planning.

Defining integration

Although it lacks a formal, universally accepted definition, the notion of 'integration' is frequently used in the refugee context. The term is often used to frame the political means for dealing with the consequences of immigration. Thus, it is used to describe the process of social change that occurs when immigrants are integrated into the host society (Favell 1999: 3). What makes the term so complex is that integration has become a popular way to conceptualise the relationship between states and immigrant populations (Favell 1999: 1–4). In Germany, continued immigration has progressively made the view of the term more complex and intensified the debate on an adequate process of integration. The recent influx of asylum seekers only further intensified the debate, yet, despite the established use of the term 'integration' in connection with refugees, there is no consensus on a definition (UNHCR 2013).

There is a substantial amount of literature on the issue of definition, identifying key indicators and evaluating the effectiveness of integration programmes, yet there is no shared definition in the academic and policy discourse or international law (see e.g. Sezer 2010; UNHCR 2013; Auswärtiges Amt 2016; HRW 2016). With the high number of people seeking refuge, the lack of a definition ensures that integration remains a politically sensitive topic (see e.g. Penninx 2003; Penninx et al. 2008; Sezer 2010). Ager and Strang (2002: 6), on the other hand, argue that 'there is sufficient consensus on the character of an integrated community', and regard the finding of a definition as a not too difficult task and a 'goal to work towards'. They further explain that the objective of the definition should be to simplify the understanding of integration, without distorting key meanings and considerations.

In a basic sense the term 'integration' is a process of combining two or more things into one. Yet there are different definitions when it comes to the social context of integration. In a social context, the term refers to a dynamic and structured process in which all members participate in a dialogue to achieve and maintain peaceful social relations (UNDESA 2005). Social integration has to be distinguished from coerced assimilation or forced integration. It is more a process where an interaction between cultures results in a cultural and psychological change including elements of coexistence, collaboration and cohesion (UNDESA 2005). The UN refugee agency defined integration in 2007 as a

> dynamic and multifaceted two-way process which requires efforts by all parties concerned, including a preparedness on the part of refugees to adapt to the host society without having to forego their own cultural identity, and a corresponding readiness on the part of host communities and public institutions to welcome refugees and meet the needs of a diverse population. (UNHCR 2007: 1)

The definition highlights that integration is a two-way process with 'distinct but interrelated legal, economic, social and cultural dimensions, all of which are important for refugees' ability to integrate successfully as fully included members of society' (UNHCR 2007: 1). In 2013, the UNHCR defined integration as 'the end product of a dynamic and multifaceted two-way process with three interrelated dimensions: a legal, an economic and a social-cultural dimension'. The report further identifies that 'integration requires efforts by all parties concerned' (UNHCR 2013: 14). An attempt to define integration was also made by the European Council on Refugees and Exiles (ECRE). ECRE considers integration as a process of change, which includes three different domains: dynamic and two-way, long-term, and multidimensional. Integration is further explained as a process, which 'requires a preparedness [of the refugees] to adapt to the lifestyle of the host society without having to lose one's own cultural identity' (ECRE 2002: 4). This definition necessitates that the host society accepts refugees as part of the national community, so they can become active members from a legal, social, economic, educational and cultural perspective.

Scholars such as Ager and Strang (2002) add to the complexity domains of integration and outline, within each domain, indicators which should be considered when attempting to analyse the success of refugee integration processes. These scholars define 'integration' as a concept with three different indicators: the achievement of public outcomes (employment, housing, education, health etc.); a social connection with the community; and a sufficient linguistic competence and knowledge. Their definition further emphasises that integration is a 'two-way' process and puts into focus the importance of social connections of all members of society. Phillimore (2012: 11–13), who has tested their work empirically, discovered that 'integration was multifaceted, bringing together activities from across Ager and Strang's domains'. Phillimore further noted that integration is multidimensional and stressed the importance of interconnectedness. She found that effective integration projects 'focused on the development of social connections between individual refugees' (Phillimore 2012: 16–19).

Scholars such as Korac (2003: 52) explain that in the context of refugee studies, integration should be understood from a more practical or functional viewpoint. Her opinion is that since the settlement of refugees is more defined and implies access to certain rights and social services, finding a definition in the refugee context should be more straightforward. And while there is a debate over the term 'integration', some scholars will embrace the idea that 'integration' remains a somewhat chaotic concept, where the word is used by many, but understood differently by most (e.g. Robinson 1998). Many scholars will see little prospect of the formation of a unifying definition and argue that it will continue to be controversial and debated, while the lack of a single, generally accepted definition will persist (Robinson 1998; Castles et al. 2001).

In order to understand the concept of integration and disclose the importance of human rights in the integration process, this chapter uses the UNHCR definition quoted above. It is one of the most frequently quoted definitions and closely related to the work of the UN on the human rights-based approach to refugee integration. This definition assumes that integration requires efforts by all parties concerned, both the refugees and the host society, including references to moral, legal and economic considerations.

Refugee integration in Germany

In Germany, even actors directly involved in the integration sector will define integration differently and approach the integration process in different ways (see e.g. BMI 2019; Bundesregierung 2019; VHS-Berlin 2019). Nevertheless, the German government has put the basic concept of integration in the newly developed guiding principle of the 2016 Integration Act (*Integrationsgesetz*). This act aims at facilitating the integration of legitimate asylum seekers and to 'support and challenge' (*Fördern und Fordern*) immigrants in their integration process. On the basis of the Integration Act, the Federal Office for Migration and Refugees (BAMF) formulated the following definition:

> Integration is a long-term process. Its aim is to include everyone in society who lives in Germany on a permanent and legal basis. Immigrants should have the opportunity to participate fully in all areas of society on an equal standing. Their responsibility is to learn German and to respect and abide by the constitution and its laws. (BAMF 2019b)

According to this definition, the goal is to give immigrants the same opportunities as the native population to participate in the economic and social spheres. While the definition states the relevance of equality and a sense of togetherness, it also makes acclimatisation to German culture and language acquisition of high importance. In fact, the integration process in Germany officially begins with the integration courses of the BAMF. These are governmentally organised, funded and compulsory language courses for asylum applicants with good prospects of remaining in Germany. The integration course is designed to enable the participants to learn the values on which German society is based (BAMF 2019b). The course is regarded as the main pillar of integration and it is divided into a language and an orientation course (BAMF 2016). It covers topics from everyday life as well as German history, culture and politics, and concludes with a final test that allows access to subsequent German language and employment training.

Identifying truly German values, however, is still controversial due to ongoing integration debates. Nonetheless, access to knowledge on German history, culture, politics and values as well as a willingness to adapt to the values is part of the course and of the requirement to receive a permanent residency permit (BAMF 2016; BMAS 2016). This means that refugees who show the potential to integrate (e.g. through learning German and familiarising themselves with the culture) will have a good chance of a right to remain (BMAS 2016; Gesley 2016). The issue, however, is that such integration policies do not take into consideration the personal situation of refugees and therefore contravene the obligation to protect refugees.

Moreover, there is potential for discrimination against refugees who cannot meet the obligations (e.g. due to psychological reasons), as those who show the potential to integrate and have a good chance of staying permanently in Germany are provided with easier and faster access to integration classes and employment opportunities, while refugees who refuse to cooperate face a reduction in benefits (Gesley 2016).

Such practices are not unusual, as there is no specific legal obligation to ensure that the rights of refugees are protected in the integration process. The level of protection is based on the sovereign states' willingness to include human rights values in their integration measures (e.g. Barbulescu 2015; RSF 2017). This means that although Germany has signed most human rights treaties and embedded them in its Basic Law, there is still no explicit law to prevent discriminatory practice in its integration policies.

Scholars argue that such a discrepancy between legal standards of human rights protection and integration policies is due to political reasons, and that EU member states have established policies that guarantee only certain basic conditions of protections and rights to reduce the incentives to seek asylum in their country (e.g. Robila 2018: 9). Moreover, countries which have traditionally been more hospitable towards refugees can be overwhelmed by a large influx and turn to discriminating against them due to economic reasons (e.g. Mandel 1997: 82–3). Mandel explains that the reason for this is that 'refugees, asylum seekers and displaced people – especially in situations of mass influx – are universally regarded with negativity as a strain upon resources and a potential threat to stability, identity and social cohesion' (Mandel 1997: 82). This is particularly likely when refugees are quite dissimilar from the host society - ethnically, racially or religiously.

Traditionally, Germany bases its principle of nationality law on *jus sanguinis* (Latin: 'the right of blood') by which citizenship is determined or acquired through the German nationality or ethnicity of one or both parents. Germany has a comparatively short history of guest workers and only a very recent reinvention as an immigration country. Nonetheless, Germany witnessed the arrival of a large number of refugees, mostly from the Middle East, between 2015 and 2017. As these people are ethnically, racially and religiously different from the general German population, the risk of Germany becoming overwhelmed by the large influx of refugees and turning towards discriminating against them is apparent.

While Germany (with France and Greece) was one of the three main destinations of refugees in 2015–18 (Eurostat 2019), policies to integrate foreigners have become a key concern for most EU member states. That said, there is little information and few studies available on successfully integrated refugees in Germany. In fact, most studies focus on how language acquisition has led to, for example, higher employment rates for refugees (Danzer and Yaman 2010). There are also studies on the connection between integration costs and positive economic impulses in the host country (see e.g. Fratzscher and Junker 2015; Bach et. al 2017; BMAS 2017). Other studies focus on measures to integrate refugees into the labour market (Bertelsmann 2015). Brücker et al. (2016) collected data from asylum seekers arriving in Germany and attempted to give an insight into values which the interviewees regarded as important. Yet no study was found that further describes successful integration or bases its findings on the experience of refugees in the integration process.

Studies don't seem to go beyond factors such as language acquisition and employment in connection with what makes integration successful (Polzer 2008; Born and Schwefer 2016). This may either be because the recent influx of asylum seekers does not yet offer statistical results, or because successful integration is not yet defined and cannot be measured beyond factors such as language acquisition or employment experience.

On the other hand, a recent study performed by the German Federal Office for Migration and Refugees (BAMF 2019a) has discovered that refugees often suffer from mental health problems and that this slows down their integration process. According to the study, women, elderly refugees and people from Afghanistan are particularly at high risk of post-traumatic stress disorder. The study further highlights that finding professional help is difficult for refugees, as they are usually only entitled to treatment for serious physical complaints during the initial period. After that, long waiting times for a therapy place and a lack of mother-tongue therapists and interpreters make treatment difficult (BAMF 2019a). Nevertheless, such troubles with the integration process are not recorded in studies that use limited perceptions to measure successful integration systems.

The recent research results on the mental state of refugees suggests that there appears to be a lack of knowledge on how sufficient integration of refugees can be best performed or encouraged, and successful integration measured beyond language acquisition or employment rates. The reasons for such a lack of knowledge seems to be the established understanding of integration in Germany and how this is influenced by concerns to preserve the national identity in times of immigration (Zimmermann 2016).

The refugee integration debate in Germany

Nearly 890,000 people fled to Germany in 2015 (Brücker et al. 2016: 1), many of whom are likely to return to their homeland, but others will remain in Germany. Some of the asylum seekers have already received a legitimate right to remain in Germany, while others have not. To integrate all those with the legitimate right and desire to remain in Germany is considered an important task. As the Commissioner for Immigration, Refugees and Integration stated, 'for many, the country that gives them protection will become a new home' (Bundesregierung 2016). The Commissioner sees Germany's obligation to provide the living conditions needed to promote their integration. Integrating those with a legitimate right to remain and work in Germany is regarded as a great social and entrepreneurial challenge, but also an opportunity (Netzwerk 2016).

This puts the German state in a difficult position, as its government has to act to integrate those with a legitimate right to remain and at the same time test society's willingness to comply with the integration regulations. One important step was the recognition of the German government that it is an immigrant country (Bundesregierung 2016). Although the government has only begun to internalise, accept and communicate this in the past years, Germany has been an immigrant country for a long time. In fact, it has been a significant destination for immigration ever since the aftermath of World War II, although 'Germany conducted a long and anguished debate over whether it could or should be considered a country of immigration' (Green 2013: 334).

Given that in Germany the integration debate is focusing on finding durable solutions where both parties – the host society and the refugee – can profit, this created a parallel debate on German cultural identity. Terms such as 'guiding culture' (*Leitkultur*) and 'welcoming culture' (*Willkommenskultur*) are frequently used in connection with the level of integration needed from the host society and the refugee. The term *Leitkultur* is a highly controversial concept. Zimmermann (2016) from the German Culture Council (Deutscher Kulturrat, an umbrella organisation of German cultural associations and contact point for communication of cultural associations with the German federal government and the EU) defines integration as 'the absorption of immigrants into an existing cultural and social structure'.

The issue, however, is that while Germany is a country with democratic values, with a history of immigration and with vast historic traditions and customs, no one seems to know what kind of culture the refugees are integrating into. It seems as if the large number of immigrants in Germany makes the political debate inevitable. In fact, the current debate is sparked by concerns to preserve German identity in a process of acculturation or cultural confrontation. The term *Willkommenskultur* makes the magnitude of the debate and a divide in the German population even more apparent. On the one hand, the term represents the positive attitude of the German population, politicians, businesses and other institutions towards foreigners, migrants and asylum seekers. It established itself as a term and concept in 2015 when the German chancellor Angela Merkel decided not to close Germany's borders to Syrian refugees and Germans welcomed the arriving refugees with food, clothes, toys and so forth (Bergfeld 2017: 80).

However, the promotion of a positive attitude towards foreigners has its limits, and the term also represents the division of the German population into those that welcome foreigners and those that are less welcoming. In 2015 the press claimed that it seemed as if 'there are two Germany's: a quiet, compassionate - and a loud, aggressive one. Two parallel worlds whose inhabitants have not yet found a way to get to the point of negotiating with each other, in what kind of society they live' (N-TV 2015). Contrary to the idea of a *Willkommenskultur*, as MacKellar (2014: 167) describes, 'one of the prices of democracy is populism, and considerable time is spent describing the rise of the extreme right'. In fact, there is a side of the German population which is more aggressive towards foreigners and, according to Amnesty International (2016), there were over 1,000 attacks on the homes of refugees and asylum seekers in 2015. While there is a *Willkommenskultur* in Germany, there is also a part of the German population that is embracing right-wing populism and statements against foreigners (MacKellar 2014: 169). This development is also noticeable in the refugee integration debate in Germany, as approval for right-wing populist values in the country has increased since 2015. The rise of right-wing populist views has also led to the election success of the right-wing Populist Party Alternative for Germany (AFD) in the German Bundestag and several state parliaments. This has brought change to the German party system and affected the debate on the integration of foreigners (Fischer and Dunn 2019: 7).

It can be argued that the German perception of 'integration' is dynamic and will further develop within a German debate on core values and culture. It constantly evolves, and in 2017 the Federal Minister of the Interior, who was then still recently elected, presented a ten-point list for a German *Leitkultur* (Die Welt 2017). He named qualities, apart from fundamental rights and fundamental principles, which he considers part of German core values. He views these rules as non-legally binding, but as 'unwritten rules of our coexistence', which can be extended by additional points. The core values mentioned include aspects of general education, the importance of productive achievement, the legacy of German history, with a special relationship to Israel, and cultural wealth. The minister added that Germany is a Christian-shaped, friendly but globally neutral state (Die Welt 2017).

The reactions to the ten-point list were mixed. Many regarded it as an invitation to further discussion, while others strongly criticised it. More importantly, it caused new discussions, and various institutions from politics and civil society saw it as a reason to publish their own lists and contribute to the *Leitkulturdebatte* (see e.g. Initiative Kulturelle Integration 2017). According to the Initiative Kulturelle Integration, the German language is key to social participation and cultural diversity is perceived as a strength. The list also regards immigration as part of German history and an element of its future.

As is visible in the complexity of the debate, the root cause of the intensity of the *Leitkulturdebatte* has various dimension which have a lot to do with German culture and history. In the aftermath of World War II many of the patriotic traditions were relinquished, and a new sense of national pride had to be created (Kulturrat 2015). The Kulturrat believes that the challenge to guiding principles in the *Leitkulturdebatte* is that values were not debated either during the unification of Germany, or in the realisation of the internal market, or during the formation of the EU (Kulturrat 2015). This, however, makes the absence of a clear definition of 'German cultural values' apparent. The Kulturrat claims that a German discussion of values, which also reflects the responsibility of Germany in the world, has not taken place and a debate on a functional life in a multicultural society is needed.

Rethinking refugee integration in Germany

When looking at the integration narrative, it becomes apparent that inflows of foreigners can leave governments searching for adequate integration policies and scholars in search of innovative approaches (e.g. Bhatia and Ram 2009; Phillimore 2012; Splitt 2015; Craig 2015; Pries 2018). One suggested path is a human rights-based approach (HRBA) to integration, which includes suggestions to use human rights standards in integration policies, initiatives and measures (see e.g. Da Costa 2006; Cholewinski and Taran 2010; Xanthaki 2016; Pries 2018). A common denominator of the scholars suggesting the HRBA is a criticism of the integration narrative and the claim that integration policies dilute human rights protection (see e.g. Da Costa 2006; Xanthaki 2016; Loszycki 2017; Pries 2018). Scholars such as Xanthaki (2016) argue that integration policies 'can only be positive, if they are consistent with the internationally recognised human rights as well as minority rights'. Such an approach, however, has not yet been further developed or implemented. So far, there is merely a scholarly discussion suggesting such an approach, and it lacks concepts of implementation or ways to incorporate the approach into existing initiatives.

Information on the realisation and practicality of an HRBA can only be found in other disciplines, such as in the development context and in relation to the Millennium Development Goals (see e.g. Alston 2005; Nelson 2007; BMZ 2008; Langford et al. 2009). When assessing available information, the most common obstacle to the practicability of an HRBA appear to be the need to use clear language when communicating the measures and goals of the approach (Robinson 2004; Cornwell and Nyamu-Musembi 2004). According to scholars, the challenge is to make 'the language and approach of human rights accessible to wider audiences' (Robinson 2004: 867–8).

The reason for communicating beyond human rights legislation and including an action plan is to prevent repoliticising and mainstreaming the human rights issue (Cornwell and Nyamu-Musembi 2004). When such measures are taken, a human rights-based perspective can add value to a context and make the relationship between the rights holder and duty bearers more visible (e.g. OHCHR 2006; Da Costa 2006; Langford et al. 2009; UNHRBA 2016; UNFPA 2017). Scholars often argue that the HRBA embodies an intrinsic rationale, acknowledging that protecting human rights is – morally, legally and economically – the right thing to do (e.g. Robinson 2004; Cornwell and Nyamu-Musembi 2004; Da Costa 2006; Langford et. al. 2009). The advantage of the use of an HRBA is seen in its ability to set out clearly who has an obligation or a duty, and exactly which obligations and duties are meant. As the obligations and duties are based on binding and publicly available human rights standards and agreements, it is argued that this can ensure the participation of all stakeholders involved (OHCHR 2006; UNHRBA 2016; UNFPA 2017).

While the discourse on the HRBA to refugee integration is still in its early stages and there is little information available on its practical feasibility, various scholars have managed to link refugee integration in Germany with the work of civil society organisations (see e.g. Ziviz 2017; Schiffauer et al. 2017; Pries 2018). In fact, research on the influx of asylum seekers in Germany from 2015 to 2017 shows that integration was largely performed through the support systems of civil society organisations (e.g. Ziviz 2017; Schiffauer et al. 2017). Scholars have found that civil society organisations were able to develop creative answers to the challenges of the integration of the arriving asylum seekers, including drawing attention to the situation, needs and rights of refugees (e.g. Schiffauer et al. 2017). Beyond that, scholars have also established that civil society organisations can focus on various models of integration, which can include the implementation of substantial humanitarian principles in the response mechanisms to the arrival of the asylum seekers, and the inclusion of human rights standards as a normative guideline for human coexistence (e.g. Pries 2018).

This notion, however, is neither new nor specific to the latest refugee influx in 2015 or to Germany. Various scholars have been arguing for decades that civil society organisations are important actors in the social integration of non-national immigrants in EU member states (see e.g. Geddes 1999; Sales 2007; Koff 2008). In fact, older research results have already pointed out that civil society organisations can increase public trust and introduce a sense of community through offering a better understanding of the refugee's situation (Koff 2008: 138). Scholars have determined that the implementation of integration policies is largely happening at the local level through civil society organisations, and that it gives them a significant influence on the outcome of the policies and the experience of the refugees (Sales 2007). Beyond that, scholars have pointed out the importance of civil society for the integration of refugees (e.g. Gesemann and Roth 2009; Han-Broich 2014; OECD 2016; Klie and Klie 2018), and argued that the first contact for refugees in the host country is often with civil society organisations and their integration projects (e.g. Braun and Nobis 2011; Schiffauer et al. 2017; Pries 2018). The main argument for civil society organisations being leaders in the integration movement both politically and socially is that governments are often late to react to immigration flows and that it is civil society organisations which can act earlier (Pries 2018). Despite the large-scale engagement of scholars with the integration work of civil society organisations in Germany from 2015 to 2017, there is little insight into the relationship of the work of the organisations with human rights values or an HRBA. This establishes that there is a need for further in-depth research on this topic.

Beyond that, it is apparent that in the German context the perception of successful integration is closely connected to language acquisition, employment and cultural values, which fuels the current *Leitkulturde-batte*. Therefore the development of approaches to integration should not only imply an analysis, discussion and confrontation with German core values of *Leitkultur* and *Willkommenskultur*, but also take the needs of the refugees into consideration. For further research, it may be useful to monitor the debate as well as identify and analyse the core parts of successful integration in Germany, and, perhaps, to put the findings in context with the life stories and the needs of refugees. This could be done through an analysis of the predominant factors of unity in aspects of successful integration; identification of core points of the debates; and interviews with refugees which take both a life story method and the comparative nature of research into consideration. The involvement of applied observational research on successful integration could be of core importance to developing durable solutions where both parties – the host society and the refugee – can profit. As the above-mentioned scientists claim, integration will become a lasting question with no definite answer. It can be determined that integration is a learning process for all the actors involved. Therefore it could be conducive to continuously observe the integration debate and compare it with findings from empirical studies and future scenario planning. This approach could lead to a valuable strategy for rethinking refugee integration in Germany.

References

Ager, A., and A. Strang (2002) *Indicators of Integration: Final Report*. Home Office Development and Practice Reports: Research, Development and Statistics Directorate, <https://webarchive.nationalarchives.gov.uk/20110218141321/http://rds.homeoffice.gov.uk/rds/pdfs04/dpr28.pdf> (last accessed 4 January 2020).

Alston, P. (2005) 'Ships passing in the night: the current state of the human rights and development debate seen through the lens of the Millennium Development Goals.' *Human Rights Quarterly* 27(3): 755–829.

Amnesty International (2016) *'Leben in Unsicherheit': Wie Deutschland die Opfer rassistischer Gewalt im Stich lässt*. Amnesty International, <https://www.amnesty.de/informieren/material-download/deutschland-leben-unsicherheit-bericht-ueber-rassistische-gewalt> (last accessed 10 October 2019).

Auswärtiges Amt (2016) 'The refugee and migration situation: what German foreign policy is doing to help.' Federal Foreign Office, <https://www.auswaertiges-amt.de/en/aussenpolitik/themen/migration> (last accessed 10 October 2019).

Bach, S., H. Brücker, P. Haan, A. Romiti, K. van Deuverden and E. Weber (2017) 'IAB-Kurzbericht 2/2017: Investitionen in die Integration der Flüchtlinge lohnen sich.' *foraus.de-Newsletter*, <https://www.foraus.de/html/foraus_4375.php> (last accessed 10 October 2019).

BAMF (2016) 'Learn German: integration course for immigrants.' BAMF, <http://www.bamf.de/SharedDocs/Anlagen/EN/Publikationen/Flyer/Lernen-Sie-Deutsch/lernen-sie-deutsch.pdf?__blob=publicationFile> (last accessed 4 January 2020).

BAMF (2017) 'Das Bundesamt in Zahlen 2017: Asyl, Migration und Integration.' BAMF, <http://www.bamf.de/SharedDocs/Anlagen/DE/Publikationen/Broschueren/bundesamt-in-zahlen-2017.pdf?__blob=publicationFile> (last accessed 10 October 2019).

BAMF (2019a) 'Die zentralen Ergebnisse des Migrationsberichts 2016/2017.' BAMF, <http://www.bamf.de/SharedDocs/Anlagen/DE/Publikationen/Kurzanalysen/kurzanalyse1-2019-fortschritte-sprache-beschaeftigung.pdf?__blob=publicationFile> (last accessed 10 October 2019).

BAMF (2019b) 'Glossar: Integration.' BAMF, <http://www.bamf.de/EN/Service/Left/Glossary/_function/glossar.html?nn=1449076&lv2=5832434&lv3=1504366> (last accessed 10 October 2019).

Barbulescu, R. (2015) 'Inside Fortress Europe: the Europeanisation of immigrant integration and its impact on identity.' *Politique européenne* 47: 24–45.

Bergfeld, M. (2017) 'Germany's *Willkommenskultur*: trade unions, refugees and labour market integration.' *Global Labour Journal* 8(1): 80–9.

Bertelsmann (2015) *Die Arbeitsintegration von Flüchtlingen in Deutschland*. Bertelsmann Stiftung, <https://www.bertelsmann-stiftung.de/fileadmin/files/Projekte/28_Einwanderung_und_Vielfalt/Studie_IB_Die_Arbeitsintegration_von_Fluechtlingen_in_Deutschland_2015.pdf> (last accessed 10 October 2019).

Bhatia, S., and A. Ram (2009) 'Theorizing identity in transnational and diaspora cultures: a critical approach to acculturation.' *International Journal of Intercultural Relations* 33(2): 140–9.

BMAS (2016) 'The Integration Act promotes rapid integration into the labour market.' BMAS, <https://www.bmas.de/EN/Our-Topics/Info-for-asylum-seekers/the-new-integration-act.html> (last accessed 4 January 2020).

BMAS (2017) 'Forschungsbericht: Abschätzung von Effekten der Integration von Flüchtlingen.' BMAS, <http://www.bmas.de/SharedDocs/Downloads/DE/PDF-Publikationen/Forschungsberichte/fb477-integration.pdf?__blob=publicationFile&v=2> (last accessed 4 January 2020).

BMI (2019) 'Warum Integration so wichtig ist.' Federal Ministry of the Interior, <https://www.bmi.bund.de/DE/themen/heimat-integration/integration/integration-bedeutung/integration-bedeutung-node.html;jsessionid=D2CC04A246366B009740D1F9592A6430.2_cid364> (last accessed 10 October 2019).

BMZ (2008) 'Development policy action plan on human rights 2008–2010.' Ministry for Economic Cooperation and Development (BMZ), <http://health.bmz.de/what_we_do/Gender_and_human_rights/Policies_and_concepts/Human_Rights_

in_German_Development_Policy_Strategy_Paper/BMZ-Strategiepapier-Health_ and_Human_Rights.pdf> (last accessed 4 January 2020).

Born, R., and M. Schwefer (2016) 'Institutional dimensions of successful labor market integration of refugees.' *CESifo DICE* (4): 82–4.

Braun, S., and T. Nobis (2011) 'Migration, Integration und Sport: Perspektiven auf zivilgesellschaftliche Kontexte vor Ort.' Pp. 9–29 in *Migration, Integration und Sport, Zivilgesellschaft vor Ort*, edited by S. Braun and T. Nobis. Cham: Springer.

Brücker, H., T. Fendel, A. Kunert, U. Mangold, M. Siegert and J. Schupp (2016) 'Warum sie kommen, was sie mitbringen und welche Erfahrungen sie machen.' *IAB-Kurzbericht*, <http://doku.iab.de/kurzber/2016/kb2416.pdf> (last accessed 10 October 2019).Bundesregierung(2016) *Einwanderungsland Deutschland*. Berlin: Beauftragte der Bundesregierung für Migration, Flüchtlinge und Integration, 2016.

Bundesregierung (2019) 'Gemeinsames Konzept von Bund und Ländern für die erfolg- reiche Integration von Flüchtlingen.' *Bundesregierung*, <https://www.bundesregierung. de/breg-de/aktuelles/gemeinsames-konzept-von-bund-und-laendern-fuer-die-erfolg- reiche-integration-von-fluechtlingen-463902> (last accessed 10 October 2019).

Castles, S., M. Korac, E. Vasta and S. Vertovec (2001) *Integration: Mapping the Field*. London: Home Office.

Cholewinski, R., and P. Taran (2010) 'Migration, governance and human rights: con- temporary dilemmas in the era of globalisation.' *Refugee Survey Quarterly* 28 (4): 1–33.

Cornwell, A., and C. Nyamu-Musembi (2004) 'Putting the "rights-based approach" to development into perspective.' *Third World Quarterly* 25(8): 1415–37.

Craig, G. (2015) *Migration and Integration: A Local and Experiential Perspective*. IRIS Working Paper Series, No. 7, University of Birmingham.

Da Costa, R. (2006) *Rights of Refugees in the Context of Integration: Legal Standards and Recommendations*. UNHCR, <https://www.un.org/ruleoflaw/files/Rights%20 of%20Refugees%20in%20the%20Context%20of%20Integration_Legal%20Stan- dards%20and%20Recommendations.pdf> (last accessed 10 October 2019).

Danzer, A., and F. Yaman (2010) 'Immigranten in Deutschland: Ethnische Enklaven schwächen die Sprachkompetenz, mehr Bildung stärkt sie.' *IAB-Kurzbericht*, <http://doku.iab.de/kurzber/2010/kb1710.pdf> (last accessed 10 October 2019).

Die Welt (2017) 'De Maizière stellt zehn Thesen zur deutschen Leitkultur auf.' *Die Welt*, <https://www.welt.de/politik/deutschland/article164132024/De-Maiziere-stellt- zehn-Thesen-zur-deutschen-Leitkultur-auf.html> (last accessed 10 October 2019).

ECRE (2002) *Position on the Integration of Refugees in Europe*. European Council on Refugees and Exiles, <http://www.refworld.org/docid/3f4e5c154.html> (last accessed 10 October 2019).

Eurostat (2019) 'Asylum statistics.' Eurostat, <https://ec.europa.eu/eurostat/statis- tics-explained/index.php/Asylum_statistics#Main_countries_of_destination:_ Germany.2C_France_and_Greece> (last accessed 10 October 2019).

Favell, A. (1999) *Philosophies of Integration: Immigration and the Idea of Citizenship in France and Britain*. Basingstoke: Palgrave.

Fischer, J., and K. Dunn (2019) *Stifled Progress: International Perspectives on Social Work and Social Policy in an Era of Right-Wing Populism*. Leverkusen: Büdrich.

Fratzscher, M., and S. Junker (2015) 'Integration von Flüchtlingen: eine langfristig lohnende Investition.' *DIW Wochenbericht*, <http://www.diw.de/documents/publikationen/73/diw_01.c.518252.de/15-45-4.pdf> (last accessed 10 October 2019).

Geddes, A. (1999) *Immigration and European Integration: Towards Fortress Europe?* Manchester: Manchester University Press.

Gesemann, F., and F. Roth. (2009) *Lokale Integrationspolitik in der Einwanderungsgesellschaft: Migration und Integration als Herausforderung von Kommunen.* Wiesbaden: VS Verlag für Sozialwissenschaften.

Gesley, J. (2016) 'Germany: the development of migration and citizenship law in postwar Germany.' *Global Legal Monitor*, <https://www.loc.gov/law/foreign-news/article/germany-act-to-integrate-refugees-enters-into-force> (last accessed 4 January 2020).

Green, S. (2013) 'Germany: a changing country of immigration.' *German Politics* 22(3): 333–51.

Han-Broich, M. (2014) 'Flüchtlings- und Migrantenintegration: eine ganzheitliche Integrationstheorie und eine erfolgversprechende Integrationsarbeit.' *Migration und Soziale Arbeit* 36(4): 350–60.

HRW (2016) 'European Union: refugee response falls short: migration, security crisis challenge divided union on rights.' Human Rights Watch, <https://www.hrw.org/news/2016/01/27/european-union-refugee-response-falls-short> (last accessed 10 October 2019).

Initiative Kulturelle Integration (2017) 'Zusammenhalt in Vielfalt: 15 Thesen zu kultureller Integration und Zusammenhalt.' *Deutscher Kulturrat*, <http://kulturelle-integration.de/thesen> (last accessed 10 October 2019).

Klie, T., and A. Klie (2018) *Engagement und Zivilgesellschaft.* Wiesbaden: Springer.

Koff, H. (2008) *Fortress of Europe or Europe of Fortresses? The Integration of Migrants in Western Europe.* Brussels: Peter Lang.

Korac, M. (2003) 'Integration and how we facilitate it: a comparative study of the settlement experiences in Italy and the Netherlands.' *Sociology* 37(1): 51–68.

Kulturrat (2015) 'Wertedebatte: eine Einführung Verfassungspatriotismus alleine schafft keine Integration.' *Deutscher Kulturrat*, <https://www.kulturrat.de/themen/integration/wertedebatte/wertedebatte-eine-einfuehrung> (last accessed 10 October 2019).

Langford, M., A. Sumner, and A. Ely Yamin. (2009). *The Millennium Development Goals and Human Rights: - Past, Present and Future.* Cambridge: Cambridge University Press.

Loszycki, L. (2017) 'Wir Flüchtlinge: Hannah Arendts Kritik der Menschenrechte angesichts der heutigen Flüchtlingskrise.' *Universität Oldenburg*, <http://openjournal.uni­oldenburg.de/index.php/forsch/issue/view/9> (last accessed 4 January 2020).

MacKellar, L. (2014) 'Reviewed work(s): *The Politics of Immigration: Contradictions of the Liberal State* by James Hampshire.' *Population and Development Review* 40(1): 166–9.

Mandel, R. (1997) 'Perceived security threat and the global refugee crisis.' *Armed Forces and Society* 24(1): 77–103.

Nelson, P. (2007) 'Human rights, the Millennium Development Goals and the future of development cooperation.' *World Development* 35(12): 2041–55.

Netzwerk (2016) *Handbuch: finden, kennenlernen, einstellen: wie gelingt die Integration von Geflüchteten ins Unternehme.* Netzwerk Unternehmen integrieren Flüchtlinge der DIHK und BMWI, <https://www.unternehmen-integrieren-fluechtlinge.de> (last accessed 10 October 2019).

N-TV (2015) 'Flüchtlinge in Deutschland: wir brauchen eine Wertedebatte.' N-TV, <http://www.n-tv.de/politik/pressestimmen/Wir-brauchen-eine-Wertedebatte-article15679241.html> (last accessed 10 October 2019).

OECD (2016) *Erfolgreiche Integration: Flüchtlinge und sonstige Schutzbedürftige'* OECD, <http://www.oecd.org/migration/erfolgreiche-integration-9789264251632-de.htm> (last accessed 10 October 2019).

OHCHR (2006) *Frequently Asked Questions on a Human's Rights-Based Approach to Development Cooperation.* OHCHR, <http://www.ohchr.org/Documents/Publications/FAQen.pdf> (last accessed 10 October 2019).

Penninx, R. (2003) 'Integration: the role of communities, institutions and the state.' *Migration Information Source*, <http://www.migrationpolicy.org/article/integration-role-communities-institutions-and-state> (last accessed 10 October 2019).

Penninx, R., D. Spencer and N. van Hear (2008) *Migration and Integration in Europe: The State of Research.* Technical Report, ESRC, <https://www.researchgate.net/publication/237539737_Migration_and_Integration_in_Europe_The_State_of_Research> (last accessed 10 October 2019).

Phillimore, J. (2012) 'Implementing integration in the UK: lessons for integration, theory, policy and practice.' *Policy and Politics*, <https://www.researchgate.net/publication/272209617_Implementing_Integration_in_the_UK_Lessons_for_Integration_Theory_Policy_and_Practice> (last accessed 4 January 2020).

Polzer, T. (2008) 'Invisible integration: how bureaucratic, academic and social categories obscure integrated refugees.' *Journal of Refugee Studies* 21(4): 476–97.

Pries, L. (2018) *Refugees, Civil Society and the State: European Experiences and Global Challenges.* Cheltenham: Edward Elgar.

Robila, M. (2018) *Refugees and Social Integration in Europe.* UNDESA Division for Social Policy and Development, United Nations Expert Group, Meeting, <https://www.un.org/development/desa/family/wp-content/uploads/sites/23/2018/05/Robila_EGM_2018.pdf> (last accessed 26 December 2019).

Robinson, V. (1998) *Defining and Measuring Successful Refugee Integration.* Proceedings of ECRE International Conference on Integration of Refugees in Europe, Antwerp, November.

Robinson, V. (2004) 'Advancing economic, social, and cultural rights: the way forward.' *Human Rights Quarterly* 26(4): 866–72.

RSF (2017) *Models of Integration in Europe.* Robert Schuman Foundation, <https://www.robert-schuman.eu/en/european-issues/0449-models-of-integration-in-europe> (last accessed 10 October 2019).

Sales, R. (2007) *Understanding Immigration and Refugee Policy: Contradictions and Continuities.* Bristol: Bristol University Press.

Sezer, K. (2010) 'Was ist Integration?' *Migration und Integration*, Goethe Institut, <http://www.goethe.de/lhr/prj/daz/mag/igd/de6964668.htm> (last accessed 10 October 2019).

Schiffauer, W., A. Eilert and M. Rudloff (2017) *So schaffen wir das: Eine Zivilgesell-schaft im Aufbruch*. Bielefeld: Transcript.

Splitt, C. (2015) 'Refugee policy of tomorrow – EKD Study: Reform of development cooperation is overdue.' *EKD Press Releases*, <https://ww.ekd.de/ english/ ekd_press_releases-pr_2015_09_25_ekdtext_122_ekd_study_reform_of_development_cooeration_ in_overdue.html> (last accessed 26 December 2019).

UNDESA (2005) 'Working definition of social integration.' UNDESA, <http://www.un.org/esa/socdev/sib/peacedialogue/soc_integration.htm> (last accessed 26 December 2019).

UNFPA (2017) *The Human Rights-Based Approach*. United Nations Populations Fund, <http://www.unfpa.org/human-rights-based-approach> (last accessed 10 October 2019).

UNHCR (2007) *Note on the Integration of Refugees*. UNHCR, <http://www.unhcr.org/463b462c4.pdf> (last accessed 10 October 2019).

UNHCR (2013) *A New Beginning: Refugee Integration in Europe*. UNHCR and European Refugee Fund of the European Commission, <http://www.unhcr.org/52403d389.pdf> (last accessed 10 October 2019).

UNHRBA (2016) *The Human Rights Based Approach to Development Cooperation: Towards a Common Understanding Among UN Agencies*. UNHRBA, <http://hrba-portal.org/the-human-rights-based-approach-to-development-cooperation-to-wards-a-common-understanding-among-un-agencies> (last accessed 10 October 2019).

VHS-Berlin (2019) 'Leitbild der Berliner Volkshochschulen.' *VHS-Berlin*, <https://www.berlin.de/vhs-neukoelln/ueber-uns/leitbild> (last accessed 10 October 2019).

Xanthaki, A. (2016) 'Against integration, for human rights.' *The International Journal of Human Rights* 20(6): 815–38.

Zimmermann, O. (2016) 'Integration wohin? Wir werden uns verständigen müssen, auch wenn es schwer ist.' *Deutscher Kulturrat*, <https://www.kulturrat.de/themen/integration/wertedebatte/integration-wohin-wir-werden-uns-verstaendigen-muessen-auch-wenn-es-schwer-ist> (last accessed 10 October 2019).

Ziviz (2017) *Wie interkulturelle Öffnung gelingt*. Ziviz, <http://ziviz.de/leitfaden-inter-kulturelle-oeffnung> (last accessed 18 December 2019).

4

The Unfolding of the Syrian Refugee Crisis in Turkey: From Temporariness to Permanency

Ayhan Kaya

THIS CHAPTER AIMS to unravel the transformation of the legal and societal status of Syrian refugees in Turkey from the state of temporariness to a state of permanency. The main premise of this chapter is that there is a parallel between the state of temporariness granted to the Syrian refugees by the Turkish government and the Islamic set of discourses and policies generated by the government in the second half of the 2000s leading to the de-Europeanisation of Turkey. The break-up of Turkey's European perspective has partly contributed to the destabilisation of the Middle East and the emergence of the Syrian crisis. It has partially resulted in the favouring of Sunni Muslim Syrian refugees on the part of central and local administrations run by the Justice and Development Party (JDP) government, at the expense of Kurdish, Alevi, Christian, Circassian and Yazidi groups originating from Syria. Favouring of Sunni Muslim Syrians by the JDP is partly similar to the ways in which some EU member states, such as Hungary, favoured Christian refugees rather than Muslim-origin refugees.[1]

Methodologically, the chapter will make use of legal texts (Law on Foreigners and International Protection enacted in 2014, Regulation on Temporary Protection issued in 2014, Visa Regulations issued by Turkey since the year 2000, either in collaboration with the EU or against EU norms), official statements by leading political figures such as President Recep Tayyip Erdoğan, Prime Minister Ahmet Davutoğlu and the then Deputy Prime Minister Numan Kurtulmuş, as well as media archives, relevant statistics and secondary literature. The speeches by political figures and legal texts will be decoded through discourse analysis.

Discourse analysis deals with the relationship between language, socio-political processes and the power relations associated with them. It is based on earlier studies by Michel Foucault, Mikhail Bakhtin and Antonio Gramsci, and seeks to combine linguistics and sociological approaches within the analysis of the discourse in order to examine the complex interactions between discourse and society. In this chapter, I will use some extracts and quotations from speeches, declarations and media statements by relevant leading political figures to decode the ways in which the Syrian refugees have so far been framed by the state actors.[2] The chapter will also benefit from the findings of two different field research experiences: the first one conducted by the Support to Life Association (Hayata Destek Derneği) in Istanbul under the supervision of the author (Kaya and Kıraç 2016); and the second one conducted within the framework of a Horizon 2020 project by a research team in Istanbul, Izmir and Şanlıurfa in the summer of 2018.[3]

The study was a qualitative and quantitative research study conducted in six districts of Istanbul in the last quarter of 2015 and the first quarter of 2016. Both Syrian refugees and Turkish receiving community members and organisations have been interviewed in one-on-one interviews, in focus group discussions and via structured questionnaires. Six districts in Istanbul, namely Küçükçekmece, Başakşehir, Bağcılar, Fatih, Sultanbeyli and Ümraniye, are run by the JDP's local government administrations, and they have been surveyed in order to identify the needs and vulnerabilities of the Syrian refugee population in Istanbul. In order to identify a random sample of the target population, in line with the requirements of statistical analysis, the districts were chosen due to their diverse geographic locations in Istanbul (four on the European and two on the Asian side of the city). These districts host the highest number of Syrians in Istanbul, often living together with other marginalised communities in the city such as Kurds, Alevis and the Roma (see Figure 4.1 below). The needs assessment study has been carried out by the Support to Life Association under the supervision of the author to collect data through a multitude of research techniques: in-depth interviews conducted by Syrian-origin researchers as well as senior Turkish researchers in each of the six districts, with key informants working in the host community, for a total of 200 individuals. These included focus group discussions (FGDs) conducted with both Syrian refugees (male and female) and the local host community members in each district (18 FGDs with Syrian refugees, 6 FDGs with host community members) with a total of 136 individuals; and household (HH) surveys conducted by Arabic-speaking Syrian assessment officers in each district, with an estimated average of 6 individuals per household, amounting to a total of 124 surveys and 744 individuals (Kaya and Kıraç 2016).

This chapter strives to analyse the factors behind the de-Europeanisation of Turkish migration and asylum policies with a specific focus on the Syrian refugee crisis, which has immense domestic and international repercussions. The chapter covers the depiction of the process of Europeanisation and de-Europeanisation that the Turkish state has gone through since the 1999 Helsinki Summit of the European Union. Subsequently, the impact of Europeanisation and de-Europeanisation processes on the transformation of Turkish migration and asylum policies will be discussed briefly, to pave the way to elaborate on the ways in which the Turkish state has managed to accommodate more than three million Syrian refugees since 2011.

In this regard, due to the fact that Turkey still keeps a geographical limitation with regard to the 1951 Geneva Convention on the Protection of Refugees – a limitation which does not let the Turkish state recognise the Syrians as refugees – Turkey has framed the Syrian refugees as 'guests', with a certain reference to the past experiences depicted in religious texts, such as the depiction of 'Ansar spirit', which will be discussed shortly. The status of guest-hood posits that Syrians are not automatically considered to be a part of the national stock. On the contrary, this status excludes them from being a part of the Turkish national identity prescribed on the basis of ethno-cultural and religious aspects (Turkish Sunni Muslim). The status of guest-hood also suggests that there is a border running between the Turks and the Syrians. It will be shown that depicting the Syrians as 'guests' has also made them even more vulnerable and exposed to some acts of ruthlessness and racism among the wider society in Turkey. Finally, the chapter will conclude with an exposure of the ways in which the state of temporariness of the Syrians has now been changing towards an admission of the state of permanency, which includes the policies and legal regulations to accommodate the Syrians in different spheres of everyday life ranging from the labour market to education.

Europeanisation and de-Europeanisation of Turkey

There is an extensive literature on the Europeanisation of Turkey since the 1999 Helsinki Summit of the European Union, where Turkey was given candidacy status. Following the decision, and even earlier than that, Turkish state actors successfully managed to democratise the country through a set of reforms and constitutional changes ranging from the abolition of the death penalty to combatting the military legacy (see e.g. Keyman and Öniş 2007; Kaya and Tarhanli 2005; Öniş 2004). In October 2005, accession negotiations started between Turkey and the EU. Once the actual negotiations had started, the adoption of the *acquis communautaire* in justice and home affairs became very important, especially with regard to the fields of asylum and immigration. Any candidate state is expected to take on this matter before full membership, as a part of conditionality. In this respect, one could speak of the transformation, or Europeanisation, of Turkish asylum and immigration policies. Turkey's desire to become a member of the EU is one of the most important factors behind the changes with regard to the reformulation of migration policy, at least at a rhetorical level. In compliance with the Accession Partnership, Turkey prepared its initial National Programme for the Adoption of the Acquis (NPAA) in March 2001, and revised it first in 2003 and then in 2008 to demonstrate its grip on the idea that it wanted to fall within the borders of Europe.

In the Justice and Home Affairs Chapter of the NPAA, Turkey committed itself to reinforcing the fight against so-called 'illegal' migration and to the adoption and best practices of admission, readmission and expulsion of migrants, with a view to preventing irregular migration in the medium term. In order to respond to these challenges, Turkey formed a special Task Force on Asylum, Migration and Border Protection which prepared the 2003 Migration Strategy Paper (Kaiser and Kaya 2015; Kirişçi 2011; Keser 2006). In the accession process, Turkey was asked to rearrange its visa policy in accordance with EU legislation, especially with the Schengen visa regime. Therefore, Turkey is expected to apply a uniform policy towards all EU citizens with regard to the visa obligation, and to adopt the Schengen negative list. Yet instead, in line with Turkey's changing foreign policy towards Middle Eastern countries in the second half of the 2000s, Turkey abolished visas for neighbouring or regional countries, such as Syria, Jordan, Lebanon and Saudi Arabia, which were on the EU's blacklist and subject to strict visa regulations. The EU also required Turkey to tighten its borders with countries such as Georgia, Iran, Iraq and Syria. However, what has happened since is quite the opposite, although the process developed a bit differently from the way it was envisaged. The convergence with EU policy priorities shows variation as applied to irregular and transit migration as well as to the rights of migrants and asylum seekers arriving in Turkey from different regions (Canefe 2016).

The JDP has generated two different cycles in relation to the Europeanisation of Turkey. The first cycle had been created during the first four years of its rule and has been called a '*virtuous circle*' due to the successful legal, political and social changes generated by the JDP. In the first cycle, one should not underestimate the growing interest of civil society actors on the boundaries of the former Ottoman Empire, such as the Middle East, the Caucasus and the Balkans, in envisaging a Europeanised, democratic, prosperous, cooperative and friendly Turkey, which could also have a *transformative effect* on these countries in the foreseeable future (Yılmaz 2011; Flockhart 2010; Börzel and Risse 2003; Keyman and İçduygu 2003). This period of Europeanisation, or the transformative power of the EU, provided Turkey and its neighbours with a vision of building peace and stability in the region. It was also the transformative power of the EU that had a strong impact on Turkey in discovering its potential as a *soft power* in the region (Kirişçi 2011; Altınay 2008).

Political stability, economic prosperity, growing Turkish Lira nationalism, based on the strong currency, strong political determination against the traditional legacy of the Turkish army, Turkey's becoming a *soft power* in the region and developing friendly relations with countries of the Middle East, North Africa, the Caucasus and the former Soviet Union, the creation of a political climate receptive to the claims of several different ethno-cultural groups in the process of preparing a new constitution, and other similar factors: these were all decisive in the consolidation of the JDP's power in Turkey as well as in the immediate neighbourhood, such as the Middle East (Kirişçi 2011). However, the potential of being a promising *soft power* was exhausted in the second cycle when Turkey's EU perspective was derailed.

The latter cycle was created after the Presidential Palace had been taken over by President Gül, one of the founding members of the JDP, in 2007, and this cycle has been called a '*vicious circle*' due to elements of growing Euroscepticism, de-Europeanisation, Islamisation, de-secularisation, nationalism, parochialism, authoritarianisation and neo-Ottomanisation of the Turkish state. Euroscepticism, nationalism and parochialism in Turkey were triggered by sentiments of disapproval towards the American occupation of Iraq, the limitations on national sovereignty posed by EU integration, the high tide of the ninetieth anniversary in 2005 of the Armenian genocide among the Armenian diaspora, the 'risk of recognition' of southern Cyprus by Turkey for the sake of EU integration, anti-Turkey public opinion in the EU countries framed by leading conservative powers, enlargement fatigue in the EU, and Israel's attacks on Lebanon in 2006. Against such a background the state elite became very sceptical of the Europeanisation process. The best way to explain the sources of such scepticism among the state elite is to refer to 'Sèvres Syndrome', which is based on a fear deriving from the post-World War I era and characterised by popular belief regarding the risk of the break-up of the Turkish state (see e.g. Öniş 2004: 12).

After 2005, the JDP withdrew from its pro-European position, as it perceived the EU no longer paid off. Actually, it was not the nationalist climax in the country which turned the JDP into a Eurosceptic party, but rather the decision of the European Court of Human Rights vis-à-vis the headscarf case *Leyla Şahin vs. Turkey*, which challenged a Turkish law banning wearing the Islamic headscarf at universities and other educational and state institutions (Saktanber and Çorbacıoğlu 2008). De-secularisation and Islamisation of the state in Turkey coupled with neoliberal governance also corresponds to the period of de-Europeanisation in the country. The JDP has developed strategies, discourses and policies in relation to the Islamisation of state and society in Turkey. These strategies refer to the societal and political alliances set up by the JDP to consolidate its electoral power. In this regard, strategic alliances with the EU, liberal democrats in Turkey and the Gülen movement were formulated (Kaya 2013). Discourses refer to the ideologies and paradigms utilised by the JDP in winning the hearts of the masses in and around Turkey. Accordingly, the JDP has produced various discourses of neoconservatism, neoliberalism, Islamism, victimisation, and anti-laicism focusing on the attempts at lifting the headscarf ban, liberating the clergy schools (Imam Hatip), changing the elementary and secondary school structure, and revising the national curriculum in education. Eventually, the JDP has formulated policies on family and social provisioning with a visible emphasis on Islam and faith-based voluntary organisations (Kaya 2015). De-Europeanisation of Turkey under JDP rule could also be interpreted as de-secularisation of the state in a way that has the potential to transform the society from a secular one to a more Islamic one. Such acts of the Turkish government encountered fierce resistance from the public during and after the massive Gezi protests, which erupted in Istanbul first, and stretched to other cities in the summer of 2013 (Hemer and Persson 2018).

As I have outlined elsewhere (Kaya 2013), the discourse of 'alliance of civilisations' deployed by the JDP paid off in the first half of the 2000s in a way that contributed to the Europeanisation of Turkey at a time when the EU had been inspired by a global vision. On the one hand, as a political party, which originally gained legitimacy with its culturalist and civilisational perspective in a period of time constrained by Huntington's paradigm of the clash of civilisations, the JDP invested in the culturalisation and religionisation of what is social, political and economic in nature by highlighting the cleavages between 'crescent' and 'cross' (Davutoğlu 2005; Yetkin 2018). On the other hand, the overwhelming use of the very same discourse by Turkey-sceptic conservative political forces such as Angela Merkel's Christian Democratic Union (CDU) and Nicolas Sarkozy's Union for a Popular Movement (UMP) has distanced Turkey from the EU due to the parochial and inward-looking polity of many EU member states, following enlargement fatigue in 2004 and then during the global financial crisis. Angela Merkel's so-called 'privileged partnership' proposal to Turkey and Nicolas Sarkozy's plans on 'Mediterranean Union' were all perceived by the Turkish political elite as unacceptable, since they were denouncing the possibility of Turkey's full membership of the EU in the foreseeable future. Such debates also prompted the Turkish public and the political elite to see the EU as a 'Christian club' (Kaya 2013).

The latter cycle, the 'vicious circle', has also been coupled with the effort of creating a *Brand Turkey*, at the expense of distancing Turkey from the EU - a brand emphasising tourism promotion, promotion of the country's culture and heritage, campaigns to attract foreign investment, immigration policies, foreign and domestic policies and the export of domestic product brands. Presenting Turkey as an emerging country of immigration was also one of the essential elements of the 'New Turkey' brand (Tecmen 2017; Zihnioğlu 2013; Kalın 2011). This is very obvious in the efforts of the Turkish Ministry of Foreign Affairs in organising the Global Migration Forum under the auspices of the UN in Turkey in autumn 2015, in order to present Turkey as the most courageous and generous country of immigration, welcoming more than three million Syrian and other refugees.

In accordance with this, Turkey opened up its borders in April 2011 to the Syrian refugees. The Turkish political elite, including then Foreign Minister Ahmet Davutoğlu, expected at that time that Bashar Asad would be overthrown within a few months and that the number of Syrian refugees entering Turkey would reach at most 100,000 people (Erdoğan 2015). Syrian refugees were announced to be 'guests' due to the fact that Turkey registered a geographical reservation to the 1951 Geneva Convention, excluding non-Europeans from its purview. In the meantime, Turkey signed the Readmission Agreement with the European Union in 2013, agreeing that Turkey would lift the geographical reservation upon full EU membership, and also that the EU would start visa liberalisation talks with Turkey upon successful implementation of the Readmission Agreement during a three-year term until the end of 2016. The signing of the Readmission Agreement partly meant that Turkey accepted the mistake made in the second half of the 2000s, that is to say lifting visas for neighbouring countries in the Middle East at the expense of de-aligning itself with EU legislation. A new Law on Foreigners and International Protection (Law No. 6458) was enacted and put into force in April 2014, and Turkey opened up its borders to Syrian refugees without seeing any need to ask for international assistance in the first place.

Opening the borders not only made it easier for refugees to enter Turkish territory, but also made it easier for armed individuals - be it the militants of the Free Syrian Army, who were partly trained and armed by the Turkish state, or recruits for ISIS coming from all around the world, including Turkey - to act freely on both sides of the Turkish–Syrian border. On the other hand, labelling the refugees as 'guests' unfortunately prepared the ground for a growing intolerance towards them among the Turkish public, especially after the electoral cycle had started in 2014, with the local elections (2014), the presidential elections (2014), the general elections (2015), the presidential referendum (2017) and finally the local elections again (2019). Guest-hood suggests that refugees or migrants are temporarily staying in the receiving country, and that they are expected to leave soon when the right time comes. However, the continuation of war in Syria is likely to transform the status of temporariness of the Syrians in Turkey and neighbouring countries to the status of permanency. The new Law on Foreigners and International Protection (2014) and the Temporary Protection Law for refugees (2014) have remained insufficient in providing basic rights for refugees such as employment, housing, education and health services. Growing racism and xenophobia against the Syrians has also been strengthened by the electoral campaign discourses of the oppositional parties, such as the Republican People's Party (CHP) and the Nationalist Action Party (MHP) (Kaya and Kıraç 2016). In other words, antiSyrian discourse has characterised the entire political scene since 2015.

Legal framework and temporary protection: guests, but not refugees!

Traditionally known as emigration countries, Turkey, Lebanon and Jordan have also become settlement and transit spaces for economic and forced migrants (De Bel-Air 2006; Pérouse 2013). Syrian refugees have been considered as 'guests' by the Turkish, Lebanese and Jordanian states. From the very beginning of the refugee plight, Syrians have been presented as if they are 'welcome' in the host states and societies on the basis of some deep-rooted values such as 'Turkish hospitality', 'Muslim fraternity', 'Arab hospitality' and 'guest-hood' traditions (De Bel-Air 2006; Pérouse 2013; Chatty 2013; El Abed 2014; Kirişçi 2014; Erdoğan 2015; Erdoğan and Kaya 2015; Baban et al. 2016). However, all these values address the temporary character of the readiness to accept refugees, or guests. To this extent, a more recent metaphor to qualify the role that the Turkish state and the pious Muslim Turks should play for Syrians in Turkey has been the *Ansar spirit* (*Ansar* is Arabic for 'helpers'). As a metaphor, *Ansar* refers to the people of Medina, who supported the Prophet Mohammad and the accompanying Muslims (*muhajirun*, or migrants) who migrated there from Mecca, which was under the control of the pagans. The metaphor of *Ansar* originally points to a temporary situation, as the Muslims later returned to Mecca after their forces recaptured the city from the pagans (Korkut 2015; Haber7 2014). Hence, the Turkish government has used a kind of Islamic symbolism to legitimise its acts in the resolution of the Syrian refugee crisis. Government leaders have consistently compared Turkey's role in assisting the Syrian refugees to that of the *Ansar*. Framing the Syrian refugees within the discourse of *Ansar* and *muhajirun* has elevated public and private efforts to accommodate Syrian refugees from a humanitarian responsibility to a religious and charity-based duty (Erdemir 2016).

The then Prime Minister Ahmet Davutoğlu, in his speech in Gaziantep, one of the most popular destinations for the Syrian refugees on the Syrian border, publicly stated that Gaziantep was a city of *Ansar*: 'Gazi[antep] is an *Ansar* city now. God bless you all' (Akşam 2014). Similarly, President Erdoğan used the same discourse in his speeches in 2014 and afterwards:

> In our culture, in our civilization, guest means honour, and blessing. You [Syrian guests] have granted us the honour of being *Ansar*, but also brought us joy and blessing. As for today, we have more than 1.5 million Syrian and Iraqi guests. (Hurriyet 2014)

The discourse of *Ansar* continued until recently. Deputy Prime Minsiter Numan Kurtuluş referred to the same rhetoric when he introduced the right to work granted to the Syrian refugees under temporary protection:

The reason why the Syrian refugees are now settled in our country is hospitality and *Ansar* spirit that our nation has so far adhered to. There are other countries that cannot do anything when encountered with a few hundred thousands of refugees. But contrary to what the rich and prosperous countries could not do for the refugees, our country did its best for the refugees as a generous host, friend, brother and neighbour. (Ajans Haber 2016)

The main common denominator of the ruling political elite is that the Syrian refugees are being portrayed and framed by means of an act of benevolence. Hence, the assistance of the state to the refugees is accomplished on the basis of charity, rather than universally recognised rights that are supposed to be granted to refugees fleeing their homelands. But the problem is that Turkey is far from naming the Syrian refugees as 'refugees'. This is why the state actors tend to cope with the issue not through universal law, but through the laws of religious charity and benevolence.

From the very beginning of the refugee flow into Turkey, Syrians have officially been called 'guests' but not 'refugees', due to the fact that Turkey officially does not accept refugees other than coming from outside its western boundaries, in accordance with the geographical limitation clause of the 1951 Geneva Convention on the Protection of Refugees. Although the geographical limitation was removed for most of the members by the 1967 Additional Protocol of the Geneva Convention, Turkey decided to keep it, together with Congo, Madagascar and Monaco. However, Turkey introduced a Temporary Protection Directive for refugees in 2014, based on Articles 61 to 95 of the Law on Foreigners and International Protection, which came into force in April 2014.[4]

Turkey has adopted its Temporary Protection Regulation from a similar European experience implemented during the Balkan refugee crisis in the 1990s – during a period when there was no Common European Asylum System, harmonised asylum rules, or structures such as the European Refugee Fund, Frontex and a European Asylum Support Office. During the Balkan refugee crisis, member states had to rely on ad hoc measures to provide an adequate humanitarian response to Bosnian refugees between 1992 and 1995 and Kosovar refugees in 1999. These practices were later standardised and embedded in the Temporary Protection Directive (Council of the European Union 2001). The directive grants almost all of the social and civil rights that refugees enjoy in Western societies.[5] Accordingly, Turkey has provided Syrians with temporary protection which consists of three elements: an open-door policy for all Syrians; no forced returns to Syria (non-refoulement); and unlimited duration of stay in Turkey.

However, those enjoying temporary protection have not been allowed to apply for individual refugee status determination, which means that they did not receive the opportunity to be resettled in a third country through the mechanisms of the UNHCR. This is why a large number of Syrians are not willing to register with the Turkish authorities, in order not to lose their right to be resettled in a third country, preferably Germany (see Figure 4.1). While an open-door policy is still being implemented, Syrians are named as 'guests' instead of 'refugees'. 'Guests' are expected to leave the host country and return to their homeland at some point.[6] Therefore the length of their stay is of a limited nature, unlike that of ordinary citizens. Using the term 'guest' instead of 'refugee' also indicates the JDP's perception of the Syrian refugee crisis, which is based on the assumption that 'guests' are people whose stay will be subject to the benevolence of the host state actors for a temporary period of time, but not on a permanent basis (Eroglu 2013).

Despite the rights granted under the Temporary Protection Directive dating from April 2013, refugees have encountered various problems in the spheres of health, education, labour market and housing in Turkey.[7] Due to the fact that there are not very reliable and sufficient official data on the socio-economic status of refugees, one cannot correctly make estimates of the number of refugee children who actually do enjoy the right to primary education, or of refugees who do have access to health care, or of those given the right to work. It is estimated that around 30–5 percent of Syrian refugees in Turkey are school-aged children. This amounts to around 993,000 children that need to be attending school. While AFAD (the Turkish Disaster and Emergency Management Authority) is providing education for children in seventy schools and the Ministry of Education is offering it in approximately seventy-five locations outside the Temporary Accommodation Centres (refugee camps; see Figure 4.1), the number of children receiving education is around 300,000, compared to the almost one million who need it. It is simply not feasible to accommodate such a high number of schoolchildren in the national education institutions in the entire country (Kılıç and Üstün 2015). Temporary Accommodation Centres were previously run by AFAD, which was first established in 2009 under the auspices of the Prime Minister's Office, and then transferred to the auspices of the Ministry of Interior in 2018.[8] When AFAD was transferred to the Ministry of Interior, its mandate on

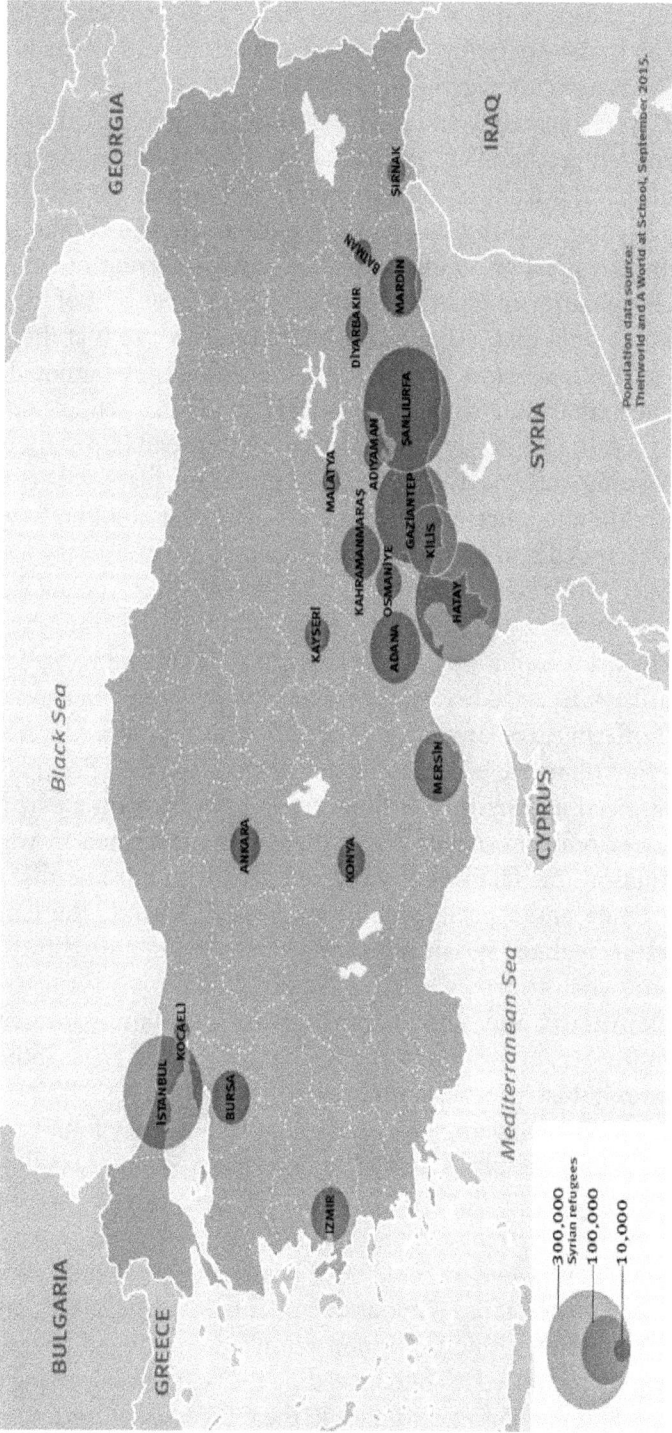

Figure 4.1 Map of Syrian refugees in Turkey
Source: Human Rights Watch.

the temporary accommodation centres was transmitted to a sister organisation, which is also operating under the same Ministry: the Directorate General of Migration Management (DGMM).[9]

Even if it were logistically and practically possible, a remarkable number of Syrian refugee families cannot register their children for school, as they send them to work in the informal labour market, mainly in the textile, construction and service sectors. Child labour as a coping strategy is a common practice among the Syrian refugees living in Istanbul. For instance, our study in Istanbul revealed that 26.6 per cent of the survey participants send their school-age children to work so that they can contribute to family income; 20.3 per cent stated that they cannot afford to pay for their education; while 14.1 per cent stated that schools do not accept them because there is not enough space for the children at the local schools. When the interlocutors were asked about the places where they send their children to work, half of those sending their children to work (26.6 per cent) stated that their children work in the textile sector (clothing, shoes, etc.) while the others work in the service sector (small shops, catering, cafés, restaurants), the construction sector and the industrial sector (furniture factories, automobile factories, etc.) (Kaya and Kıraç 2016).

There is also anecdotal evidence that there is only one pharmacy left in Istanbul offering free-of-charge medication to refugees, due to the allegations that pharmacies are not being reimbursed by AFAD, which has been the lead agency in coordinating the government's efforts to respond to the refugees' needs.[10] It can easily be imagined in what a difficult situation this fact might leave refugees with chronic diseases, pregnant women and especially children. Besides, despite the temporary protection regime, Syrian refugees seem to have limited freedom of movement when it comes to lucrative holiday resorts: Syrians were told to leave Antalya and, now, also Muğla, two provinces located on the Turkish Riviera, in order not to damage the large business interests of the tourism industry (Spiegel Online 2014).

The first group of Syrian nationals coming into Turkey found refuge when crossing into the province of Hatay on 29 April 2011. Following the escalation of local conflicts in Syria, the JDP government declared an open-door policy for Syrian refugees in October 2011 (Table 4.1). Accordingly, Turkey allowed Syrians holding a passport to enter the country freely and even treated those without documents in a similar welcoming way; it guaranteed the principle of non-refoulement; offered temporary protection, and committed itself to providing the best possible living conditions for and humanitarian assistance to the refugees (İçduygu, 2015).

Table 4.1 Changing number of Syrian refugees in major cities, 2014–19

City	November 2014	21 July 2017	2 August 2019
İstanbul	330,000	495,027	547,943
Gaziantep	220,000	336,929	445,748
Hatay	190,000	397,047	432,436
Şanlıurfa	170,000	433,856	429,735
Mardin	70,000	96,062	87,507
Adana	50,000	165,818	240,376
Kilis	49,000	127,175	116,317
Mersin	45,000	153,976	201,887
Konya	45,000	79,139	108,419
Kahramanmaraş	44,000	93,408	90,073
Ankara	30,000	80,279	93,120
Bursa	20,000	114,498	174,865
Batman	20,000	20,181	22,392
Şırnak	19,000	15,080	15,019
Kocaeli	15,000	34,957	57,745
İzmir	13,000	113,460	145,123
Osmaniye	12,000	46,157	50,295
Antalya	10,000	458	1,786
Kayseri	9,500	62,645	79,161
Diyarbakır	5,000	30,405	33,245
Adıyaman	2,500	27,084	25,549
Samsun	1,230	4,540	5,852
Niğde	1,100	3,848	4,674
Aydın	1,000	8,806	7,922

Source: Ministry of Interior, Directorate General of Migration Management, <http://www.goc.gov.tr/icerik6/gecici-koruma_363_378_4713_icerik> (last accessed 11 December 2019).

Notes: For a detailed account of the number of the Syrian refugees in Turkey see the website of the UNHCR, <http://data.unhcr.org/syrianrefugees/country.php?id=224> (last accessed 11 December 2019). According to the figures of 21 November 2015, the total number of registered Syrian refugees in Turkey was 2,181,293. The number of those living in the twenty-two refugee camps around the Turkish–Syrian border is more than 220,000. In August 2019, according to the same UNHCR sources, the total number of registered Syrian refugees was 3,079,914.

However, the number of Syrian refugees who leave Turkey for Europe increased drastically in 2014 and 2015. A majority of refugees going to EU countries either sailed from Turkish coasts to the Greek islands, or crossed Turkey's borders with Greece and Bulgaria (UNHCR 2015). The perils of the sea journey - shipwrecks with many missing and dead – did not deter many Syrian refugees. Some were prepared to make this journey at all costs. The situation changed, though, after the agreement made between Turkey and the EU on 18 March 2016, resulting in stricter surveillance of the Aegean coasts by the Turkish security forces, and thus a decline in the number of refugees trying to cross the sea (Collett 2016; Spijkerboer 2016).

Apparently, Syrian refugees are discontented with their status in Turkey. Amnesty International (2014) reported that they 'remained unsure of what they could expect in terms of support from the Turkish authorities and how long they would be welcome'. However, even if it is true that some of the Syrians have lost hope of going back home and cannot envisage a future in Turkey due to growing racism, misery, exploitation, domestic political problems and an unstable political climate, one should not forget that a very small minority of the Syrians who managed to travel across the Greek islands had spent a short period of time in Turkey prior to their journey to Greece. More than 80 per cent of the Syrians who settled on the Greek islands reported that they only spent a few days in Turkey to get prepared for their journey into Greece. Only 20 per cent of those reported that they had spent more than six months in Turkey prior to their journey to Greece (UNHCR 2015).

Many Syrian refugees in Turkey have already lost hope concerning the ending of armed conflicts in their homeland. Due to the ambiguous status granted to them under the Temporary Protection Regulation, most of the Syrian children cannot enrol in proper education; men and women were granted the right to work as recently as February 2016; they have been exploited in the labour market; they are being exposed to xenophobic attitudes; and they are not able to apply for permanent residence (Öner and Genç 2015).

The Transatlantic Trends Survey of the German Marshall Fund of the United States (GMF) carried out in 2014 provides further evidence for the worsening perceptions of immigrants in Turkey.[11] According to this survey, 42 per cent of the Turkish population think that there are too many foreign-born people in Turkey, a 17 percentage-point increase over 2013. Moreover, 66 per cent of the respondents from Turkey support more restrictive policies towards refugees. In the World Values Survey covering fifty-one countries, Turkey is ranked in thirteenth place – third on the European continent – in terms of intolerance towards immigrants and foreign workers. The results from the Life in Transition Survey II (LITS2), conducted in 2010, named Turkey as the most intolerant nation among thirty-four European and Asian countries, tying with Mongolia. Although negative perceptions about immigrants have increased in 2013 and there is strong support for restrictions of Turkey's policies towards refugees, this issue had not yet transferred into the political sphere in 2014. Then, only 4 per cent of Turks said that immigration was Turkey's most important problem (Erdoğan 2014).

The framing of the refugee reality by state actors as an act of benevolence and tolerance has also shaped public opinion in a way which has led to the exposure of some racist and xenophobic attitudes vis-à-vis refugees. This is why it is not a surprise that Turkish society has witnessed several lynching attempts, stereotypes, prejudices, communal conflicts and other forms of harassment performed against Syrians (Gökay 2015; Togral-Koca 2016). The massive increase in the number of refugees outside camps and the lack of adequate assistance policies towards them has aggravated a range of social problems. Refugees experience problems of adaptation in big cities, and the language barrier has seriously complicated their ability to integrate into Turkish society. There are several problems the Syrians have been facing in everyday life. There is now a growing concern about underage Syrian girls being forced into marriage, as well as fears that a recent constitutional court ruling decriminalising religious weddings without civil marriage will lead to a spread of polygamy involving Syrian women and girls (Kirişçi and Ferris 2015). The sight of Syrians begging in the streets is causing particular resentment among local people, especially in the western cities of Turkey. There have also been reports of occasional violence between refugees and the local population. In turn, this reinforces a growing public perception that Syrian refugees are associated with criminality, violence and corruption. These attitudes contrast with local authorities' and security officials' observations that in reality, criminality is surprisingly low and that Syrian community leaders are very effective in preventing crime and defusing tensions between refugees and locals (Kirişçi and Karaca 2015).

Discursive shift from temporariness to permanency

As soon as it turned out that framing the refugees as 'guests' was not sustainable in terms of accommodating their urgent needs, as well as of coming to terms with the increasing resentment among the local populations vis-à-vis the refugees, Turkey first introduced a Temporary Protection Directive for refugees in 2014, as we have seen.

Following the implementation of the Temporary Protection regulation, which still frames the refugees with a state of temporariness, some discursive shifts were witnessed in the media with regard to the state actors' changing position on the permanent character of at least some of the Syrian refugees in Turkey. These discursive shifts have so far mainly emphasised the permanent nature of the issue: introduction of work permits in early 2016, incorporation of pupils into public schools, creating quotas for Syrian students in higher education institutions, granting citizenship to Syrians, and some statements from political figures such as President Erdoğan and Deputy Prime Minister Numan Kurtulmuş. Comparing the Turks living in Germany and the USA with the Syrians living in Turkey, in a meeting with journalists, President Erdoğan referred to the need for granting citizenship to the Syrian refugees residing in Turkey:

> Today, a Turk can go to Germany and become a German citizen; [a Turk] can go to the U.S. and become an American citizen; why can't the same be possible for people living in our country?[12]

This statement brought about a big commotion in Turkey, as it made Turkish citizens conclude that all the Syrians would be granted citizenship immediately. Due to the disturbance of the public in general, Deputy Prime Minister Kurtulmuş had to announce that the Ministry of Interior was working on a proposal, implicitly meaning that the government was considering granting citizenship to those with cultural and economic capital:

> Our citizens should be comfortable. We have not yet completed the proposal about granting citizenship to the Syrians. The Ministry of Interior is working on the proposal. There are so many skilled people [among the Syrians] who can make contributions to Turkey. To this effect, we can propose some criteria. When there is nothing concrete, some oppositional groups are trying to create chaos for the sake of opposition; and these groups are gossiping about the uncertain things as if everything is clearly laid out by the government. These are all incorrect.[13]

However, it is still not clear what the Turkish state actors mean by granting citizenship. Anecdotal evidence indicates that those Syrians with economic and cultural capital are more likely to be granted citizenship than those whose standing is precarious, who seem to be instrumentalised by the ongoing neoliberal forms of governance for the establishment of a model of precarious work for non-citizen workers (Canefe 2016; Baban et al. 2016). As of March 2019, the total number of Syrians who had been granted Turkish citizenship was 79,894.[14] This number had become 92,280 by August 2019.[15]

According to the findings of the RESPOND field research conducted in Istanbul, Izmir (Aegean coast) and Şanlıurfa (at the Syrian border) in the summer of 2018, Turkish citizenship is mostly granted to those who are young, educated, skilled, employed, multilingual, Turkish-speaking and with a lower- or upper-middle-class background. It is also common practice to be granted Turkish citizenship through marriage with a Turkish citizen. However, those of Kurdish ethnicity, are old, are unemployed, or have a working-class background and no qualifications are much less likely to be granted citizenship. A middle-class 19-year-old Arabic- and English-speaking male working as a translator in the private service sector in Izmir explained his experience of being asked by the local authorities in Izmir whether he wants to be granted Turkish citizenship:

> I did not apply for citizenship but they called me in my working place for appointment one day, and they said that I was eligible to be granted citizenship. We went to get it, prepared the documents, and now we are waiting for the Turkish ID cards to come. No one in my family applied, but it was granted to all of us. Maybe because of my father's job. He works in an insurance company. Though he is not a university graduate person, he works in a good company. (Interview, 5 August 2018, İzmir, Karabağlar, 5_SRII)

Another young person from İzmir recounted a similar story about her experience with being granted Turkish citizenship. This middle-class 24-year-old Arabic-, English- and Turkish-speaking female working in a migration-related NGO in İzmir said the following:

> First we got residence permits in Izmir. A year later, we were given ID cards [temporary protection status]. Now, we are Turkish citizens. We were granted citizenship like 8 months ago. As my father is a teacher working here, they permit such qualified Syrians like teachers, doctors, engineers to become citizen. My father applied for citizenship, and the whole family became Turkish citizens. (Interview, İzmir, 30 July 2018, 9_SRII)

However, it is quite rare to come across someone who is granted Turkish citizenship, or who is willing to apply for it. During the field research, we came across others who have received, or heard about others receiving, phone calls from authorities asking them whether they want to return to Syria. Our experiences in the field show that there is a group of Syrians with a particular ethnic profile that is expected to return to Syria, that is, Kurds. A Kurdish-origin 23-year-old married woman from Afrin, with a son and residing in İzmir, said the following when asked about what makes life meaningful for her:

> We do not have any future [here], some went abroad, they were able to succeed. My sister-in-law told me that they received a phone call from someone asking them whether they want to return to Syria. I am saying there is no house, no job, no equipment. Where could we go? How can they call us to ask whether we want to return to Syria? I give you our property over there, just you go, how can you go, how can you work there? If you are young, you cannot go there at all, if you are a woman, you may be captured on the way, even before arriving in Afrin, they would be raped. In fact, I want to go, return, all of us want to go back, why do I pay such a high rent here, only 100 TL remains us from our salary, unfortunately, there is no saving left for us. I do not know what we would do, we do not have a future, we are not able to move back or forth, we are stuck here. (Interview, 17 August 2018, İzmir, 13_SRII)

It has become obvious that the Turkish state is more engaged now in integrating refugees into social, economic and political spheres of life as well as in trying to engage the local municipalities in taking responsibility in the integration of migrants and refugees. Due to the lack of space in this chapter, I could not go into details of the activities undertaken by the state actors, local municipalities and the civil society organisations in Turkey for the integration of refugees and migrants. The International Organization for Migration (IOM) has recently been working with a group of scholars on preparing policy recommendations for the integration of migrants, in collaboration with the DGMM. Hence, one could argue that the refugee crisis has also brought about some substantial changes in the mindset of the state actors, together with international organisations such as the IOM, to prepare a solid integration policy in Turkey, which is still in progress. Anecdotal evidence shows that these attempts increased in the aftermath of the Refugee Deal signed between Turkey and the EU on 18 March 2016.

Conclusion

This chapter has argued that the Syrian refugees' state of temporariness is now turning into a state of permanency. This shift partly depends on the Europeanisation of migration and asylum policies in Turkey, partly on the instrumentalisation of the Syrians in the labour market, and partly on the government's demographic concerns. Whatever the reason is, one thing is very clear: Syrian refugees have made Turkish state actors work on policy recommendations for the integration of migrants, which is imperative for the improvement of the conditions of the Syrians as well as other migrants. Syrians are exposed to various difficulties in everyday life in Turkey, not only because of the lack of a permanent legal status, but also because of the fact that the absorption capacity of Turkey is not enough to accommodate more than three million refugees. It is exactly these problems which, in the end, prompt some refugees to leave Turkey at the expense of risking their lives at the border.

Turkey has many challenges ahead, with regard not only to the integration of refugees but also to the reenactment of democracy in the aftermath of the failed coup of 15 July 2016. Societal and political polarisation within the country has become evident since the #occupygezi movement of June 2013, and the refugees are also becoming more and more exposed to such divides. There is growing popular resentment against the Syrian refugees, which has become even more detectable since the Turkish government explicitly announced that a number of Syrian refugees will be granted Turkish citizenship. The level of popular resentment increased even more in southeast Anatolia among the Kurdish- and Alevi-origin local populations due to rumours that the government is becoming more likely to demographically instrumentalise Sunni Muslim Arabs to counterbalance the ethno-nationalist and centrifugal claims of the Kurds. One could argue that the most feasible scenario for Turkey coming to terms with the social, political and economic implications of the Syrian refugees is to align itself with the European Union and the Europeanisation process, which has already brought about many progressive elements in the liberalisation of migration, asylum and integration policies on the basis of universal rights and values.

Evidently, the task for Turkey is a difficult one, but the task of the European Union is not easy either. The refugee crisis is reinforcing the growth of populist movements in the EU - a development which had already been triggered by the financial crisis and neoliberal forms of governmentality. So far, the EU has been relying on the Turkey–EU refugee deal signed on 18 March 2016 to bring down the number of refugees trying to go to EU countries as well as the number of border deaths. Thomas Spijkerboer (2016) has even found that the deal has also been instrumental in breaking the business model of smugglers. The message of the deal to refugees is that 'getting on a boat in Turkey, and endangering lives in the process, is not worth the risk given that there is a legal and safe pathway through resettlement' (Spijkerboer, 2016).

According to the 18 March agreement, irregular migrants who arrived in the Greek islands from Turkey after 20 March 2016 would be sent back to Turkey. In return, the EU was to resettle one Syrian refugee from Turkey to the bloc for each Syrian that Greece returned to Turkey. In return, Turkey was to receive up to 6 billion euros, visa-free travel and fast-track negotiations on EU accession.[16] The deal has been considered 'unlawful' or 'unethical' by many observers who claim that the EU has become very silent on the undemocratic acts of the Turkish government, to make sure that the deal will be implemented by the Turkish state.[17] Whether the deal is unlawful or unethical according to international law, what is essential is to keep Turkey on the right track to reinforce the Europeanisation process and the continuation of the accession negotiations. Hence, the introduction of visa-free travel for Turkish citizens has a strategic importance in making sure that Turkish civil society will continue to find a strong appeal in the European accession process, which is still the most essential element for the alignment of the migration, asylum and integration policies in Turkey.

Notes

Part of the research for this chapter was undertaken as part of the Horizon 2020 research and innovation project RESPOND (Multilevel Governance of Mass Migration in Europe and Beyond) under Grant Agreement Number 770564. As a member of the Turkey team, I would like to express my gratitude to the other members of the team (Aslı Aydın, Susan Rottmann, Ela Gökalp-Aras and Zeynep Şahin-Mencütek) who carried out the interviews with the Syrian refugees.

1. For more discussion on Viktor Orbán's political discourse on the Syrian refugees see Guardian (2015); see also <http://helsinki.hu/wp-content/uploads/Asylum-2015-Hungary-press-info-4March2015.pdf> (last accessed 7 November 2016).
2. For further detail on discourse analysis see Wodak (2009).
3. That is, the Horizon 2020 Project RESPOND (Multilevel Governance of Mass Migration in Europe and Beyond), Grant Agreement Number 770564.
4. Despite the geographical limitation of its refugee regime, Kirişci (2014: 8) asserts that 'with 45,000 applications in 2013, Turkey became the fifth largest recipient of individual asylum seekers among forty-four industrialized countries'.

5. For the text of the Geneva Convention and Protocol relating to the Status of Refugees see <http://www.unhcr.org/3b66c2aa10> (last accessed 11 December 2019).

6. For a similar discursive marking of Syrians as 'guests' see Korkut (2015).

7. For the official text of the Temporary Protection Regulation see Directorate General of Migration Management (2014).

8. For more detail on the history and organisational structure of AFAD see <https://en.afad.gov.tr/about-us> (last accessed 21 December 2019).

9. For a full account of the number of people residing in the temporary accommodation centres until the delivery of their organisation to the DGMM in October 2018, see the official internet page of AFAD, <https://www.afad.gov.tr/barinma-merkezlerinde-son-durum> (last accessed 21 December 2019).

10. It was later reported by the public servants in a workshop that the security forces in Istanbul revealed that thousands of medicines were illegally marketed by smugglers after being taken from pharmacies using the refugees' identities. Following this incident, AFAD took a radical decision to have strict surveillance of the trafficking of medicine and to authorise only one pharmacy to process the medication for the refugees under temporary protection.

11. For more detail on the survey carried out by the GMF see <http://www.gmfus.org/turkey> (last accessed 11 December 2019).

12. For news coverage about President Erdoğan's discourse on the Syrians being granted citizenship, or dual nationality, see Hurriyet Daily News (2016).

13. For the deputy prime minister Numan Kurtulmuş's speech on granting citizenship to the Syrians see Sabah (2016).

14. See <https://multeciler.org.tr/turkiyedeki-suriyeli-sayisi> (last accessed 6 May 2019).

15. See <https://t24.com.tr/haber/suleyman-soylu-vatandaslik-verilen-suriyelilerin-sayisini-acikladi,833262> (last accessed 10 August 2019).

16. For a detailed account of the current state of the agreement see the 'Letter from President Juncker to the President and the Members of the European Council on progress in the implementation of the Facility for Refugees in Turkey', 17 October 2016, <http://europa.eu/rapid/press-release_STATEMENT-16-3465_en.htm> (last accessed 11 December 2019). On the other hand, as opposed to what Jean-Claude Juncker said in his statement, some claim that the agreement has failed and resulted in the deterioration of the state of refugees in the Greek islands. See Karnitschnig and Delcker (2016).

17. For a detailed account of the European response to the refugee crisis, see Toygür and Benvenuti (2016).

References

Ajans Haber (2016) 'Bakanlar Kurulu sonrası Kurtulmuş'tan açıklama' ['Kurtulmuş's speech after the Council of Ministers'] 11 January, <http://www.ajanshaber.com/bakanlar-kurulu-sonrasi-kurtulmustan-aciklama-haberi/325379> (last accessed 8 November 2019).

Akşam (2014) 'Davutoğlu: Gazi şehir artık Ensar şehridir' ['Davutoğlu: Veteran city is now Ansar city'], 28 December, <http://www.aksam.com.tr/siyaset/davutoglu-gazi-sehir-artik-ensar-sehirdir/haber-367691> (last accessed 7 November 2019).

Altınay, H. (2008) 'Turkey's soft power: an unpolished gem or an elusive mirage?' Insight Turkey 10(2): 55–66.

Amnesty International (2014) *Struggling to Survive: Refugees from Syria in Turkey.* EUR 44/017/2014, <https://www.amnesty.org/en/documents/EUR44/017/2014/en> (last accessed 10 December 2019).

Baban, F., S. Ilcan and K. Rygiel (2016) 'Syrian refugees in Turkey: pathways to precarity, differential inclusion, and negotiated citizenship rights.' *Journal of Ethnic and Migration Studies*, 43(1): 41–57, <https://doi.org/10.1080/1369183X.2016.1192996> (last accessed 10 December 2019).

Börzel, T., and T. Risse (2003) 'Conceptualizing the domestic impact of Europe.' Pp. 57–82 in *The Politics of Europeanization*, edited by K. Featherstone and C. M. Radaelli. Oxford: Oxford University Press.

Canefe, N. (2016) 'Management of irregular migration: Syrians in Turkey as paradigm shifters for forced migration studies.' *New Perspectives on Turkey* 54: 9–32.

Chatty, D. (2013) 'Guests and hosts: Arab hospitality underpins a humane approach to asylum policy.' *The Cairo Review of Global Affairs* 19 (22 April), <http://www.auce-gypt.edu/GAPP/CairoReview/Pages/articleDetails.aspx?aid=335> (last accessed 20 December 2019).

Collett, E. (2016) 'The paradox of the EU–Turkey refugee deal,' *Migration Policy*, March, <http://www.migrationpolicy.org/news/paradox-eu-turkey-refugee-deal> (last accessed 22 September 2016).

Council of the European Union (2001) 'Council Directive of European Temporary Protection.' *Official Journal of the European Communities*, L 212/12 (7 August), <https://eur-lex.europa.eu/LexUriServ/LexUriServ.do?uri=OJ:L:2001:212:0012:0023:EN:PDF> (last accessed 8 August 2019).

Davutoğlu, A. (2005) *Stratejik Derinlik: Türkiye'nin Uluslararası Konumu* (Strategic Depth: Turkey's International Position). İstanbul: Küre.

De Bel-Air, F. (2006) *Migration and Politics in the Middle East: Migration Policies, Nation Building and International Relations.* Beyrouth: IFPO.

Directorate General of Migration Management (2014) *The Temporary Protection Regulation in Turkey*, <https://www.refworld.org/docid/56572fd74.html> (last accessed 21 December 2019).

El Abed, O. (2014) 'The discourse of guesthood: forced migrants in Jordan.' Pp. 81–100 in *Managing Muslim Mobilities*, edited by A. Fabos and R. Osotalo. London: Palgrave.

Erdemir, A. (2016) 'The Syrian refugee crisis: can Turkey be an effective partner?' *Foundation for Defence of Democracies*, 16 February, <http://www.defenddemoc-racy.org/media-hit/dr-aykan-erdemir-the-syrian-refugee-crisis-can-turkey-be-an-effective-partner> (last accessed 3 October 2016).

Erdoğan, E. (2014) *Unwanted, Unwelcome: Anti-Immigration Attitudes in Turkey.* Working Paper, German Marshall Fund of the United States (10 September).

Erdoğan, M. (2015) *Türkiye'deki Suriyeliler* (Syrians in Turkey). Istanbul: Istanbul Bilgi University Press.

Erdoğan, M., and A. Kaya (eds) (2015) *14. Yüzyıldan 21. Yüzyıla Türkiye'ye Göçler* (Migration to Turkey since the 14th Century). Istanbul: Istanbul Bilgi University Press.

Eroglu, D. (2013) 'The making of asylum policies in Turkey: analysis of non-governmental organisations, political elites and bureaucrats.' PhD thesis, University of Essex.

Flockhart, T. (2010) 'Europeanization or EU-ization? The transfer of EU norms across time and space.' *Journal of Common Market Studies* 48(4): 787–810.

Gökay, B. (2015) 'The making of a racist myth.' *Ottomania* (15 January), <http://www.fabrikzeitung.ch/the-making-of-a-racist-myth/> (last accessed 11 December 2019)

Guardian (2015) 'Editorial', 6 September, <https://www.theguardian.com/commentisfree/2015/sep/06/the-guardian-view-on-hungaryand-the-refugee-crisis-orban-the-awful> (last accessed 6 November 2019).

Haber7 (2014) 'Cumhurbaşkanı Erdoğan: Bizler Ensar sizler muhacir' ['President Erdoğan: we are *Ansar*, you are *muhacir*'], 7 October, <http://www.haber7.com/ic-politika/haber/1208342-cumhurbaskani-erdogan-bizler-ensar-sizler-muhacir> (last accessed 4 October 2019)

Hemer, O., and H. A. Persson (eds) (2018) *In the Aftermath of Gezi: From Social Movement to Social Change?* Cham: Palgrave

Hurriyet (2014) 'Erdoğan Suriyeli sığınmacılara seslendi' ['Erdoğan addressed at the Syrian refugees'], 8 October, <http://www.hurriyet.com.tr/erdogan-suriyeli-siginmacilara-seslendi-27342780> (last accessed 7 November 2019).

Hurriyet Daily News (2016) 'Erdoğan details dual citizenship for Syrians', 11 July, <http://www.hurriyetdailynews.com/erdogan-details-dual-citizenship-for-syrians.aspx?pageID=238&nid=101428&NewsCatID=341> (last accessed 21 December 2019).

İçduygu, A. (2015) *Turkey's Evolving Migration Policies: A Mediterranean Transit Stop at the Doors of the EU.* IAI Working Paper 15/31, Rome (September).

Kaiser, B., and A. Kaya (2015) 'Transformation of migration and asylum policies in Turkey.' Pp. 94–115 in *The Europeanization of Public Policies: A Scorecard*, edited by A. Güney and A. Tekin. Abingdon: Routledge.

Kalın, I. (2011) 'Soft power and public diplomacy in Turkey.' *Perceptions* 16(3): 5–23.

Karnitschnig, M., and J. Delcker (2016) 'Europe's refugee bomb: EU–Turkey deal "falls dramatically short," says one of the architects of the plan.' *POLITICO*, 18 October, <http://www.politico.eu/article/europes-refugee-time-bomb-merkel-turkey-deal-news/> (last accessed 11 December 2019)

Kaya, A. (2005) 'Cultural reification in Circassian diaspora: stereotypes, prejudices and ethnic relations.' *Journal of Ethnic and Migration Studies* 31(1): 129–49.

Kaya, A. (2013) *Europeanization and Tolerance in Turkey: The Myth of Toleration.* London: Palgrave

Kaya, A. (2015) 'Islamisation of Turkey under the AKP rule: empowering family, faith and charity.' *South European Society and Politics* 20(1): 47–69, <https://doi.org/10.1080/13608746.2014.979031> (last accessed 11 December 2019).

Kaya, A., and A. Kıraç (2016) *Vulnerability Assessment of Syrian Refugees in Istanbul.* Report, Support to Life Association, <http://eu.bilgi.edu.tr/media/files/160621_Ist_NA_Report.pdf/> (last accessed 11 December 2019).

Kaya, A. and T. Tarhanli (eds) (2005) *Türkiye'de Çoğunluk ve Azınlık Politikaları: AB Sürecinde Yurttaşlık Tartışmaları* (Majority and Minority Policies in Turkey: Citizenship Debates on the way to the EU). Istanbul: TESEV.

Keser, H. (2006) 'Justice and home affairs: Europeanization of Turkish asylum and immigration policy in the light of the Central and Eastern European experience.' *Ankara Review of European Studies*, 5(3): 115–30.

Keyman, E. F., and A. İçduygu (2003) 'Globalization, civil society and citizenship in Turkey: actors, boundaries and discourses.' *Citizenship Studies* 7(2): 219–34.

Keyman, E. F., and Z. Öniş (2007) *Turkish Politics in a Changing World: Global Dynamics and Domestic Transformations*. Istanbul: Istanbul Bilgi University Press.

Kılıç, B. K., and K. Üstün (2015) *Turkey's Syrian Refugees: Towards Integration*. Istanbul: Seta.

Kirişçi, K. (2011) 'Turkey's "demonstrative effect" and the transformation of the Middle East.' *Insight Turkey*13(2): 33–55.

Kirişçi, K. (2014) *Syrian Refugees and Turkey's Challenges: Going Beyond Hospitality*. Working Paper (May), Brookings Institute.

Kirişçi, K., and E. Ferris (2015) *Not Likely to Go Home: Syrian Refugees and the Challenges to Turkey – and the International Community*. Turkey Project Policy Paper, No. 7 (September), Brookings Institute.

Kirişçi, K., and S. Karaca (2015) 'Hoşgörü ve Çelişkiler: 1989, 1991 ve 2011'de Türkiye'ye Yönelen Kitlesel Mülteci Akınları' (Tolerance and Conflicts: Massive Refugee Flows to Turkey). Pp. 295–314 in *14. Yüzyıldan 21. Yüzyıla Türkiye'ye Göçler* (Migration to Turkey since the 14th Century), edited by M. Erdoğan and A. Kaya. Istanbul: Istanbul Bilgi University Press.

Korkut, U. (2015) 'Pragmatism, moral responsibility or policy change: the Syrian refugee crisis and selective humanitarianism in the Turkish refugee regime.' *Comparative Migration Studies* 4: 2, <https://doi.org/10.1186/s40878-015-0020-9> (last accessed 11 December 2019).

Öner, A. Ş., and D. Genç (2015) 'Vulnerability leading to mobility: Syrians' exodus from Turkey.' *Migration Letters* 12(3): 251–62

Öniş, Z. (2004) 'Turkish modernization and challenges for the new Europe.' *Perceptions* (Autumn): 5–28.

Pérouse, J. -F. (2013) 'La Turquie face aux soubresauts migratoires dans un contexte de crise.' *Confluences Méditerrannée* 4(87): 85–93.

Sabah (2016) 'Hükümetten Suriyelilere Vatandaşlık açıklaması' ['Turkish government details citizenship to Syrians'], 15 July, <http://www.sabah.com.tr/gundem/2016/07/14/hukumetten-suriyelilere-vatandaslik-aciklamasi> (last accessed 21 December 2019).

Saktanber, A., and G. Çorbacıoğlu. (2008) 'Veiling and headscarf skepticism in Turkey.' *Social Politics: International Studies in Gender, State & Society* 15(4): 514–38.

Spiegel Online (2014) 'Antalya verweigert syrischen Flüchtlingen Aufenthalt.' Spiegel Online, 8 November, <http://www.spiegel.de/panorama/tuerkei-syrische-fluechtlingeduerfen-nicht-in-antalya-bleiben-a-1001851.html> (last accessed 6 September 2016).

Spijkerboer, T. (2016) 'Fact check: did the EU–Turkey deal bring down the number of migrants and of border deaths?' *Border Criminologies*, 28 September,

<https://www.law.ox.ac.uk/research-subject-groups/centre-criminology/centreborder-criminologies/blog/2016/09/fact-check-did-eu> (last accessed 11 December 2019)

T24 (2019) 'Süleyman Soylu vatandaşlık verilen Suriyelilerin sayısını açıkladı' ['Süleyman Soylu announced the number of Syrians granted Turkish citizenship'], 2 August, <https://t24.com.tr/haber/suleyman-soylu-vatandaslik-verilen-suriyelilerin-sayisini-acikladi,833262> (last accessed 21 December 2019).

Tecmen, A. (2017) 'Nation branding and right to brand/brand Turkey.' *Research and Policy on Turkey* 2(1): 76–89.

Togral-Koca, B. (2016) 'Syrian refugees in Turkey: from "guests" to "enemies"?' *New Perspectives on Turkey*, 54: 55–75.

Toygür, İ., and B. Benvenuti (2016) *The European Response to the Refugee Crisis: Angela Merkel on the Move*. IPC-Mercator Policy Brief (June).

UNHCR (2010) Geneva Convention and Protocol relating to the Status of Refugees. <http://www.unhcr.org/3b66c2aa10> (last accessed 11 December 2019).

UNHCR (2015) *The Sea Route to Europe: The Mediterranean Passage in the Age of Refugees*. 1 July, <http://www.unhcr.org/5592bd059.html> (last accessed 11 December 2019).

Wodak, R. (2009) *The Discourse of Politics in Action: Politics as Usual*. Basingstoke: Palgrave Macmillan.

Yetkin, M. (2018) '"Cross vs. crescent" again? Seriously?' *Hurriyet Daily News*, 12 June, <http://www.hurriyetdailynews.com/opinion/murat-yetkin/cross-vs-crescent-again-seriously-133156> (last accessed 30 August 2019).

Yılmaz, G. (2011) *Is There a Puzzle? Compliance with Minority Rights in Turkey (1999–2010)*. KFG Working Paper Series, No. 23.

Zihnioğlu, Ö. (2013) *European Union Civil Society Policy and Turkey: A Bridge Too Far?* New York: Palgrave Macmillan.

5

The Middle Eastern Refugee Crisis and the So-Called Islamic State: Motivations of Iraqi Yazidis for Migrating to Europe

Karel Černý

Introduction

THIS CHAPTER FOCUSES on refugees from the Yazidi minority in Iraq and their motivations for migrating to Europe. It is a case study based on field research conducted in March 2016 in the territory of the Kurdish regional government in northern Iraq, and it presents preliminary findings from the field. The chapter is based on more than thirty in-depth semi-structured interviews with refugees (internally displaced people, IDPs), both inside and outside refugee camps, and it discusses the many and complex motivations that the refugees take into consideration when making decisions about their past migration inside Iraq and especially about possible future migration to Europe. This study presents the perspective of the Yazidi refugees themselves, which is in some respects unique to this religious minority, but findings also contribute to the more general discussion about the many motivations of refugees from war zones in the contemporary Middle East.

The main research question is why the Iraqi Yazidis want to migrate to Europe (a synonym for Europe is usually Germany). The answer is seemingly simple since we can assume that the obvious reason is the military attack on the Yazidi communities by the so-called Islamic State in 2014.[1] Or we can claim similarly that the main reason is the military conflict in Iraq at that time. However, the Iraqi Yazidis did not directly run away from their villages to Europe; most of them took refuge in the territory of the autonomous region of Iraqi Kurdistan instead. Also, Iraqi Yazidis were emigrating to Europe beforehand, both those from Iraq (Sinjar) and those from autonomous Kurdistan. So such a mono-causal explanation does not fit the complex reality of the Yazidi migration to Europe. In fact, this chapter uncovers a rather complex set of motivations for migrating to Europe, and as a result provides the reader with a multi-factor explanation of the phenomenon.

It should also be clear to the reader from the start that the field research focused on the motives for migrating to Europe, not on the motives for staying in some other parts of Iraq or returning home. However, we consider those issues as strongly interconnected in order to understand the complex decision-making process about possible migration. Last but not least, the interviews were carried out with Iraqi Yazidis in the territory of the autonomous Kurdistan region in northern Iraq, not with those Yazidis who had already successfully emigrated to Europe. As a consequence, the research design does not allow us to generate hypotheses about the possible differences between those Yazidis who were motivated to migrate, although they never did, and those who actually made the step and migrated. Again, research into the issue would help us to understand the actual complexities of migration better, and we consider it an important topic for further research, beyond the scope of this chapter.

The structure of the chapter is as follows. First, it briefly introduces the relevant theoretical and methodological concepts employed in the research. Second, it provides a brief overview of the Iraqi Yazidis, including their geographical distribution, religious beliefs and societal organisation. After this contextual information, it briefly provides historical background to the genocide of 2014, especially in terms of shifting boundaries between various political actors and communities, and the consequent growing political instability and unpredictability of Nineveh Province. The last main section of the chapter deals with the many and complex motivations of Iraqi Yazidis for leaving Iraq for Europe; this section is then followed by conclusions.

Interpretative sociology and social constructivism show us that people act not according to how the world is objectively, but according to their own subjective understanding of it, according to how they grasp and interpret this world. A person's subjective perception of the world is thus a kind of intermediary between the objective world on the one hand and action in this world on the other. These subjective interpretations, however, tend to be shared collectively within one society, and are constantly being (re)negotiated and passed on from person to person. Individuals are thus not as a rule in any way original and authentic in how they read the world in which they live (Berger and Luckmann 1999). Iraqi Yazidis weigh the option of leaving for Europe in the light of how they subjectively understand the society and land that they live in. These subjective views are also the individual and more general motives that we discover in our analysis. Yet what this refers to is nothing other than the 'push factors' that are already well known in migration theory, factors that lean in favour of leaving Iraq or specifically the autonomous region of Iraqi Kurdistan (see Ritchey 1976).

However, we did not focus that much on other dimensions of migration theory and we did not systematically cover the 'pull factors'. In other words, we did not research into the question of how the potential migrants (refugees) subjectively access their preferences in terms of where to migrate. Also, we did not cover the related topic of how they evaluate possible obstacles on their imagined migration journey. Finally, it is important to stress that we have interviewed potential migrants, who might or might not migrate in the end. The reader should keep this in mind throughout the analysis.

Field research and data collection were carried out in March 2016 in Kurdish northern Iraq (Dohuk Province) using more than thirty semi-structured in-depth interviews. The interviews usually lasted ninety minutes and respondents were asked about the reasons and circumstances that led to their becoming refugees. The interviews also explored the refugees' strategies for the future, including the possibility of going to Europe. The interviews were conducted with Yazidi refugees both inside and outside refugee camps, and translators were recruited from the Yazidi community to interpret. Contact with respondents and access to the field were obtained with the aid of 'gatekeepers', who enjoy a high level of trust amongst Yazidi refugees. Interviews were also conducted with Yazidis who had been living in Dohuk Province for a long time and were not refugees. Many of the in-depth interviews were conducted with Yazidi academics, activists and top political and religious figures. Interviewing was concluded as soon as the sample was 'theoretically saturated', that is to say, when further interviews began to provide the same content over and over and offered no additional value for understanding how the respondents ended up as refugees and what reasons exist for migrating to Europe. In order to ensure the safety of respondents, the names of some of them will not be given in full.

The interviews were analysed according to the logic of 'grounded theory', the aim of which is to build a theoretical explanation based on empirical data. Three types of coding were used: open (to uncover basic motives for migration), axial (to cluster the basic motives under more abstract and general categories) and selective (to propose basic causal relations among the categories). The study was thus based on a qualitative research design, working with a large amount of data on a small number of persons. The study is thus aimed not at generalisations about the Yazidi population, but at generalisations that can be applied in the construction of a theory about the causes of Yazidi migration to Europe (see Strauss and Corbinová 1999; Hendl 2005).

The Yazidis in Iraq

The unique religion of the Yazidi people and the unusual way in which they order their society, which is based on both tribalism and a caste system, make them one of the most fascinating minorities in Iraq, but also one of the least studied and most shrouded in myth. Out of a population of more than 600,000, more than half a million Yazidis live in the largely Kurdish region of northern Iraq and speak the Kurdish *kurmanji* dialect. They follow a monotheistic religion unlike any other (Kubálek 2016), and they believe that they are the inheritors of the oldest religion in the Middle East, the roots of which stretch back to ancient Mesopotamia and Persia. They also believe that they are the authentic pre-Kurds, the true followers of a pre-historical Kurdish religion that the other Kurds abandoned under pressure from Islam. Now they also believe, with renewed conviction, that they are the eternal victims of persecution by the majority (Açikyildiz 2010; Domle 2013).

Yazidism is a religious syncretism. It originated in its current form when a group of Arab Suffi Muslims in the mountains of northern Iraq encountered Kurds who were followers of various pre-Islamic cults (Kubálek 2015). The earliest foundations of Yazidism were formed by proto-Iranian religions. The Yazidi practices of praying to the Peacock Angel as a symbol of the deity, and of viewing the sun, stars and basic elements such as water and fire as sacred, all date from that period, and Yazidi teachings about reincarnation and the strict division of their society into castes originated in early Mesopotamia. Conversely, Yazidism's most recent formative layer comes from Islamic mysticism, which was introduced into Yazidism by the prominent twelfth-century reformer Sheikh Adi (the practice of fasting, the cult of saints, and the ascetic fakirs all date from this period). Yazidism also contains elements of classical mythology, Christianity and Judaism (Açikyildiz 2010).

The Yazidis' knowledge of the teachings of their religion is somewhat limited and rather more intuitive in nature; religious tradition is passed on orally, it is not recorded in any sacred books, and there is no formal theology. Yazidism cannot, however, be narrowly interpreted as a religious system, as it also involves a specific way of regulating interpersonal relations and a specific culture. It is thus much more than just a religion in the narrow sense of the word (Kubálek 2007a; 2007b; 2007c; 2015). Yazidism is above all a specific approach to ordering society that is based on a caste system. Two castes form the religious aristocracy (*sheikhs* and *pirs*), and all other Yazidis belong to the lowest caste, the *murids* (Açikyildiz 2010).

Historically, the majority of Yazidis have always been centred in a peripheral, rebellious and conservatively orientated region, located near the Sinjar Mountains, approximately a hundred kilometres west of Mosul (Kubálek 2016). This remote region in the Iraqi province of Nineveh has, however, experienced for centuries escalating pressure from the in-migration of non-Yazidis and forced conversions. While this area was for centuries the demographic centre of the Yazidi people, in the summer of 2014 the majority of them were driven out of Sinjar by Daesh (the so-called Islamic State). The Yazidis' spiritual and secular authorities continue to be based in the town of Ain Sifni in the Shekhan District, located further north, while their main shrine and pilgrimage site are in nearby Lalish. Both it and Sinjar are areas that have been subject to territorial disputes between Iraqi Kurds and the central government in Baghdad since the 1990s. There was also a group of Arabic-speaking Yazidis residing in an ethnic enclave in the twin towns of Bahzani and Bashiqa, near Mosul, until the enclave was attacked by the so-called Islamic State. After 2014, most of the Iraqi Yazidis fled from the Islamists into the Kurdish Dohuk Province and are now IDPs. Approximately sixty-six thousand of them then became refugees and left for Europe, most of them heading for Germany and Sweden (Kubálek 2016).

Yazidis in Nineveh province:
the background to the attack by the Islamic State

The story of Yazidi migration to Europe after the genocide of 2014 needs to be told in a proper historical context to make sense. To put it in other words, history matters if we are to understand the contemporary motivations of Iraqi Yazidis for leaving Iraq. Since the era of the Ba'ath Party regime, through the 2003 toppling of the Saddam Hussein regime, and until the expansion of the so-called Islamic State, most Iraqi Yazidis have been living in an unstable environment, characterised by a constant bordering and re-bordering (conflicts of the Arabs versus the Kurds, central government versus the provincial government versus the autonomous Kurdish government, locals versus the newcomers, those connected to state power versus those excluded).

For Iraqi Yazidis the American-led invasion of Iraq that toppled the dictatorship of Saddam Hussein in 2003 marked the start of fundamental changes in their lives. Iraq drew up a constitution in 2005 that gave official recognition to ethnic and religious minorities and established Iraq as a federation, within which the Kurds were granted extensive autonomy (Laurens 2013; Salloum 2013). After the dictatorship was dismantled, however, the Yazidis were unable to integrate into what became a rapidly disintegrating Iraqi society. Nor were they able to obtain adequate representation in the new political system or state institutions. This was one of the reasons why the state failed to effectively protect Yazidis against everyday discrimination and multiplying attacks from Islamic radicals long before the emergence of the Islamic State (Maisel 2008).

After 2003, the position of the Yazidi minority was further complicated not just by the spiralling sectarian conflicts between Sunni and Shiite Arabs, but also by the conflict between the central Arabic government and the autonomous Kurdistan Regional Government, which sought greater independence while laying claim to a substantial section of the disputed territories in Nineveh Province, where the majority of Yazidis were living. The disputed territories are the main factor, and a unique one, contributing to the destabilisation of Nineveh Province and the rise of the Islamic State and attacks on defenceless Yazidis. While the Iraqi constitution requires that a referendum be held to determine the fate of the disputed territories, the referendum has never taken place. A chronic legal and administrative vacuum consequently surrounds this issue. The Kurdistan Regional Government (in Erbil), the Federal Government (in Baghdad) and the Provincial Government (in Mosul) have been passing the buck amongst themselves as to which of them is responsible for the fate of the population residing in the disputed territories. The opaque division of responsibility on this issue has led to administrative chaos and the absence of any single authority assuming responsibility for investment, the development of infrastructure and the protection of minorities.

Nineveh Province has suffered as a result of being ignored by the Federal Government. Once a prosperous province with a diverse economy, after 2003 Nineveh became one of the poorest provinces in Iraq, saddled with a small budget, collapsing infrastructure and surging unemployment. Its problems were further exacerbated by an influx of IDPs from other parts of Iraq. By 2008, Nineveh was home to the largest number of IDPs in the country; they fled there because the province was able to offer them some safety. This put added pressure on the province's already strained infrastructure and a shortage in the supply of goods. If that were not enough, Nineveh was hit by an extreme drought (2009 and 2010), so that crop production in the agricultural region shrank by 47 per cent, and there were not enough water sources to meet the needs of agricultural production and household consumption (UN Habitat 2015: 3).

Moreover, Nineveh Province was the region within Iraq that was impacted most by Saddam Hussein's Arabisation campaigns, which then hindered the province's development after 2003. The forced deportation of local Kurds (including Yazidis) and, conversely, the resettling in Nineveh of Arabs from neighbouring provinces, who were loyal to Saddam Hussein's regime, gave rise to persistent tensions between the different communities. Since then there have been ongoing legal disputes over land and property belonging to Kurds and other minorities that was destroyed or confiscated by the state under Saddam Hussein and handed over to new Arab settlers to secure their support. The mainly Arabic army of Saddam Hussein also committed war crimes in the 1980s, primarily against Kurds and Yazidis, during which a million inhabitants were deported from their traditional towns and villages, chemical weapons were used on civilians, and more than one hundred thousand people were killed or remain unaccounted for. For this reason, members of minorities remain distrustful of federal security forces to this day. These skeletons from the past began tumbling out of the closet after 2003 and contributed to the escalation of sectarianism (Recchia 2012).

Nineveh Province is also, however, an illustration in miniature of the larger, more general collapse of the Iraqi state and the radicalisation of its society. The collapse of the state and radicalisation are the reasons why there were so many defenceless minorities, who ended up located in the province in close proximity to growing numbers of militants. The latter were driven into Nineveh from the neighbouring Anbar Province, which became too dangerous for them after the 2007 American surge in Iraq and the birth of the Sahwa (Awakening) Movement. The weakness of state institutions and security forces together with the absence of any political will to protect minorities are other factors that left minorities vulnerable. In the resulting political and security vacuum it was easy for the Islamic State to establish itself, and unlike its predecessors (e.g. Al Qaeda) it had not only an ideological motivation for wiping out minorities but also the capacity to genuinely carry its objectives through (Kikoler 2015).

Security forces present in Nineveh Province were not independent, but followed a sectarian logic. The Shiite-led federal army in particular looked on the primarily Sunni population of Nineveh as an alien occupying force. The frustrations of Sunni Arabs were amplified when, after taking to the streets to demonstrate against corruption and lawlessness, they were dispersed by the army and the Shiite militia in 2012. Sunni extremists, including the Islamic State, used this to their advantage and were able to establish themselves in Nineveh not just because of the weakness of institutions but also because of the frustrations felt by the population (Khalaf 2016; Jírů 2015). At the same time, people began to seek protection from the militias that were forming along ethnic, religious and party lines and offered some kind of security amidst a collapsing state, which left a power vacuum in its wake that was filled by rival militias, resulting in even greater chaos. It is little surprise that it was the Islamic State that after years of instability and lawlessness promised to restore security and order (Kikoler 2015).

The absence of rule of law moreover gave rise to a culture of impunity. After 2003, Sunni and Shiite extremists grew used to the fact that the state never carried out any investigations or sought accountability from anyone. It was clear to perpetrators and victims alike that the state was neither willing nor able to protect its citizens. And it was also the corrupt armed forces of the state that helped to create this culture of impunity. A lack of security was something that everyone had to contend with. Yet it was minorities in particular who were the most vulnerable because they had no backing from state forces and did not have militias of their own (Kikoler 2015).

In this context, the Islamic State seized the provincial capital of Mosul while the Iraqi army collapsed across Nineveh in the summer of 2014. An attack on Sinjar followed, on 3 August 2014. After capturing the plains of Sinjar, the Islamists also temporarily seized the Yazidi enclaves in Bashiqa and Bahzani, near Mosul (Kubálek 2016). All that remained defended against the Islamic State was the poorly accessible Sinjar Mountains, where the Yazidi resistance entrenched itself (Khanki 2015: 16). The total number of people murdered in Yazidi regions is not yet known and estimates of the number of victims vary. Only with the liberation of Yazidi regions will the true scope of the catastrophe become clear (Tariq 2015). All Yazidis, without exception, were driven from their homes, and out of the community of four hundred thousand who lived in Sinjar, almost no one is left there. The Islamists also destroyed the Yazidi shrines (UNHRC 2016; Yazda 2016).

All the above suggests there is little if anything left that Yazidis could return to, and many of them have thought of leaving their homeland in search of a better life. Let us now move forward and look at the specific characteristics of Yazidi migration, aimed primarily at Europe. The following pages will outline the primary motives Yazidis list for making or refusing the choice to migrate. These show how complex the choice of migration is even for people in such a dire situation.

The primary motives for migrating to Europe

This section presents the main findings of the interview-based research, indicating the primary motives Yazidis most often take into account when considering whether or not to migrate to Europe.

Insufficient aid, unsuitable conditions

One of the most visible signs of the collapse of the Iraqi state, which has become unable to perform its basic functions and see to the needs of its citizens, is the inadequate capacity of its refugee camps. Even two years after the Yazidis fled their homes, the demand for space in refugee camps in Iraq was still greater than the supply. And the shortage of space had even begun to increase. Initially, most refugees managed to find accommodation outside the camps – with relatives, in public buildings, in buildings still under construction or in rented flats. Many of them have now exhausted their savings and therefore, much later on, are seeking places in camps and humanitarian assistance.

The lack of space available in the refugee camps means that they suffer from *overcrowding* and that the material conditions in the camps are poor. Refugees living in the camps complain most about a *shortage of water, toilets, and showers*. The people in these camps are from a conservative society, but facilities and resources have to be shared by families who do not know each other, and this generates conflicts between already frustrated refugees. The refugees are also dejected at the shortage of electricity, though the ordinary population of Iraqi Kurdistan is also hit with power outages. The refugees complain too of a lack of *health care*, which they have to seek out themselves in private clinics, and as a result even refugees who may at first have been self-sufficient financially can end up in debt and dependent on assistance from others. Finally, the refugees complain about the unsuitable tents and infrastructure in the camps (unpaved muddy roads, the absence of any connections to the outside world, few schools and teachers).

The refugees thus believe that their basic life needs are not being met, and in their view the situation is not improving but deteriorating. The typically unbearable conditions in the camp were summed up by sixty-six-year-old farmer Guri Ibrahim: 'This is no life.' As Khary B. Husien, a representative of the Kurdistan Regional Government responsible for Yazidi affairs, said in Dohuk: 'A person can endure weeks or months in the modest provisional conditions of the camps. But not years. That is why people see emigration to Europe as a rational alternative to languishing in the camps.'

There are too many frustrated and traumatised people living in the overcrowded camps and they are there for too long a time, with too much forced free time and too little space to move around in. The most common frustrations the refugees feel are hopelessness and a sense of having lost control over their own lives. A typical comment in this respect was made by Nawaf, an uneducated worker and father of seven children: 'Yazidis have no future here. The only hope is that God will help us. There is no one else on the horizon.'

People in the camps complain about the lack of educational opportunities, and as a result there is a risk that a 'lost generation' will grow up in the camps that will be at a lifelong disadvantage compared to their peers in other Iraqi groups. There is a shortage of teachers, the primary schools are too full, and levels of schooling above primary education are not available. Young people note also how impossible it is to actually study in the overcrowded tents. As twenty-three-year-old Nayla Abdullah says:

After we had to escape from the front line, where various forces were chaotically shooting at each other, and then also pass through four Arabic villages we did not know, I've become an irrevocably different Nayla. I used to study extremely well. I love physics, chemistry, and English. But now my grades are declining. I don't enjoy anything. The worst though is my relationship with my younger siblings. They want to play in the tent and they have no respect for the fact that I need to study. And worst of all is my dad, who is pressuring me to do better. One time he even took away my cell phone because of it.

Another problem is the lack of playgrounds for children, sports and free-time facilities for youths, and community centres for adults. As a result refugees often complain that they suffer from depressing boredom. Older people were accustomed to working hard in the fields or earning their living in some other way from morning to night all their lives, and now they have to sit around with their arms crossed. This is an entirely new, unbearable and dehumanising experience for them. Refugees want to work not just because of the income but also to escape from the traumas they've experienced, claiming work allows them to take their minds off their troubles for a while. As Qaro, a sixty-year-old semi-literate herder, told us:

> My dream is to return to my village, feel safe there, work and live like before. But there's nothing more difficult than starting over. Nothing will be the way it was before. But God is great. I hope he will help us.

A specific problem among young refugees is the *marriage crisis* and related sexual frustrations. Most young people do not have the resources to become independent and enter into a marriage. Young lovers eloping outside the camp has thus become a common cause of controversy. Nevertheless, premarital sex is taboo and a family's honour rests on its ability to protect the purity of its female members.

According to respondents, not enough aid is distributed in the camps. As a result they have to compete with each other for what insufficient resources are available. This feeds conflicts between them, not cooperation. The outcome is chronic tension between members of different families, villages and tribes within the camps. In situations of shortage and collapsing state institutions, people will turn to traditional communities and kinship groups for protection.

Another important consequence is that tension against the outside also grows as frustrations swell into looting and protests against the Kurdish Regional Government, which is regarded as incompetent and corrupt. The poor distribution of aid is blamed not just on corruption but also on the politicisation of aid through clientelism. There are recurring complaints that families with ties to the Kurdistan Democratic Party receive better and faster aid from the government. People without connections are worse off. And those worst off are refugees suspected by the government of sympathising with the Kurdistan Workers' Party (PKK). They purportedly never get any aid at all.

Tribal wars in the camps: anonymity and disintegration

The camps are surprisingly anonymous. Many people have to live together within a small space, but their close physical proximity to each other is accompanied by efforts to maintain a social distance from each other. As a statement by one middle-aged refugee typically illustrates:

After two years we only know the people living in the adjacent tents. They are good people. We are friends with each other, even though we'd never seen each other before. Other than that we and some compatriots from our town who also fled here try to support each other.

The younger generation speaks the same way. For example, a former soldier in the Iraqi army, Dawoud Hassan, claims that he has not found a single friend among people from other villages or tribes even after a year in the camp:

Everyone is respected most by the others when they're in their own place. In their home where they belong. The tension between people from different villages and tribes would go away if we could all return home again as soon as possible.

Yazidis were accustomed to living in cohesive villages and towns organised around family and tribal kinship relations and solidarity. Yazidis from the largest caste, *murids*, were equally accustomed to being able to seek advice and assistance from family confidants from the *pir* and *sheikh* castes with whom they had a personal tie. The refugee crisis, however, threw this traditional and functional arrangement into disarray. Members of the same family, village or tribe are now scattered across the territory of Kurdistan and Europe. They are cut off from each other. The refugee crisis also separated *murids* from their *pirs* and *sheikhs*. People now have no one they can turn to trustingly with requests for help, support and protection.

By the same token, because traditional Yazidi communities are scrambled across different overcrowded camps they have to live in close proximity to members of alien families, villages and tribes. All this is complicated by a language barrier (a minority of Yazidis speak Arabic, most of them speak one of two mutually incomprehensible Kurdish dialects) accompanied by different mentalities. The most sensitive issue is that old and unresolved animosities exist and persist between villages and tribes that in the camps are forced to live in close physical proximity. When they were geographically separated from each other, these animosities did not play any major role, and it was not difficult for people in feuding families, villages or tribes to avoid each other. And there were always tribal chiefs or religious authorities that could be turned to, as they were prepared to mediate in such conflicts.

The overcrowded camps, however, create a new situation. The physical proximity of members of feuding families, villages and tribes is amplified when the people are suffering from psychological trauma and faced with material shortages, and are moreover forced to compete with each other for access to resources. This deepens the traditional social cleavages of Yazidi society. This tension can then give rise to rapidly escalating 'tribal wars'. Nevertheless, many refugees claim that they reject these conflicts. For example, university student Nayem Khujily claims he always asks men acting aggressively: 'If you're really such a hotshot, why are you sitting here in a camp? Why aren't you instead chasing the Islamic State out of our villages so that we can all go back home?'

The vicious cycle: refugee migration generates more migration

Once the process of Yazidis migrating to Europe started, this triggered changes that make the migration of more refugees easier, and add to it. These are changes that have an impact on those who stayed behind in Iraqi Kurdistan. There are several such self-reinforcing mechanisms. For example, a *'brain-drain'* occurs as doctors, teachers and business people leave first. The rest of the population then becomes aware of a shortage of services and job opportunities and is forced to also begin thinking about emigrating. There is also a *demonstration effect* produced by the example of the migration not just of these elites but also of the many Syrian refugees, who have used Iraqi Kurdistan as a transfer station from which to move on to Europe since 2011.

'Chain migration' is another mechanism that comes into play. A typical case is that of forty-something Heydar who comes from a Yazidi community in Bashiqa. He accompanied his eldest son, aged twenty-two, as far as Istanbul, showing their last photographs together on his mobile phone. There he paid for his son to travel across the sea and along the 'Balkan route':

> My son likes it in Germany, he's learning the language, going to school, and doing sports. He looks content, like other Germans, we're in touch thanks to the internet. My wife and I and our younger children hope to join him in time.

The effect of chain migration was amplified among Iraqi Yazidis after 2014 by the existence of the Yazidi diasporas that formed in Germany and Scandinavia after World War II.

The current wave of migration is contributing to a *transformation of traditional views* on emigration. The idea of emigrating abroad used to be unthinkable for conservative Yazidis. Doing so came with the risk of losing family ties, and emigrants with no access to Yazidi shrines and spiritual leaders could lose their Yazidi identity, partly owing to the fact that the Yazidi faith is not fixed in writing in any sacred books. Another sensitive issue is that it is taboo to marry partners outside the Yazidi community, which is something that happens abroad. There is currently a pragmatism, however, that undermines these traditional feelings, as saving individual lives has become the priority. Sheikh Shamo, a Yazidi MP in the Kurdish parliament, commented:

> Emigrating abroad also represents a fatal risk for a religious or ethnic minority. A Christian can go to a church anywhere in the world. Similarly, a Muslim can go to a mosque anywhere. But the Yazidi shrines and sacred territory are only in Kurdistan. Only there can they fully practise their faith and rite. Migration saves the individual, but it can culturally destroy the community.

The highest religious authority of the Yazidis, Khurto Hajji Ismail, based in Shekhan, expressed a similar ambivalence in our interview:

> I personally do not support migration and I do not agree with it. More people are drowning today in the Mediterranean Sea trying to get to Europe than are being killed by the Islamic State. People left to their own fate in Europe are at risk of quickly losing their faith. I, however, cannot forbid people from migrating. I can only give them warning. After all, my two sons have been living in Sweden since the 1990s. That would be a little hypocritical, don't you think?

Nevertheless, even opponents of migration are not consistent in their motives. For example, Selim, a teacher, asked at the end of our interview about opportunities to study in the West, even though before that he had floridly held forth on how emigration is unpatriotic. Nawaf, a semi-literate labourer who was unable to imagine life elsewhere than in his village, claimed in turn that his children could live anywhere in the world. And Professor Othman, one of just two former Yazidi ministers in the federal government in Baghdad, has possessed what could be described as Yazidi life insurance in the form of dual citizenship since the 1990s, even though he discourages others from emigration. There is a thin line between these contradictory attitudes towards emigration. This line cuts not just through the community, however, but through individuals. People are thus torn between the longing 'to live like they used to' and a desire to find safety for themselves and their children.

*Complex economic crisis and the collapsed central state:
growing tension between locals and refugees*

The exodus of Yazidis who had been residing in the autonomous Kurdish Region occurred when the region was struck by economic decline resulting from a combination of factors: an enormous surge in expenditures on defence owing to the war with the Islamic State; a simultaneous surge in state expenditure to take care of refugees; a slump in oil and gas prices on the world market; the departure of foreign investors and humanitarian organisations; and a halt on transfers to regional authorities from the federal budget. All this has badly hurt the economy and generated tensions between the local Kurdish majority and (not just) Yazidi refugees. The result is a sense of insecurity and a lack of safety, which increase the motivation for leaving and going to Europe.

Amidst rising unemployment, refugees have to compete with local Kurds for jobs. Locals believe that in 2014 they selflessly provided the refugees with assistance, but no one is helping them now. While the declining aid from federal and international agencies continues to be channelled to refugees, locals themselves cannot request aid and it is their impression that the only people shopping in the stores are refugees. In this context they are beginning to see the refugees as the source of their problems. They blame them for the inflation-driven rise in the prices of groceries, gas, electricity, services and rents. The inflation was genuinely caused by an increase in demand resulting from the growing number of people in the region, which was due to the influx of refugees. Similarly, refugees are accused of putting extra strain on an already insufficient and inadequate infrastructure, which manifests itself in traffic jams in the cities and daily power outages.

The Yazidis blame the Baghdad government for allowing its large army to collapse at Mosul without engaging the Islamic State in combat in the summer of 2014. The Iraqi state thus abandoned its basic function of physically protecting its citizens. As soon as a state is unable to maintain the monopoly on violence in its territory, it collapses and ceases to be a state. According to Yazidis, however, Iraq exhibits other symptoms of a dysfunctional and collapsing state. A traumatised and vulnerable minority has no faith that this kind of state would be willing and able to protect them in the future in an increasingly turbulent region.

The most common direct complaint is that in the first weeks of the humanitarian catastrophe the central government promised the refugees effective humanitarian aid. According to the Yazidis, however, even two years later they have yet to receive such aid. As Guri Ibrahim, a charismatic sixty-year-old, put it:

> Life is much worse in the camps than the government promised us and we therefore expected. In 2014 Baghdad immediately promised every family a grant amounting to a million Iraqi dinars. This was supposed to help get us through the first months without a home. But most of us are scraping by and haven't seen anything of that yet.

The third problem that is connected with the weak central government is the absence of efforts to investigate war crimes committed against Yazidis. Yazidi university professor and journalist Khidher Domle noted that the refugees would not return home until their trust in the state, the enforceability of law, and justice are restored. Unless those responsible for the genocide are named, brought before a court and punished, it is impossible to imagine that either Arab or Kurdish neighbours will ever regain trust in the legal system. Izz Ad-Din Saleem Baqesri, a former MP in the parliament of the autonomous Kurdish Region, adds on behalf of the Yazidi community:

> The main reasons Yazidis are fleeing to Europe are not economic. In their eyes Europe's wealth lies in its ability to uphold the law and justice. To them Europe seems safe because they can be sure that there no one will be able to take their property, land, work, wife, or life with impunity. No one in Iraq however will guarantee them that kind of legal protection.

The last problem mentioned is that there has been no effort on the part of the central government yet to begin reconstruction of the destroyed Yazidi regions that have now been liberated. No funding in the state budget has been earmarked for this reconstruction and the Yazidis have not even been presented with any plan for reconstruction. The central government has thus not offered the Yazidis any hope or prospects for the future or sent them any signal that it is concerned about their future and envisions them as part of Iraq.

Distrust of the local government and own elites:
private vs collective interests

The Yazidis also lost their trust in the Kurdistan Regional Government during the refugee crisis. Yazidis regard the much-repeated promise of Kurdish leaders in the summer of 2014 that the Kurdish Peshmerga would protect them instead of the collapsed Iraqi army as a betrayal by their leadership. The basic reason for the Yazidis' distrust was the surprising and still incomprehensible withdrawal of the Peshmerga, without warning, from the entire front line that was defending the Sinjar region at that time. The Yazidis believe that this withdrawal was a response to a well-prepared, secret and organised command that came from the highest ranks of the Kurdish Democratic Party. They see this as an unjustifiable and inexplicable betrayal. On the morning of 3 August 2014, Yazidi villagers discovered to their horror that no one was protecting them from the Islamists. The only ones waging battle with the rapidly advancing Islamic State were the rearguard of the receding Peshmerga and, primarily, the Yazidis themselves, though they had no weapons.

The Yazidis thereby came to understand that the Kurdish Peshmerga are not a national army defending the public interest, but a party militia that in Dohuk Province and Erbil is subordinate to the Democratic Party of Kurdistan, which is controlled by the Barzani tribe, and in Sulaimani Province operates under the Patriotic Union of Kurdistan, controlled by the rival Talabani tribe. While there are no doubt members of the Peshmerga, Yazidis included, who are willing to patriotically lay down their lives for Kurdistan, the Peshmerga as such defend the private interests of party structures. Conditions within the ranks of the Peshmerga moreover reflect the general problems of dysfunctional Kurdish institutions: rampant clientelism, corruption and discrimination against minorities. As Dilman Hamid, a young Yazidi geologist, told me:

> My family aren't refugees, we come from Dohuk in Iraqi Kurdistan. But because of the corruption and discrimination there we are leaving for Europe anyway. One uncle of mine went to Germany back in 2007. Another uncle served with the Peshmerga for a long time. But he received little pay and it was not enough to support his family. And the risks in battles and the discrimination were too great. So, fed up, he left for Germany too.

The most sensitive issue is the role of the Kurdish Marxist guerrillas (PPK/YPG), who came from neighbouring Syria to the aid of the Yazidis after they were attacked by the so-called Islamic State. They managed to evacuate a portion of the fleeing Yazidis surrounded in the mountains by setting up a humanitarian corridor. With this, however, the Kurdish Regional Government politically lost Sinjar to its Marxist Kurdish rivals from Turkey and Syria. As a result, Kurdish leadership in northern Iraq does not support Yazidi refugees who want to go back home to the already liberated Sinjar area.

Dejected refugees from the ranks of the vulnerable minority are in need of functional self-organisation and representation in order to be able to orientate themselves in a new situation, to lobby for their interests and to distribute aid among themselves. Nevertheless, the Yazidis are lacking in respected elites at the very time they need them most. The Yazidis' trust in their political and tribal elites, unlike religious elites, collapsed rapidly in response to the events surrounding the attack from the Islamic State.

Controversy in particular surrounded the role of the party and tribal elites during the Islamic State's assault on Mosul and then Sinjar. Weeks and months before the attack, these elites allegedly persuaded the other residents of Sinjar not to flee because the Kurdish Peshmerga would protect them. They did so at the request of the Democratic Party of Kurdistan. The most sensitive issue, however, is that contrary to these assurances, and without giving civilians any warning, as soon as the Peshmerga made their coordinated withdrawal from the front lines, tribal chiefs and political frontmen in the Kurdish Democratic Party secretly fled their homes. They were the only ones among Yazidis who had information about the Peshmerga's withdrawal and the advance of the Islamic State.

A related criticism directed at the Yazidi elites in connection with the dramatic events of 2014 contends that the Islamic State on one side and the Kurdish Peshmerga on the other at that time were not the only ones who had weapons. In Khanke, young illiterate Gulistan spoke to me about this, as others listened in nodding:

> We don't just blame the genocide on the Kurdish Peshmerga, who despite all the promises left us in the lurch. We were also betrayed by Yazidis in the Kurdish political parties. They had weapons too. But instead of using them to protect their own people they ran away just like the Peshmerga. The Peshmerga may not have wanted to die on our behalf. That was however the duty of our leaders.

In general, the refugees believe that the elites allowed themselves to be *co-opted* by the political and economic system of Iraqi Kurdistan. They are able to build their careers in the party and in business because they exchanged their loyalty to the Yazidi community for loyalty to the Kurdish Regional Government. The refugees claim that the elites are not performing the role they are supposed to and are shirking the traditional obligations to the community that they have always had and that derive from their position in the community. As forty-five-year-old Piruz Othman said:

> Tribal chiefs do not help us at all with life in the camp. Our chief is living comfortably in the city of Zakho, where he fled. But because we're from a different political party from his, he never visits us. He either ignores us entirely or he even has the gall from time to time to ask us for help. Us, who are scraping by and have absolutely nothing.

The very same criticism is directed at the top tiers of the Yazidis' political leadership. Their highest secular authority is the Mir. He is living in an opulent residence in Shekhan District that is surrounded by a high wall. He ranks, however, above their main spiritual leader. According to a translator named Shiwan, unlike his popular predecessor, he is failing entirely to perform his function:

> He's been keeping a low profile during the refugee crisis. He's nowhere to be seen. He won't receive Yazidi delegations at his residence. He doesn't appear in the media. He doesn't drawn attention to the suffering. He doesn't travel the world and ask for help. The religious leaders are doing all this instead of him. People are angry because he's only looking after himself, and so the world is forgetting us.

Shiwan adds that the Mir is working on his career in the Kurdish Democratic Party. In Kurdistan a career and connections in politics are reportedly the precondition for success in business – the very opposite of Europe, where property and economic power are the main precondition for success in politics.

Distrust of Arab neighbours and the Muslim majority: betrayal and historical trauma

The Yazidis' distrust of their Arab neighbours makes it difficult for them to go back to the towns and villages they come from even after they are liberated. Yazidi refugees view the Arabs as traitors for siding with the Islamic State during the dramatic events of the summer of 2014. As sixty-year-old Guri Ibrahim said:

> The Islamic State fighters came from other places so they didn't know their way around our area. They didn't know exactly where the Yazidis were living and how to find us. Former friends among our Arab neighbours betrayed us. First they showed the Islamic State where we were and how to reach us. Then when we ran away they looted our homes and raped our women. And sometimes they were even more brutal than the Islamists.

This distrust also exists in relation to those Arab neighbours who did not align themselves with the Islamic State but did not run away from them either. Refugees in a camp in Khadia told me:

> It will be hard for us to return to our homes. We experienced unspeakable sufferings there and lost loved ones. So we hate that place. But our Arab neighbours go on living their life comfortably and are not running away from the Islamists. That's impossible for us to understand. Is it that they like the Islamists being there?

Other refugees speak about how the chasm that emerged between the Yazidi and Arab communities altered their everyday behaviour and habits. For example, Qaro, a farmer and the father of ten children in the camp in Khanke, says:

> After the attack, Arabs ran off with my only tractor and looted all the property on my farm. Before, I used to wear Arab clothing. Now I'll never do that again, I'll go around as a Kurd. I won't have the same clothes on me as the ones my neighbours robbed me in.

It is the shared opinion among Yazidi refugees that it would be difficult if not impossible to go home and restore old friendships and live side by side again. There are also voices among them calling for weapons, blood and revenge. The Yazidis' distrust of their neighbours is amplified by the fact that there have never been any investigations into war crimes in Iraq and the government has made no effort to mediate tensions between former neighbours. If the government does not identify the exact culprits among the Arab villagers and try them in court, the

Yazidis will start to think in terms of collective guilt, and then they will begin to call for collective punishment. They'll look at ethnic cleansing as necessary if they are to return home and a sense of safety and basic justice is to be restored.

Fear of the Islamic State is not the only obstacle to returning home. The Yazidis fear the spread of radical Islam in general, and they even speak fearfully about Islam itself. A former MP in the post-Saddam central government in Baghdad, Mamo Othman, told me:

> It is by no means just about the Islamic State. In our view, defeating them doesn't solve anything. The problem with Islamists is more long standing and runs deeper. After the American invasion in 2003 we were brutally attacked by Al Qaeda. Now it was by their reincarnation in the form of the Islamic State. But who knows what crazies are going to emerge next? And might it be even something worse? As long as the Islamists can't accept the plurality that exists among humankind, Yazidis and other minorities in Iraq will not feel safe.

A separate, but related issue is the strong sense of discrimination. Yazidis repeatedly complained of having long been subject to systematic discrimination from the majority society across all the country's institutions: military, economic and political. They believe this discrimination is not the result of government practice or ideology, but rather the product of traditional tribalism and the recent Islamic revival. Mathew Barber, director of a Yazidi non-governmental organisation called Yazda, commented:

> Kurds here will talk long and floridly about how we are all human beings. How we are all brothers and sisters. They will swear blindly that they have never discriminated against anyone. And then they will get up and without blinking go join in a pogrom.

In the eyes of many Yazidis, all of Islam shrivelled into a violent ideology after 2014 - and all Muslims became dangerous terrorists. Khero, a refugee who after arriving at a camp immediately joined a Kurdish Peshmerga battalion, said to me:

> In the view of Muslims we Yazidis are unbelievers (*kafir*) just like you Europeans. But in reality they are the ones who have strayed from God. We are the believers, they are the unbelievers. We believe in God, they have lost God.

This discourse used by Yazidi refugees is strikingly similar to the rhetoric of Islamophobia in use in Europe today.

The Islamic State is moreover effective at provoking and building on Yazidi fears of Islam because its propaganda and actions are consistent with the logic of Yazidi identity, historical experience and collective memory. The killing that is currently being done in the name of Islam provokes a sense of dread among Yazidis that is amplified by historical experience and memory, in which the Yazidis are framed as constantly the defenceless victims. This self-image has gained renewed strength and meaning in response to the latest genocide. Deep within Yazidi collective memory there is a dark story about seventy-two genocides[1] committed against the Yazidi minority since the dawn of time.

Conclusions

It is possible to identify many basic motives that Yazidi refugees have for migrating to Europe. To sum up, they are as follows: there is a lack of material aid in (and outside) the camps, which bolsters a feeling amongst the refugees that they are being ignored by the international community and their own government; the social conditions in the camps are poor, especially given the extensive amount of forced free time the refugees have and the absence of any meaningful activities; and there is poor distribution of aid, which generates conflicts among the refugees as they have to compete for the scarce resources. Traditional cleavages in Yazidi society have been strengthening along the lines of tribal or regional identities, and in the overcrowded conditions of the camps there is growing anonymity and disintegration, while old conflicts are being relit. There is a vicious cycle whereby the current and growing tides of emigration themselves serve to encourage others to emigrate. Iraqi Kurdistan is experiencing an overall economic crisis that only exacerbates tensions between the Kurdish majority population and refugees; refugees have a distrust of the Iraqi central government because the state is dysfunctional and unable to properly look after their needs or to physically protect its minorities against extremists; they also have a distrust of the Regional Government of Kurdistan, which is seen as corrupt and as manipulating the interests of minorities. The Yazidis also no longer have any trust in their own elites, who failed them during the refugee crisis by putting their own interests before the interests of the community; the Yazidis no longer trust their former Arab neighbours, whom they accuse of varying degrees of collaboration with the Islamic State; and the Yazidis no longer have trust in the majority Iraqi society that follows Islam (this also includes the additional issue of everyday discrimination).

The Yazidis' motives for emigrating to Europe can generally be summed up under three types of loss of trust: (1) loss of trust in state institutions; (2) loss of trust in majority society; and (3) loss of trust in their own elites and in the ability of the Yazidi community to defend (and organise) itself. State institutions (of the Iraqi state and Kurdish Regional Government) are accused of failing to protect Yazidis against extremists over the long term, and after the Yazidis were attacked by the Islamic State these institutions failed to help the victims. In addition to this, the Yazidis lost trust in Muslim majority society (which is represented by their Arab neighbours, fellow Kurds and the media). The majority is now seen as rapidly radicalising in the name of Islam or nationalism, however much a role in fuelling the tensions and distrust is in fact played by old property disputes and crimes from the time of Saddam Hussein, or by more traditional and newly revived tribalism. The most sensitive finding, however, is the fact that the Yazidis lost their trust in both their tribal and their political authorities (though not in their religious authorities) while at the same time, in response to the many dilemmas the refugee crisis gave rise to, traditional Yazidi society began to disintegrate: splitting into supporters and opponents of emigration; dividing up into traditional tribal and regional cleavages as they are forced to compete for the scarce amount of aid provided to them; established gender roles being disrupted; and growing conflicts due, in part, to the marriage crisis.

There is thus not just one cause but multiple causes explaining Yazidi migration. The three main motives outlined above are essential, but in themselves not a sufficient motive for emigration. Majority society's radicalisation would not in itself generate a sense that there exists a direct mortal threat, if the state institutions were capable of tackling the growing atmosphere of impunity in society and were able to physically protect minorities against the majority and extremist organisations. Similarly, the collapse of state institutions alone would not have led to a direct sense of immediate danger if the collapse had occurred in a tolerant and open society, and if the minorities were not systematically being threatened by anyone. Finally, Yazidi refugees would probably not be emigrating abroad if the functions of the failing state institutions had been successfully taken up by the Yazidi elites and a self-organised Yazidi society, which could itself have assumed responsibility for the post-war reconstruction of Sinjar, restored the rule of law and, above all, created effective and independent Yazidi militias (with all the associated risks this would entail) to defend the Yazidis against the radicalising majority

Notes

This chapter was supported by the Czech Science Foundation (GAČR) through Project No. 20-24833S. The Project title is 'A Case Study of the Middle Eastern Refugees: Iraqi Yazidis'.

1. In the early sections of the chapter I use the wording 'so-called Islamic State' to stress a critical distance from the worldview of the extremists and the way they use the classical Islamic concepts to legitimize their political project.
2. The number seventy-two was constantly cited by Yazidis during the interviews. This is not a factual historical figure, but a symbolic way of expressing a large number.

References

Açikyildiz, Birgül (2010) *The Yezidis: The History of a Community, Culture and Religion.* London: I. B. Tauris.

Berger, Peter, and Thomas Luckmann (1999) *Sociální konstrukce reality* [*The Social Construction of Reality*]. Brno: CDK.

Domle, Khidher (2013) 'Yazidis: a deep-rooted community in an unstable present.' Pp. 66–78 in *Minorities in Iraq: Memory, Identity and Challenges*, edited by Saad Saloum. Baghdad: Masarat.

Hendl, Jan (2005) *Základy kvalitativního výzkumu* [*Basis of Qualitative Research*]. Prague: Portál.

Jírů, Lucie (2016) 'Role kmenů v Iráku: od Osmanské říše po Islámský stát' ['The role of tribalism in Iraq: From the Ottomans to the Islamic State']. Pp. 47–87 in *Význam kmenové společnosti v 21. století*, edited by Karel Černý and Břetislav Tureček. Prague: Nakladatelství Lidové noviny.

Khalaf, Farida (with Andrea C. Hoffmann) (2016) *The Girl Who Beat ISIS: My Story.* London: Square Peg.

Khanki, Kovan (2015) 'Crimes and sexual abuse committed against Ezidies.' *Lalish* 40: 16–24.

Kikoler, Naomi (2015) *Our Generation is Gone: The Islamic State's Targeting of Iraqi Minorities in Ninewa.* Washington, DC: United States Holocaust Memorial Museum.

Kubálek, Petr (2007a) 'Periodizace dějin jezídismu.' *Kurdové a Kurdistán*, available at: <http://kudrove.ecn.cz /clanky.shtml?x=1973933> (last accessed 12 December 2019).

Kubálek, Petr (2007b) 'Problémy studia dějin jezídismu.' *Kurdové a Kurdistán*, <http://kudrove.ecn.cz /clanky.shtml?x=1973934> (last accessed 12 December 2019).

Kubálek, Petr (2007c) 'Chronologie dějin jezídů.' *Kurdové a Kurdistán*, <http://kudrove.ecn.cz /dokumenty.shtml?x=1972745> (last accessed 12 December 2019).

Kubálek, Petr (2015) 'End of Islam, end of time: an eschatological reading of Yezidism.' *Archiv Orientální* 83(3: 569–98.

Kubálek, Petr (2016) 'Jezídi.' Pp. 120–50 in *Ve stínu islámu*, edited by Jiří Gebelt. Prague: Vyšehrad.

Laurens, Henry (2013) *Arabský Orient za časů Ameriky*. Prague: Academia.

Maisel, Sebastian (2008) *Social Change Amidst Terror and Discrimination: Yezidis in the New Iraq*. Middle East Institute Policy Brief, No. 18, August.

Recchia, Francesca (2012) 'From forced displacement to urban cores: the case of collective towns in Iraqi Kurdistan.' *Architexturez South Asia*, <http://architexturez.net/doc/az-cf-123984> (last accessed 14 January 2020).

Ritchey, Neal (1976) 'Explanations of migration.', *Annual Review of Sociology*, (2): 364–404.

Salloum, Saad (2013) *Minorities in Iraq: Memory, Identity and Challenges*. Baghdad: Masarat.

Strauss, Anselm L., and Juliet Corbinová (1999) *Základy kvalitativního výzkumu: postupy a techniky metody zakotvené teorie*. Boskovice: Albert.

Tariq, Peshkafty (2015) 'Liberation of Shingal: hope and disappointment.' *Lalish* 41: 7–8.

UN Habitat (2015) *Emerging Land Tenure Issues Among Displaced Yazidis from Sinjar, Iraq: How Chances of Return May Be Further Undermined by a Discrimination Policy Dating Back 40 Years*. November, <https://unhabitat.org/emerging-land-tenure-issues-among-displaced-yazidis-from-sinjar-iraq.pdf> (last accessed 12 December 2019).

UNHRC (2016) *'They Came to Destroy': ISIS Crimes Against the Yazidis*. New York: United Nations, 2016.

Yazda (2016) *Yazda Report on Humanitarian Aid and Development Opportunities in Sinjar: Caring for IDPs While Rebuilding and Facilitating Returns*. Dohuk: Yazda Organization.

6

Current Migration Trends in Russia: The Role of the CIS Region Twenty Years after the Collapse of the Soviet Union

Maria Apanovich

Introduction

THIS CHAPTER PROVIDES an overview of the migration trends in the Russian Federation from the 1990s to the 2010s in the context of the drastic change in the political, economic and social aspects of the country. Because there are few sources of data available for this period, it is difficult for researchers to derive full knowledge of the migratory processes. However, various laws were passed during the period, which indicate the architecture of the migration policy in the 'new' Russia. This chapter focuses on the Migration Policy Concept (hereafter: the Concept) which was adopted in 2012 as an action plan until 2025, and on criticism of it. The last part of the chapter gives an overview of the most recent adjustment of the Concept in November 2018.

The Concept is analysed in order to determine the difficulties faced in the implementation process as well as its potential for improvement. In the context of international globalisation, the importance of several factors allowing migrants to enter Russia increased: the mutual recognition of qualifications, diplomas and other educational documents; the creation of conditions for the admission of highly qualified foreign professionals in accordance with the requirements of the country's economy; and related innovations in the field of education for the training of specialists with foreign citizenship. The Russian Federation still relies mainly on the available labour force of the Commonwealth of Independent States (CIS) countries that are specified in the articles of the Concept. In order to accommodate the diverse range of labour migrants from different countries, the chapter also provides a set of recommendations based on the findings of the Concept review. First, in order to accommodate open global migration, the information and administration connected with education must be simplified. Second, it is necessary to compile a list of professions needed for the development of the national economy and Russian society that can be open to migrants. The expansion of technological potential is directly connected to the availability of labour. In modern economies, this problem is solved with the help of not only internal potential but also the external potential of foreign employees.

This chapter first provides a description of the major characteristics of international migration of the pre-collapse stage of the Soviet Union. Emigration and immigration flows were under the control of the services of the Soviet apparatus that were responsible for them. According to Ivakhnyuk (2011: 5–7) 'the country's external borders were completely closed, and there was "strict control over people's movement"'. The intensity of migration among the Soviet republics is comparable to the current external flows of migrants.

Registration of migrants

During Gorbachev's *perestroika*, immediately before the collapse of the Soviet Union, limitations on free movement were abolished and liberal reforms were introduced in the economy. In addition, the number of short-term migrations abroad and the amount of emigrations to Western countries increased, mainly from among members of certain ethnic groups and their families. The late 1980s were also marked by 'the emergence of the first flashpoints of ethnic conflict in some of the USSR republics, which caused the first flows of forced migrants unfamiliar to the USSR. People were saving their lives by escaping from Azerbaijan, Armenia, Georgia and Tajikistan' (Ivakhnyuk 2008: 227–8).

It is important to highlight that the description of migration trends in the Russian Federation should take into account the mechanism of the data collection and estimation. The rules and methodology of data collection have changed several times, mainly between 1995 and 2009. The decrease in immigration that started in 1996 was one cause of the methodological change in how to define the notion of 'migrant'. To clarify, before the new rules on mandatory registration of the place of residence and place of stay (Rules of Registration, 1995) came into effect, citizens of the USSR and Russia were considered migrants if they had changed their place of residence (or stay) for a period of over forty-five days, excluding trips made for medical treatment, recreation and vacations. For foreigners, the time threshold was three months. Thus, the statistics include both short-term and long-term migrants and migrations (external and internal).

As a result, the number of registered migrants increased, even though some were internal citizens of the country and followed the local system of population registration (*propiska*). They had to be registered in the 'new' place if they moved for labour or family reasons. In 1995, new rules of registration were adopted in the practical implementation of the law on freedom of movement, which had been put into force two years earlier. Residents of Russia were allowed to keep their *de jure* registration at their place of residence and simultaneously register at their place of stay at another location. Access to the labour market, the social security system and all public goods at the place of stay were no longer restricted. The *propiska* system was an effective mechanism that the local police authorities used to control the movements of citizens, but in terms of a data source sometimes recorded unreal 'persons' in the statistics. The difficulty of the data is in the possibility of having *propiska* at one place but actually living in the other place. In cases when the person lived in a different place from the *propiska*, he or she could register himself or herself there, but there are cases when a person did not notify the authorities and then the *propiska* and real address are different.

Furthermore, 'registration at a place of stay' did not imply the statistical registration of migrants. Migrants were allowed to register in this category for 180 days. If a person intended to 'overstay', he or she had to be registered at a place of residence and be deregistered from the previous one, which complicated bureaucratic issues and confused migrants. Finally, after only one year, the time limit on temporary residence was abolished by the Constitutional Court, and the period of stay became unlimited. However, the statistics do not include migrants who were previously registered, which further problematises research into this period. When we observe the data, this means that we can clearly see tendencies, but we should keep in mind that the numbers of the database are not absolute. For example, certain migrants, especially low-qualified labour migrants, went to the 'black market of registration' and were not counted by the official statistics.

The next change in the rules of registration occurred in 2000, when foreign citizens could only register for a residence permit, which was difficult to obtain. This measure forced migrants to register at their place of stay. Consequently, the statistics for the period from 2000 to 2005 show a decrease in the flow migrants. Yet the change in the data can be explained mainly by the data collection approach of the national statistical office. In contrast, during the period from 2007 to 2009, some categories of migrants from post-Soviet areas were counted twice because of the simplified procedure used to apply for Russian citizenship. Migrants with national passports arriving from the former Soviet republics were initially counted as 'migrants', who obtained a residence permit and registered at their place of residence. When they successfully applied for Russian citizenship under the simplified procedure used during that period, they had to be registered again, even though they already had a Russian passport. At this time, the Russian Federation followed the liberal practice of deregistration. The rule that the certificate of deregistration at the former place had to be provided in order to be registered at the new place was abolished. In this respect, the coordination and exchange of data between the different entities played an important role so that a person was not counted twice. For example, if a particular local district had 1,000 migrants from Tajikistan, some of them would have been counted twice (due to the complexity of the system), while some might have not been counted at all. Instead of 1,000 migrants we could easily have fewer than 850, which in turn means not only that the data is unreliable but, in real life, that the state cannot correctly plan social or administrative support for these people. The most significant result of these errors in the data is the incorrect planning of activities on the local level to accommodate migrants. In the case of a small town, plans could be made in terms of budget and social (plus administrative) costs to accommodate 1,000 migrants coming every year, while in real life the number of migrants might be as many as 1,500 or as few as 500.

Migration flow characteristics in the period after the change of state borders

Immediately after the collapse of the Soviet Union, two major trends emerged: immigration (mainly from the post-Soviet areas) and emigration (mainly to Western countries, such as Germany, the US etc.). Both trends are significant because they substantially alter both the causes of migration and the number of migrants. The changes in borders and the creation of new countries in post-Soviet areas influenced every part of human life - economic, political and social. The formation and development of new countries, such as Kazakhstan, Uzbekistan, Belarus and Ukraine, followed their own path. Although all these territories were former Soviet republics, they had specific opportunities and obstacles to development that differed and set various conditions for both inward or outward migration.

The second most dramatic aspect of the collapse of the Soviet Union was the economic crisis and the unemployment that many former Soviet republics faced in the early 1990s. From the migration point of view, these years show the largest and most dramatic flows of migration between the 'new' states in the region. Hundreds of thousands of migrants left their homes in many of the former Soviet republics and moved to Russia, Ukraine, Belarus and Moldova. Although the majority were labour migrants, others moved from the new countries because they did not belong to the local ethno-cultural community, while some moved for family reasons or because of other ties with Russia.

Poverty, unemployment and unbelievably low living standards in their countries of origin stimulated labour migration from the former Soviet republics. According to the Russian statistical agency Rosstat, the estimated numbers increased from 129,000 in 1994 to 213,000 in 2000, 702,000 in 2005, and more than one million in 2006. According to researchers:

> Long-term immigration tallied up to only 280 thousand persons, while the inflow of migrant workers was estimated at 1.1 million persons. Out of the 17.8 million immigrants who arrived in Russia between 1981 and 2009, only 135 thousand came from countries other than the former USSR. The figure for emigration was about 11.6 million: 10.2 million to the Post Soviet Space countries and 1.4 million to countries outside the region. (Zayonchkovskaya and Vitkovskaya 2009: 231)

The majority of those migrants can be classified as economic migrants. The next interesting aspect is ethnic migration, such as the emigration of native Russians as minority groups from Kazakhstan in the late 1990s, or from Kirgizstan. In those cases emigration helped not to provoke ethnic conflicts in the parts of the countries where society was more homogeneous.

The most interesting part of the statistics data is the structure of the migration. We need to divide flows into emigration and immigration. Looking at emigration structures, the tendency was rather clear, as the 'opening' of the borders after the authoritarian regime of 'check and control' allowed a huge wave of emigration, mainly to Western countries. Among the most popular destinations were Germany, the USA, Israel and France. At the same time, the wave from the new countries (Kazakhstan, Tajikistan, Kirgizstan etc.) remained significant and is still an important source of emigration.

The beginning of the 1990s could be characterised as the period of ethnic conflicts in the countries of the former USSR republics. The issue of ethnicity did not appear suddenly, and many of the conflicts were in fact latent internal ones that had been more or less effectively managed by the Soviet authority. The break-up of the USSR brought the process of rebordering, and with the change of borders the independence status of the republics sparked the majority–minority question. In some of the new states ethnic Russians appeared to be a minority that could not feel comfortable there. This is the case in Kazakhstan or Kirgizstan, from where the majority of ethnic Russians migrated back to Russia. The older generations of citizens there (aged 50+) still speak Russian, while younger generations know only the national language well, and some probably speak English better than Russian. As such, Russia is still a popular destination for ethnic Russians from the newly formed states, but much less so for ethnic Kazaks or Kirgiz with no language or cultural ties with Russia.

Although indicators of immigration differed from period to period, this was largely due to the changes in data collection procedures (that is, how statistics was recorded). Certain peaks or 'surges' (Zayonchkovskaya and Vitkovskaya 2009) of immigration to Russia occurred, which were particularly evident against the background of the subsequent rapid decrease (by almost 50 per cent) in registered immigration that started in 1995 and lasted until 2007. On average, the annual inflow of immigrants to Russia was less than 500,000 from 1996 to 2000, while from 1991 to 1995 there were more than 906,000 migrants per year. A small increase in immigration began in 2007, which also seems related to the peculiarities in the collection of statistics rather than changes in the migration flows.

In the 1980s and 1990s, the immigration rates rose and fell, beginning at 6.4 per 1,000 people. With the collapse of the Soviet Union, there was a decrease to 4.7 per 1,000 people, and in the mid-1990s, the statistics office registered the maximum immigration rate at 7.7 per 1,000 people. This increase was due to the intensification of the migration process during that period, as described above. In addition, Russia also changed its migration policy to reach a more or less stable architecture, and immigration rates decreased to 1.2 and 1.9 per 1,000 inhabitants by 2008. In the same period, the emigration rate did not change drastically, and it was never higher than 1.0 per 1,000 inhabitants. As the well-known Russian researcher Zhanna Zayonchkovskaya (2003) argues, if we compare the tendencies of the Soviet and post-Soviet periods, we can see that the proportion of internal migration (among the Soviet republics) was the same as that of international net migration of the post-Soviet period. It is clear that international migration to Western countries added to migration flows, but still the flows of migration of the countries of the post-Soviet space are the most important and significant for Russian migration policy.

The most significant region of immigration in the Russian Federation was the post-Soviet space. Around 95 per cent of all migrants to Russia in the 1990s and early 2000s were from this region. The Russian Federal Statistics Office recorded that from 2001 to 2005, emigration to 'far abroad' was about 50 per cent of the total outflow. The term 'far abroad' (Zayonchkovskaya 2003) is used for countries outside the post Soviet space. However, emigration to the post-Soviet space was always significant in the total flows. On average, the percentage of migration to other parts of the world never exceeded 21 per cent of the migration turnover in Russia, and it has now fallen to 8 per cent (that is, 92 per cent of migration occurs within the borders of the post-Soviet space). Almost 99 per cent of the net immigration to Russia is from the countries of the former Soviet Union.

It is important to highlight some changes in the migration flows, such as motives, forms and directions of migration. According to data from the national statistical offices of the CIS countries, from 2000 to 2007, the percentage of departures to Kazakhstan comprised about 50 per cent of the outflow from Uzbekistan, 15 per cent from Kyrgyzstan and 20 per cent from Russia. Moldova and Ukraine also had a considerable exchange of migration with countries outside the Former Soviet Union (FSU); there was a particularly large amount of emigration to Southern and Western Europe. On average, from 2000 to 2007, immigrants from the other CIS countries comprised over 92 per cent of the total inflow, and about 72 per cent of all emigrants moved to the countries of the CIS (Ivakhnyuk 2008). Russia witnessed several waves of emigration. The first one started in the late 1980s and proceeded just after the collapse of the Soviet Union. Among the great receiving countries of that period were the following: Germany (570,000 Russian emigrants, or 57 per cent of total Russian emigration in the 1990s), Israel (256,000, or 25.6 per cent of total emigrants) and the US (112,000, or 11.2 per cent of total emigrants) (Zayonchkovskaya 2001).

State migration policy

The break-up of the Soviet Union appeared to be a crucial moment not only for the country but also in the lives of ordinary citizens. The migration system that had emerged many years earlier continued to exist in a new format. There was an urgent need for new reforms in the migration policy, which occurred in several stages. In the development of the current Russian migration policy, the first stage occurred in the period from 1991 to 1999, the second from 2000 to 2006/7 and the third from 2006/7 to 2012. The fourth stage began in 2012, and a new stage is planned to begin in 2025.

The first stage of Russian migration policy (1991 to 1999) was characterised by the lifting of the so-called 'Iron Curtain' and the liberalisation of the rules of entry and exit to and from the country, which triggered a significant wave of emigration. In many ways, the intensification of the process of Russians' emigration abroad was facilitated by the creation of programmes for return or re-emigration in countries such as Germany and Israel. According to various estimates, in the 1990s, 1.3 to 1.5 million people left Russia and the CIS with no plan to return (Tangi 2012).

In the late 1990s and 2000s, the flows of ethnic migration were replaced by the outflow of intellectual cadres from the country. The catalysts were the political and socio-economic transformations that were taking place in Russia. Reductions in the budget primarily affected the allocation of funds for research and development, which caused many of the best graduates to immigrate to the US, Canada, Germany and other countries. Simultaneously, however, because of the liberalisation of the policy of admission to the country, Russia became a major receiving state. According to statistical data provided by Rosstat, from 1992 to 2002, migration into Russia increased by more than five million people.

Undoubtedly, this rapid change in the country's demographic composition led to the development of new migration law in the Russian Federation. As part of a liberalised migration policy, Russia adopted the standards and norms of international documents: the Universal Declaration of Human Rights of 1948 and the International Covenant on Civil and Political Rights of 1966, which include fundamental human rights such as the right to freedom of movement and choice of residence within each state. The Bishkek Protocol, which included visa-free travel for CIS citizens in the territory of the signatories, was adopted in 1992. The Moscow agreement on mutual recognition of visas was adopted in the same year.

A difficult stage in the transformation of the post-Soviet space caused a massive flow of refugees and internally displaced people (IDPs). Because of economic instability and local ethno-cultural conflicts in the territory of the former Union republics, there were more than 25 million ethnic

Russians, as well as representatives of titular nations of Russia, who constituted the main stream of returnees in those years (Rybakovsky 2003). Consequently, in 1992, the Russian Federation agreed to the UN Convention on the Status of Refugees and its 1951 Protocol.

The next important step was the institutionalisation of the statehood and sovereignty of the Russian Federation. On 6 February 1992, the Law on Citizenship of the Russian Federation was adopted, which recognised as citizens all persons who permanently resided in the territory of the country. This law was accompanied by a simplified procedure for acquiring Russian citizenship for citizens of newly formed states, which contributed to the intensification of the immigration process. This example was followed by the CIS countries, which accepted the relevant regulatory and legal acts.

A new service was then created. The Federal Migration Service (FMS), which was based on the Committee on Population Migration under the Ministry of Labour and Employment, was established specifically to deal with the entire range of issues related to the movement of people. The initial task was to establish a hierarchical, vertical structure of regional units in order to build a clear, functioning model. In this connection, two fundamental federal laws were adopted to address forced migration, which determined the status of refugees and IDPs. As a result, in the 1990s, Russia accepted almost two million refugees and IDPs from the CIS countries, as well as from the countries of the former socialist camp.

In the field of labour migration, the decrees of the president in 1993 regulated the mechanisms for issuing permits to employers in order to attract foreign labour by creating immigration control posts. To counteract illegal migration, the Government of the Russian Federation adopted a resolution 'On measures to prevent and reduce uncontrolled external migration', which set the regulations and procedures for foreign citizens and stateless persons. In general, the new legislation aimed at addressing the problems of dealing with forced migration in the first half of the 1990s, which was unsystematic and situational.

At the beginning of the 1990s in Russia, a transition occurred from a planned management system to a market system. This transition did not bypass the issue of migration, and programme-orientated methods of political management were quite common. In 1992, the 'Migration' programme was developed and tested. It included an expert assessment of the migration situation in Russia, the tasks of the country's migration policy, and practical measures to assist in resettlement, housing and the socio-cultural provision for migrants. The programme was implemented for two years. During this time, accumulated problems were resolved and the situation of IDPs and refugees was improved, primarily through the creation of a regulatory framework. This programme was replaced by the Federal Migration Program (FMP), which was in place until 2002. The FMP included targeted social assistance to the families of forced migrants through the territorial bodies of the FMS of Russia, and the inclusion of these migrants' children in the Russian secondary education system. The employees of the FMS resolved various problems, including those related to psychological stress on people due to forced change of residence.

At the same time, the process used to control international migration in the post-Soviet space (i.e. by the Consultative Council on Labour, Migration and Social Protection of the Population of the CIS States) was being developed. The CIS Intergovernmental Agreement on Cooperation in the Field of Labour Migration and Social Protection of Migrant Workers was concluded, based on the work of the Council, in 1994. To simplify control over the migration process, in the 1990s, offices of the FMS of Russia were established in Kyrgyzstan, Tajikistan, Armenia, Turkmenistan, Lithuania and Latvia, which improved the interactions with authorities in other countries and provided solutions to individual problems in the countries of origin of migrants.

The first non-governmental organisations that provided assistance to migrants also emerged in the 1990s (e.g. the Forum of Relocation Organizations, the Committee for Assistance to Refugees, the Civic Assistance Organization etc.). The aim of these organisations was to help refugees and IDPs without funding from the state. One of the main problems during that period was the lack of coordination between the activities of public authorities and non-state bodies. Consequently, there is a lack of data about the existence of an effective mechanism for the political management of migration processes. Political decisions taken in the field of migration regulation during the first period were ill-considered and situational. Programmes for the adaptation and integration of migrants did not exist. The streams of visitors were mainly from the CIS countries, so they knew the Russian language, and initially they were well integrated into society.

The second stage can be identified as the early 2000s (from 2000 to 2006/7). This period was characterised by an increase in ethnic migration combined with an increase in illegal and unregulated migration. The global trend to securitisation was reflected in the tightening of the Russian Federations migration policy, and in Russia's withdrawal on 30

August 2000 from the agreements in the Bishkek Protocol, with the subsequent adoption of a new law that significantly complicated the procedure for acquiring Russian citizenship. The introduction of the new provision of the Government of the Russian Federation in 2002, which was then repeatedly edited and supplemented, significantly limited the legal framework for the legalisation of foreign citizens.

In 2001, there was a discussion at governmental level on the next FMP for the period from 2002 to 2004. Experts and scientists worked on the project, but because of the high demand for funding, the programme was not adopted. According to the preliminary plans, most of the funds were to be spent on social assistance to migrants and their adaptation to living in Russia. Instead of that programme, in the same year, the Concept of Demographic Development to 2015 was adopted, which has become an important policy tool in the field because of the absence of a similar concept in the migration regulations.

The role of the FMS was then diminished, and several of its functions were distributed among various authorities. In October 2001, the Ministry of the Federation was terminated, and in accordance with the Decree of the President of the Russian Federation, a new FMS was established within the Ministry of Internal Affairs of the Russian Federation. In the transition to the Ministry of Internal Affairs priority was given to resolving the issues of illegal migration and criminalisation. Both labour migration and issues involving the integration of migrants were prioritised by the ministry.

According to Vladimir Volokh, Head of the Department of the Issues of Refugees of the FMS in 2002–5:

> the institutional reform of 2002, connected with the prevailing ideas about the possibility of solving the problems of illegal migration only by tightening the migration policy, resulted in negative consequences, as a result of which the population's migration became associated with the public solely with crime . . . The inefficient management of migration processes by internal affairs agencies was one of the factors that led to the growth of illegal migration, the increase in corruption and the emergence of 'shadow' services for migrants organized by mediators and officials, as well as numerous violations of migrants' rights, anti-migrant sentiment and inter-ethnic clashes. (Volokh 2011: 951)

Another attempt was made to reform the sphere. The FMS developed the Concept for the Regulation of Migration Processes of the Russian

Federation, which was approved by the Russian government in 2003. Because of the tightening of migration legislation and the simultaneous increase in corruption, the number of illegal migrants sharply increased during the period under review. Consequently, at the supranational level, the Council of Heads of Government of the CIS established in 2004 the Joint Commission of the States, in which members of the association cooperated in combatting illegal migration. In 2007, the Council of Heads of Members of the CIS formed the Council of Heads of State and adopted the Declaration on the Agreed Migration Policy of the Member States, which included the participants in the CIS. It should be noted that this measure did not bring the desired result.

Characteristic of the stage under consideration is the stabilisation of the socio-economic situation in the country and the need to increase the number of labour migrants. Because of changes in the system of secondary education and secondary specialised education, the internal labour market lacked workers with specialised skills, so labour migrants, mainly from the CIS countries, were sought to fill such positions. However, the migration policy still included securitisation. Migrants from the CIS countries and Central Asia wanted to cross the border into the Russian Federation. The number of migrant workers in the grey sector of the economy increased. According to the established rules, legal registration was costly both financially and in terms of labour. The main objective of this category of migrants was to channel as much money as possible to their homeland to support their families. With the increase in the flow of migrants from Uzbekistan, the Kyrgyz Republic and Tajikistan, labour migration acquired a pronounced cultural character. According to the results of surveys carried out by the Centre for Migration Studies, 85 per cent of migrants from these countries were Muslim believers' (Tyuryukanova 2007).

Hence, Russian society was confronted by a new phenomenon: the fear of the loss of cultural, national and religious identity because of the influx of migrants, which led to the emergence of migrant phobia, domestic nationalism and decreased tolerance of others. Because of the increased flow of foreign cultural migrants from the 2000s, Russia began to pay special attention to the preservation and dissemination of the Russian language in the post-Soviet space, as well as the restoration and maintenance of ties in the form of intensive relationships with compatriots abroad. The promotion of re-emigration and repatriation is always closely related to the political and cultural context. A separate, significant role was assigned to Rossotrudnichestvo, a state agency that has the key responsibilities forn supporting compatriots abroad, popularisation of the Russian language and culture abroad and public diplomacy, and the programme of 'voluntary resettlement of compatriots' (Ryazantsev 2007).

The potential of return migration

The Programme for Compatriots was initiated in 2006 by presidential decree. It was based on the idea of using the potential of Russian-speaking migrants and migrants with the same or similar cultural and historic backgrounds. The term 'compatriots' is used to describe migrants born in the Soviet Union or countries in the post-Soviet space. The Russian state enumerated the key regions or cities where this category of migrants could live. They benefited from state support in transportation and information about the job market in the region. The most appealing cities, such as Moscow or St Petersburg, were not included in this programme. The preliminary targets were small or middle-sized towns that had experienced internal emigration. The rationale was that international migrants would maintain a balanced population and might even foster population growth.

The first stage started in 2007. Since then, the government has modified the conditions of the programme several times, the most recent of which was in 2013. Currently, forty-eight regions participate in the programme. For migrants who move to certain territories (marked as priorities in the programme), their financial support is up to 240,000 roubles or approximately 3,500 to 3,800 euros. According to the statistics of the Ministry of Internal Affairs, which is currently responsible, the numbers of migrants are the following: 29,462 in 2011; 56,874 in 2012; 34,697 in 2013; 106,319 in 2014; 183,146 in 2015; and 146,585 in 2016.

To facilitate a return to the country that is culturally similar to the immigrants 'home country', the state programme 'On Measures to Promote the Voluntary Resettlement of Compatriots Living in the Russian Federation to the Russian Federation Living Abroad' (hereafter: 'Compatriots') was set as one of the priorities of the Concept and a measure for improving the management of migration within the Russian Federation. The national Compatriots programme was first implemented at the subnational (regional) level of government and subsequently extended. Despite the potential for its practical implementation, many contradictions in this programme were revealed. For example, some visiting compatriots did not want to move to the region specified by the programme, and sought other locations.

The third stage took place in the period from 2006 to 2012. In this stage, an important shift occurred in the sphere of labour migration. There was a reduction and sometimes even a partial abolition of bureaucratic obstacles in the legalisation of foreign labour migrants and their employment in the territories of the country. The laws adopted in this field from 2002 to 2004 made the bureaucratic procedure difficult for both legal migrants and employers. According to Galina Vitkovskaya (2006: 41), 'as a result of the restrictive policy of the previous stage, about 90% of foreign labour migrants were illegal immigrants during that period'. The informal sector of the economy, especially the illegal employment of migrants, hindered the progressive development of the economy.

In a report tabled at a meeting of the State Duma in 2006, experts noted the need to improve the legislation in order to attract qualified and highly qualified specialists to the country, and simultaneously reduce the emigration of the best personnel from the country. The changes to the existing legislation included simplifying both the process of extending the term of stay of labour migrants in the country and the process of obtaining work permits.

Since 2010, regular amendments to the legislation have greatly simplified the procedure for hiring highly qualified migrants. In addition, 'patents' were introduced, which in the first year enabled the removal of more than one million migrants from the shadows and raised more than three billion roubles in revenue. A 'patent' is a legal document that is equal to a work permit restricted to a particular field. For example, if a man wishes to work in the construction industry, but it is difficult to find a job online in the home country, he can buy a 'patent' (so already investing in the place where the future job will be) and arrive in the territory of the Russian Federation with documents (the permit) ready for work in a particular field. When he arrives, he can search for a particular position in the labour market. This variant is certainly a facilitation for the employer, who does not cover expenses on the permit documents, but at the same time it is a risk for the worker, in case he cannot find a job position when he has already covered the expenses. The number of 'patents' and the fields where they can be used are fixed by the state.

To solve the accumulated problems associated with migration, it became necessary to develop a concept for the migration policy of the Russian Federation, on which work continued from 2005 to 2012. A wide range of experts from the state and civil society was involved in the development of the policy. With the adoption of the Concept of the Migration Policy of the Russian Federation, the next and the fourth stage in the management of migration flows began. The current Concept offers a range of measures and programmes, which will be implemented until 2025, but it also requires serious revision.

The main critique of the Concept with regard to the issues connected to migration from the post-Soviet space consists of the following: in the field of labour migration, which has the most significant numbers, around 90 per cent of migrants are from the CIS countries. However, there is an increase in the migration of illegal labour. CIS countries currently have non-visa regimes with Russia, which facilitates criminal and illegal elements in migrating to the shadow economy. According to a 2015 report by the Foundation Migration XXI Century 2015), the FMS and the Ministry for Interior Affairs (its predecessor) published limited data on this question. Hence, the estimate of this segment of the migrant population ranges between 3.5 million and 15–20 million people. Unfortunately, this lack of statistics data prevents researchers from accurately estimating the migration potential of the country.

A significant segment of the shadow economy and illegal migrants affects the social situation in the country, particularly the issue of national security. Opinion polls have shown negative attitudes towards different categories of migrants and in some cases hostility, which peaked in 2013 and 2014. In 2016, the prevalence of such attitudes had returned to the level in 2011 (see Levada Center Surveys). The image of migrants in Russian society makes it easier to 'blame' them for any instability in society and the economy. Furthermore, there is a lack of 'real' effective integration policies. The Concept claimed to be effective, and the action plan included a project on the formation of integration centres. From 2013 to 2014, pilot projects were started in the Tambov, Orenburg and Komi regions. However, they failed to be implemented. The government had proposed a poor financial mechanism to sustain the pilot. According to the action plan, migrants who were 'eager to integrate' had to pay their own expenses, and most cannot pay these. The majority of the participants at the centres were labourers or low-qualified migrants from Uzbekistan, Tajikistan and Moldova, who migrated to earn a living and to send money to their families in their home countries.

The effectiveness of the Compatriots programme discussed earlier seems difficult to estimate. The initiative in 2007 was successful, but its implementation still needs improvement. Although recent data shows a positive tendency, the mechanism is neither obvious nor simple to follow from the perspective of the 'migrant-to-be'. A lot of paperwork is required, and in some cases, the 'moving process' has taken more than 18 months. In the migrants' home countries, it is not always easy to obtain the necessary information on how to emigrate. Some scholars reported cases in which people had completed the process but faced difficulties on the border. In the process of migrating, some migrants were asked to show documents that were not required by the local offices in the countries of origin. The process needs more information, support and transparency.

Estimates of the need for immigrant labour force are required. The Concept states that migrants from the CIS countries and the development of the Compatriots programme are priorities. Nevertheless, the action plan does not specify the type of labour force that is needed. A detailed request by the Russian labour market could facilitate the process and strengthen the effectiveness of the migration policy. The most recent development of the Migration Concept appeared to happen during the Congress of the Compatriots when the president voiced the adjustments needed to the document issued in 2012. These were adopted legally in the Presidential Decree on the Migration Policy 2019–25. This document appeared to be an attempt to 1adjust policy to the changes in the migration flows and state approaches to migration in 2012, and to answer some criticisms of the previous concept.

To highlight some new aspects of the current document: first, some emphasis was given to internal migration. A comparison of the period of Soviet Union migration and post-Soviet migration shows clear and intense international migration flows (cross-border migration), but the late 2010s were also characterised by increased migration between the Russian regions. As the 2019 Concept states, internal migration flows from 2012 to 2017 have added 10 per cent to overall figures, which is already significant, and local migration programmes should take this into consideration. Second, the Compatriots program overview of 2012–17 has shown that this can be an effective tool to deal with an ageing population and population decline in some regions. Co-native inflow is perceived as a good channel of labour migration, as the analysis of the flows has shown that mainly working and not elderly people move through the programme. Third, in terms of structure, migration policy seems to have improved based on the principal changes of the period 2012–17 and what has already been achieved before.

Conclusions

Analysis has shown that the management of the migration process is a complex issue that requires not only regulatory and legislative ground-work but also control of the traffic of people to achieve planned rates of migration. The formation and development of this sphere in Russia show that the migration process has altered gradually from liberalisation to strict requirements, and has concerned issues of attracting and stimulating the migration of certain groups of people. The first three stages of migration policy development up to 2012 were characterised by the predominance of the state-centrist approach, which is reflected in the goals and projects being implemented. The management of migration processes was based on agreements and treaties at the international, supranational and national levels. Certain regulations and migration programmes were applied at regional and local levels. In fact, we could argue migration policy began to function effectively only between 2007 and 2011, despite the previous attempts at different mechanisms and positive practices. The current Concept of Migration policy emphasises the importance of labour migration for the development of the state's economy and ignores the cultural aspect. Therefore, there is a significant need for normative support of labour migration to Russia, beyond the Compatriot programme that favours co-ethnics living abroad.

Legal acts, surveys and statistics

About attraction and use in the Russian Federation of a foreign labor: the decree of the President of the Russian Federation from 16 December 1993, No. 2146. Legal system, ConsultantPlus, <http://www.consultant.ru/document/cons_doc_LAW_38978> (last accessed 5 May 2017).

CIS statistics, <http://www.cisstat.com/migration> (last accessed 8 September 2019).

Concept of the state migration policy of the Russian Federation 2019–25, <https://www.garant.ru/hotlaw/federal/1226782> (last accessed 18 October 2019).

Concept of the state migration policy of the Russian Federation until 2025, <http://www.garant.ru/products/ipo/prime/doc/70088244> (last accessed 5 May 2017)

Levada Center Survey, <http://www.levada.ru/2013/07/03/otnoshenie-k-migrantam> (last accessed 1 May 2017).

Levada Center Survey, <http://www.levada.ru/2013/07/03/trudnosti-ponimaniya-migrantov> (last accessed 1 May 2017).

Levada Center Survey, <http://www.levada.ru/2014/08/26/natsionalizm-ksenofobiya-i-migratsiya> (last accessed 1 May2017).

Levada Center Survey, <http://www.levada.ru/2016/10/11/ksenofobiya-vtoroj-svezhesti> (last accessed 1 May 2017).

On citizenship of the Russian Federation: Federal Law No. 63 of 31 May 2002 (as amended on 31 December 2014). Legal system, ConsultantPlus, <http://www.consultant.ru/popular/civic> (last accessed 5 May 2017).

On the concept of the demographic development of the Russian Federation for the period until 2015: the order of the Government of the Russian Federation from 24 September 2001, No. 1270-p. Portal Garant.ru, <http://base.garant.ru/183768/#ixzz3Rqs8N8ar> (last accessed 5 May 2017).

On the concept of regulation of migration processes in the Russian Federation: Order of the Government of the Russian Federation No. 256-r of 1 March 2003. Legal system, ConsultantPlus, <http://www.consultant.ru/document/cons_doc_LAW_113093> (last accessed 5 May 2017).

On the Federal Migration Service of Russia: Presidential Decree of 14 June 1992, No. 626. Portal Garant.ru, <http://base.garant.ru/6314016> (last accessed 5 May 2017).

On forced migrants: Federal Law No. 4530-I of the Russian Federation of 20 December 1995 (as amended on 25 October 2013)./ Legal system, ConsultantPlus, <http://www.consultant.ru/document/cons_doc_LAW_154882> (last accessed 5 May 2017).

On the improvement of public administration in the field of migration policy: Presidential Decree of 23 February 2002, No. 232. *Rossiyskaya Gazeta*. Official page of presidential decrees, <http://kremlin.ru/acts/bank/17875> (last accessed 4 January 2020).

On the legal status of foreign citizens in the Russian Federation: Federal Law of the Russian Federation of 25 July 2002, No. 115. *Rossiyskaya Gazeta*. Legal system, ConsultantPlus, <http://www.consultant.ru/document/cons_doc_LAW_37868> (last accessed 4 January 2020).

On measures to assist the voluntary resettlement of compatriots living abroad in the Russian Federation: Presidential Decree No. 637 of 22 June 2006. *Rossiyskaya Gazeta*. Legal system, ConsultantPlus, <http://www.consultant.ru/law/doc/ukaz637/> (last accessed 4 January 2020).

On measures to introduce immigration control: Presidential Decree of 16 December 1993, No. 2145. Legal system, ConsultantPlus, <http://www.consultant.ru/document/cons_doc_LAW_2859> (last accessed 5 May 2017).

On the migration registration of foreign citizens and stateless persons in the Russian Federation: Federal Law of the Russian Federation of 18 July 2006, No. 109. *Rossiyskaya Gazeta*. Legal system, ConsultantPlus, <http://www.consultant.ru/document/cons_doc_LAW_61569> (last accessed 4 January 2020).

Opinion Poll Center Survey, <http://fom.ru/Nastroeniya/11566> (last accessed 1 May 2017).

References

Foundation Migration XXI Century (2015) Foundation of the Civil Initiatives & Foundation Migration XXI Century round table on the Concept of Migration Policy, May, <https://komitetgi.ru/news/events/2258> (accessed 20 May 2017).

Iontsev, V. A., and I. V. Ivakhnyuk (2005) 'International migration of the population in Russia at the turn of the 20th and 21st centuries.' *International Economics* 1–2: 47–8.

Ivakhnyuk, I. V. (2008) 'A new model of labor migration management from the CIS countries in Russia.' *Scientific Bulletins of the Belgorod State University. Series: History. Political Science* 8(10): 226–32.

Ivakhnyuk, I. V. (2011) *Prospects for Russia's Migration Policy: Choosing the Right Path.* Moscow: Max Press.

Ryazantsev, S. V. (2007) *Labor migration in the CIS and Baltic countries: trends, consequences, regulation.* Moscow: Formula Prava.

Rybakovsky, L. L. (2003) *Migration of Population: Theory Issues.* Moscow: ISPI RAS.

Tangi, A. de (2012) *The Great Migration: Russia and the Russians after the Fall of the Iron Curtain.* Moscow: The Russian Political Encyclopedia.

Tyuryukanova, E. V. (2007) 'The impact of migration on the labor market.' *Domestic Notes*4: 56–70.

Vitkovskaya, G. S. (2006) 'Infrastructure as a factor hindering illegal migration in Russia.': *Legal Almanac of the Ministry of Internal Affairs of Russia: Professional* 4: 40–2.

Volokh, V. A. (2011) 'Modernization of migration policy and legislation in the sphere of labor migration.' *Law and Politics* 6: 943–9.

Zayonchkovskaya, J., and G. Vitkovskaya (2009) *Post-Soviet Transformations: Reflection in Migrations.* Moscow: Adamant.

Zayonchkovskaya, Z. A. (2001) 'Migration trends in the CIS: the results of the decade.' Pp. 173–86 in *Migration in the CIS and the Baltic: Through Differences of Problems to the Common Information Space,* edited by G. Vitkovskaya and J. Zayonchkovskoy. Moscow: Adamant.

Zayonchkovskaya, Z. A. (2003) 'Emigration to far abroad.' *World of Russia* 12: 145–50.

7

The North Amazon Border:
Haitian Flow to Brazil and New Policies

Tânia Tonhati and Leonardo Cavalcanti

Introduction

A globalising world is a world of networks, flows and mobility. It is also a world of borders. (Rumford 2006: 163)

A S CLEARLY STATED by Rumford (2006), the global world can no longer be defined and understood as it was by contemporary social theorists such as Bauman (2000), Appadurai (1996), Castells (1996) and Urry (1999; 2003) in the 1990s. These scholars were emphasising a world in *motion*, a world composed of motion (Knowles 2017). Bauman shows the world as a 'liquid modernity'; for Appadurai (1996) and Urry (1999; 2003) the world was best viewed as made up of flows, while Castells (1996) shows a world interconnected through networks. While the world in the global era cannot be framed on the 'old' modernity pillars, not all the pillars were totally demolished. In fact, more recently, scholars have started to argue that it is not possible to imagine a borderless and deterritorialised world (Smith and Guarnizo 1998), as the basic ordering of social groups and societies still requires categories and compartments (Harvey 2006). The border emerges, then, as an analytical concept and idea, which has strongly structured social relationships (Ingold 2008).

This chapter, then, intends to understand contemporary borders, on the basis of a case study of the recent migration flow of Haitians to Brazil, from 2010 to 2015. We shed light on how the North Amazon Brazilian border, long forgotten by the Brazilian government, has become a place of negotiation, resilience and, especially, political attention in this decade. Since 2010, Haitians have moved from being a few dozen immigrants in Brazil to become the main immigrant group in the formal labour market in the country in 2013, overtaking the classic migration flows to Brazil, such as the Portuguese (Cavalcanti et al. 2015). The unexpected presence of this migratory flow in the country, mainly through the North Amazon border, has caught the attention of the Brazilian government, resulting in a search for new policies and strategies to 'control' and 'regulate' this flow and the border (e.g. by creating new regulations and even extending this border beyond its national territory). In this vein, such a phenomenon has also caught our academic attention, as Brazilian migration scholars. We propose in this chapter an analysis of Brazilian migration policy, especially in terms of managing migratory flows and the negotiation of borders.

Throughout the 1990s, social analysis wanted to explain a world which was undergoing a number of changes. Global capitalism was destabilising the less industrialised countries, the industrial sectors of industrialised countries had been globally relocated, the division of labour had become more and more global, and the technological revolution of transportation and communication was deeply transforming human relationships. All these changes, along with global political transformations such as decolonisation, the universalisation of human rights, and the expansion of social networks which facilitated migration flows and the formation of transnational links (economic, political, religious, social, familial and emotional), constituted the complexity of this 'new' world. It became the agenda of social analysis and needed to be understood and explained (Knowles 2017; Robertson 2011).

Scholars reflecting on this new social context named it 'globalisation',' postmodern' or 'network and informational society' (Giddens 1991; Harvey 1999; Castells 1996). The dominant debate in social science was focused on the phenomena of flows and connections between distant locations, the construction of networks, and the compression of time and space as well as the growing perception of the world as a place without borders, questioning the nation-state as the model that organises social relations (Giddens 1991; Castells 1996; Harvey 1999). In this context, the terms 'international', 'global', 'transnational', 'multinational' and 'cosmopolitan' are often used synonymously to explain the new social relationships. In order to overcome the terminological confusion, some scholars such as Portes (2001: 186) have suggested differentiating the terms 'international', 'multinational' and 'transnational'. By 'international' Portes refers to the activities of the nation-state; 'multinational' concerns large-scale formal institutions; and 'transnational' is any activity initiated and sustained by non-institutional actors, whether organised groups or networks of individuals from different countries.

Although the transnational approach has been widely used in academia, and is regarded as a useful term for describing and analysing the exchanges involving migration in this 'new' global world, many scholars have pointed to the confusion surrounding the concept, and the diverse ways in which it is used (Smith and Guarnizo 1998; Vertovec 1999; 2009; Sinatti 2008). While seeking to define 'transnational', some scholars initially came up with the idea of 'autonomous space' from which both the sending and receiving nation-states are excluded (Kearney 1995), or the emergence of 'translocalities' (Appadurai 1996), which challenges the territorial basis of the nation-state. Such perspectives were termed transnationalism *'from above'*, as the nation-state had become fragile due to the emergence of 'the transnational capital, global media, and emergent supra-national political institutions' (Smith and Guarnizo 1998: 3). Some of the economic activities that fall within the category *'from above'* are mapped by Portes et al. (1999: 222) and include 'multinational investments in Third World countries, development of the tourist market of locations abroad, agencies of home country banks in migrant centres', all being highly institutionalised activities.

These writers also identify political activities which belong to *'from above'* transnationalism, for example: 'consular officials and representatives of national political parties abroad, dual nationality granted by home country governments, immigrants elected to home country legislatures', and finally, there are the socio-cultural activities *'from above'* such as 'international expositions of national arts, home country major artists perform[ing] abroad, regular cultural events organized by foreign embassies' (Portes et al. 1999: 222). These transnational activities have been examined within the terms 'globalisation', 'network societies' and 'cosmopolitanism (Castells 1996; Beck and Beck-Gernsheim 2014).

However, Smith and Guarnizo (1998) identify how transnational activities also happen *'from below'*: the literature on this highlights the 'decentering local resistances of the informal economy, ethnic nationalism and grassroots activism', and it is consequently seen as an expression of 'subversive popular resistance' (Smith and Guarnizo 1998: 3). In this vein, concepts of cultural hybridity, multi-positional identities, border-crossing by marginal others, and transnational business practices by migrant entrepreneurs are seen as successful and liberating practices carried out by ordinary people to escape the control and domination of transnationalism *'from above'* (Appadurai 1996; Kearney 1995; Portes et al. 1999). A number of activities are considered *'from below'*, for example:

Economic: informal cross-country traders, small businesses created by returned immigrants in the home country, long-distance circular labour migration; **Political:** home town civic committees created by immigrants; alliances of immigrant committees with home country political associations; fund raisers for home country electoral candidates; **Socio-cultural:** amateur cross-country sport matches, folk music groups making presentations in immigrant centres, priests from the home town visit[ing] and organiz[ing] their parishioners abroad. (Portes et al. 1999: 222)

Analysing transnational activities *'from below'*, Smith and Guarnizo (1998) add that 'transnational practices do not take place in an imaginary "third place" (Bhabha 1990) abstractly located "in between" national territories' (Smith and Guarnizo 1998: 6). For them, the image of transnational migrants as deterritorialised, free-floating people should be questioned. They argue that, even though it is a fact that intermittent spatial mobility, dense social ties and intense exchanges by migrants across national borders have reached unprecedented levels, this has also nurtured the formulation of metaphors of migration as a boundless, uprooted and, therefore, liberating process (Smith and Guarnizo 1998: 11). However, such assumptions are groundless and disregard the constraints, inequalities, policies, obligations and opportunities that constitute the migration experience (Knowles 2017).

In a similar vein, 'border thinking' as argued by Rumford (2006) emerges as one way of thinking about the 'new' global scenario described above. 'Border thinking' goes beyond the narrow debate about a borderless world, but is not just about looking at the rebordering of an increasingly security-conscious world, which has happened particularly since 9/11. In fact, authors such as Rumford (2006: 164) argue that 'borders can be created, shifted, and deconstructed by a range of actors' in diverse contexts, and the consequences are no longer matters affecting only nation-states; they now strongly affect the everyday lives of ordinary people. In this sense, as argued by Knowles (2017), mobility based on flow and network theories 'conveys an unreal ease with which people and things move from place to place.' She argues that:

once we engage with mobility empirically . . . it becomes clear that the things to which mobility thinking is applied (people, objects, images, money and so on) do not just flow. They bump awkwardly along, navigating obstacles, generating friction, and forging pathways as they move this way and that, their trajectories anything but as smooth as the term flow implies. (Knowles 2017: 490)[1]

Thus, the sociological turn from notions of 'flow', 'motion' and 'mobility' towards the paradox produced by globalisation and the concepts of 'bordering' and 'rebordering' guide this chapter. Nonetheless, it is important to note that, as has been argued by Robertson (2011: 4), 'borders and mobilities are not antithetical, and that they must, and do exist together'. This chapter, thus, frames its axes of analysis on: (1) the process of bordering: 'remembering' a forgotten border; and (2) the politics of mobility (asylum seekers and humanitarian visas). The research was based on a case study of the recent migration of Haitians to Brazil, from 2010 onwards. It aims to shed light on how the North Amazon border, long forgotten by the Brazilian government, media and academia, has become a place of negotiation, resilience and, in particular, political attention.

Data and methodology

This chapter is part of a larger research project that was carried out by the International Migration Observatory of Brazil (OBMigra), Brasília University, between 2014 and 2016, called 'Haitians' migration and the labour market in Brazil', funded by the National Council of Technological and Scientific Development (CNPQ), the International Organization for Migration (IOM) and the Labour Ministry (MT). The methodological framework consisted of different stages and techniques. First, it analysed several databases of Brazilian government institutions which are responsible for migration to Brazil. From the Ministry of Labour (MT), information was gathered based on authorisations granted to Haitian immigrants by the National Immigration Council (CNIg), and also data from the 'Annual Social Information Report' (RAIS) which indicates the presence of immigrants in the Brazilian formal labour market. The project also analysed databases of the 'National System for Registration of Foreigners' (SINCRE) and the database of 'Asylum Seekers' from the Federal Police Department (DPF), which is part of the Ministry of Justice (MJ). Finally, it analysed a database from the Ministry of Foreign Affairs (MRE) regarding visas granted to Haitians from the Brazilian consulate offices. The quantitative analysis of these data was undertaken in Brazil and the information analysed helped to better understand the new migrant flow to Brazil. The databases provided information on the migrants' main entry into the country, the visas applied for, their demographic and socio-economic profiles and their main labour activities.

The second stage of the research involved an extensive data collection exercise of secondary sources in national and local newspapers, usually of online news (e.g. *Folha de São Paulo, Estado de São Paulo, Revista Época, O Globo, Agência Notícias do Acre* (AC), *Jornal da Fronteira* (AC) etc.) about Haitians in Brazil. The news items were separated by year, which helped to uncover the unprecedented importance of this theme between 2010 and 2015. The third and final stage of the research was the main empirical research which was carried out over ten months (March 2015 to December 2015), divided between Brasília (Distrito Federal) and Curitiba (Paraná). Ninety in-depth (semi-structured) interviews were conducted, seventy with Haitians (forty-seven men and twenty-three women) and twenty with community and religious leaders and members of government. Two focus groups were also conducted, one in each city. The data collected in the first and second stages of the research strongly informed the analysis and the findings presented in this chapter. A subset of the interviewees were selected, namely those that met the criterion of having entered Brazil through the North Amazon border.

Brazil and global migration

Brazil has played an important role in the steady increase of people's mobility, more specifically migration, in the global era. Nevertheless, Brazilian migration (inflows and outflows) is still largely invisible, academically and politically, compared with that of other countries or areas of the globe.

Historically, up to the second half of the 1980s, Brazil had a traditional demographic image as a country that had been a major recipient of a diverse migrant population (Patarra 2005; Sales 1991; 2000). Between 1874 and 1930 was the historical period with the greatest intensity of immigration flows into Brazil. This intense flow was the result of various factors in Europe and Brazil. In Europe, the expansion of capitalism, the mechanisation of agricultural activities, population pressure on the demographic transition and low shipping costs, and in Brazil, the need for labour and the idea of a racial civilising project that proclaimed a desire to 'whiten' the Brazilian population (Seyferth 1986), were among the decisive factors for the immigration flow (Solé et al. 2011).

At that time, according to Levy (1974), about 4.07 million migrants entered the country, invited by the Brazilian government, who subsidised their passage. They were mostly Italians, Portuguese, Spaniards and Germans, and later, Japanese, who became an important migrant group. These migrants were a vital labour force for the coffee and cotton plantations and for the industrialisation of the country, mainly in São Paulo and the southern states of Brazil (Paraná, Santa Catarina and Rio Grande do Sul) (Solé et al. 2011).

However, from the 1930s, and especially post-World War II, the immigration flows reduced dramatically, not only for Brazil, but for all South American countries. Unlike many other countries, which had a strong emigration flow to northern countries such as the United States and Europe to meet the standard requirements of Fordist reproduction of capital in full expansion in these areas, notably through the *Bracero* programme in the US and guest-worker programmes in Europe (e.g. Germany, Switzerland, France and so on), Brazil contained migration almost entirely within its own borders (Sales 2000). Due to the profound regional inequalities within Brazil, migration occurred from the poorest northern areas to the richest industrialised states in the south and southeast, particularly São Paulo, and from rural areas into the cities (Solé et al. 2011; Piscitelli 2008). Although there is data recording the entry of approximately 1.1 million migrants into the country between 1940 and the late 1970s (Levy 1974), this figure is considered by demographers to be very low, and consequently this historical period has been characterised by the country's minimal participation in international migration, given the small volume of both inflows and output (Patarra and Baeninger 1995; Oliveira 2013).

This scenario began to change, albeit slowly, in the 1970s, when many of those opposed to the military dictatorship (which lasted from 1964 to 1985) went to live abroad, usually in exile. Nonetheless, this did not represent a significant migration flow as most of the people returned from exile to Brazil when the dictatorship ended (Sales 1991; 2000). But towards the late 1980s, Brazilians' mobility abroad gradually increased, and there is a general consensus in the literature on Brazilian migration that the first massive wave of emigration happened from the mid-1980s to the 1990s (Patarra 2005; Sales 1991; 2000; Margolis 1994; 1998; 2013; Piscitelli 2008; Solé et al. 2011; Padilla 2006; Oliveira 2013).

As suggested by Sales (2000), the numbers clearly indicate and confirm this trend. Carvalho (1996) has estimated that there was negative net migration in the 1980s of approximately 1.5 million people, who mainly went to the US. This represents the departure of almost 1 per cent of the country's total population (Sales 2000). In the 1990s, the balance remained negative, and the migration flows became more diverse, reaching countries besides the United States, such as Japan and European countries. The Brazilian official statistics institute (IBGE 2010)[2] confirms that between 1991 and 2010, 23.8 per cent of the Brazilian migration flow was to the USA, 13.4 per cent to Portugal, 9.4 per cent to Spain, 7.4 per cent to Japan, 7 per cent to Italy and 6.2 per cent to the UK. This survey also provides information on age, gender and the Brazilian states the most people migrated from. Regarding gender, 53.9 per cent were women and 46.1 per cent men, they were between twenty and thirty-nine years of age, and were mainly from the states of São Paulo and Minas Gerais.

Brazilian emigration has become an important issue for the media and academics. According to Sales (1994), news of Brazilians being prevented from entering the US has emerged as one of the main images of Brazilians abroad. The main topics discussed by the national media are: the living and working conditions of the Brazilian population abroad; remittances of Brazilian migrants; the detention, imprisonment and deportation of Brazilians; documentation problems or crossing irregular borders; and Brazilian involvement in human trafficking, sexual exploitation or prostitution (Póvoa Neto 2006). While the national media focus their attention on topics that produce 'good' headlines, scholars are trying to understand why this flow began in the mid-1980s and continued into the 1990s and 2000s, and why Brazilians migrate to particular countries such as the US, Japan and some European countries.

The main hypothesis concerns the Brazilian economic and political crisis in the 1980s and 1990s, called the 'triennium of disillusionment' (Sales 2000: 2). Later, other explanations were added. In the case of the US, scholars consider that North American cultural imperialism intensively penetrated Brazilian society and contributed to the migration, as well as the formation of social networks (Beserra 2003; Margolis 2013). Regarding the other two important Brazilian migration flows, to Japan and European countries, particularly Portugal, theories on returning or counter-current migration and colonial historical ties have been the key explanations (Padilla 2009; Tsuda 2003).

However, from 2008 onwards, Brazilian migration faced new challenges and dynamics. Due to the world economic crisis that started in the US in 2008, which soon spread and deeply affected Europe, and because of Brazilian economic growth (up to 2015), the country could no longer be described as a global player that only exported its population (Solé et al. 2011). Indeed, Brazil has consolidated itself as a country with a large number of emigrants and has begun to form a greater second generation abroad (Assis 1999; 2014; Margolis 2013; Siqueira 2009), as well as recently facing a large number of returnees (Fernandes and Knup 2012; Fernandes and Castro 2013; Hirano 2005). In addition, since 2010, it has become a destination for new immigrants, particularly Haitians (Cavalcanti et al. 2015; Tonhati et al. 2016).

The arrival of the Haitians in Brazil and the continued inflow during this decade was totally unanticipated by the Brazilian authorities, and soon there was a strong need to understand this new migratory group (Silva 2015; Handerson 2015a). Thus, research was carried out to respond to questions related to Haitians in Brazil, such as: what led the Haitians to migrate to Brazil? Who are the Haitian migrants in Brazil? How do they travel to Brazil? What is their migration status? Moreover, what kind of jobs are they doing here? (See Silva 2012; 2013; 2015; Cavalcanti et al. 2015; 2016.) These inquiries have become the focus of a number of academic studies, discussed in the next section.

Haitian migration to Brazil

In January 2010, Haiti was recovering from three hurricanes that hit the country in 2009, when a massive earthquake of 7.3 on the Richter scale struck the country. The capital of the country, Port-au-Prince, was hit extremely hard and it was estimated that 80 per cent of buildings in the city were seriously damaged, including schools, hospitals, police stations and the presidential palace itself. In addition to infrastructure damage, approximately 230,000 Haitians lost their lives and 1.5 million were left homeless by the earthquake (Giraldi 2012; Handerson 2015a; 2015b). As a result of this devastating scenario, many countries offered material help (medicine, food, temporary shelters). Nonetheless, it was not enough to stop numerous people from migrating to other countries. Migration increased after the earthquake, even though migration had always been strongly constitutive of Haitian society (Handerson 2015b). In this context, questions emerged about what led the Haitians to migrate to Brazil. The academic literature developed some arguments.

The first main hypothesis linked the Haitian migration to Brazil with the MINUSTAH (United Nations Stabilization Mission in Haiti). In 2004, Haitian president Aristide was forcibly removed from the country by the US military, supported by France. After Aristide left power, the Haitian Supreme Court president, Bonifácio Alexandre, took command of the country and requested assistance from the United Nations to contain the country's political crisis, which had also become very violent. The United Nations Security Council (UNSC) then established the Interim Multinational Force (MIF) and, in April 2004, the Council approved Resolution 1542, giving rise to MINUSTAH led by Brazil.

The MINUSTAH along with other Brazilian non-governmental organisations (e.g. Viva Rio, ActionAid, Pastoral da Criança, the Support Group for AIDS Prevention) carried out a number of social and humanitarian projects, such as: helping with the construction of a hydroelectric power plant on the Artibonite River in the south of the country; encouraging the production of vegetables in the Kenscoff region; funding by the Brazilian Cooperation Agency (ABC) and the Brazilian Ministry of Sport in partnership with the United Nations Children's Fund (UNICEF) to promote programmes which encouraged the practice of sports during school activities; and the contribution by the Brazilian women's secretary and health ministry to the development of a national programme aimed at the prevention of gender violence in Haiti (Moraes et al. 2013; Zeni and Filipim 2013; Fernandes and Castro 2014). These authors suggest that the measures contributed to creating in Haiti a positive image of Brazil. Furthermore, the economic growth of Brazil at the beginning of this decade nourished the idea of '*Brezil pa peyi blan*' (Brazil as a 'white' country) (Handerson 2015a). According to Handerson:

> '*Peyi blan*' is a category with various meanings. In some cases, it can be understood as '*peyi etranje*' (foreign country), '*peyi lòt bò dlo*' (country beyond the sea). It is expressed and used among those residing in Haiti and abroad to describe industrialized and economically developed countries, which are mostly composed of a significant white population, but not necessarily. In addition, in a '*peyi blan*' people earn in '*lajan*' diaspora, meaning in US dollars and euros. (Handerson 2015a: 374)[3]

The more empirically engaged studies, such as the one developed by Handerson, showed that in fact the first flow of Haitians to Brazil did not intend to stay in Brazil. They intended to go to French Guiana and from there maybe to France. According to Handerson (2015a), French Guiana would work as a place of passage, a 'couloir' or corridor. There, the Haitians planned to seek asylum and, once they had acquired permission to stay, most of them intended to travel to France, and maybe later to the US and/or Canada. In fact, French Guiana was considered a '*peyi etranje*' and not a '*peyi blan*'. The Haitians called the countries of passage '*ti peyi*' (small country, in the socio-economic sense). These countries represented only the beginning of the mobility process, but played a very important role in the Haitians' mobility. It is necessary to have a visa from a '*ti peyi*' country and the passport pages filled with stamps before applying for a visa of a '*peyi blan*' country such as the United States, France or Canada.

It is common in Haiti for people to travel to the Dominican Republic and Panama several times a year before subsequently applying for an American, French or Canadian visa (Handerson 2015a). In this sense, their migration can be seen as non-permanent, as it was believed that it would facilitate being granted a visa.

In addition to the positive image given by the MINUSTAH, and the fact that Brazil was a corridor to French Guiana, which are seen as the two strongest arguments for the great Haitian flow to Brazil, other reasons listed include:

> 3) the public and international position of openness and hospitality of the Brazilian Government towards the Haitians; 4) the diffusion among Haitians (in Haiti and abroad) that the Brazilian Government was encouraging Haitian migration to the country, having an interest in Haitian labour to build the World Cup stadiums (even if it was not true); 5) the propaganda of the image of Brazil as a 'racial paradise', without discrimination, particularly in the imagination of those who suffered such discrimination in the Dominican Republic and Ecuador; 6) the information that in Brazil the migrant earns housing and food (it is not a fact), in addition to salary, which was supposed to range from U$ 2,000 to U$ 3,000 monthly (not true either). (Handerson 2015a: 44)[4]

It was in this context that the Haitian migration flow to Brazil increased steadily from 2010 onwards. It was estimated that about 7,000 Haitian migrants passed through the Triple Border – Brazil, Colombia and Peru – between 2010 and 2013, and there are between 35,000 and 40,000 in Brazil, between 15,000 and 17,000 in Suriname and 33,500 in French Guiana (Granger 2007: 291). More recent data from the International Migration Observatory of Brazil (OBMigra) shows that between 2010 and 2015 the Brazilian Federal Police, which is responsible for the Brazilian borders, registered the entry of 72,406 Haitians into the country. The same database shows an increase in the number of foreigners entering via the state of Acre (43,000), which is linked to the massive numbers of Haitians entering through this border (Oliveira 2016). It is in this new scenario that the North Amazon border, long forgotten by Brazilian authorities and policies, has become an enormous national and international issue, reaching the news as well as political and academic agendas.

The new and unexpected presence of the Haitian migratory flow into the country, through the North Amazon border, attracted the attention of the Brazilian government, which resulted in a call for new policies and strategies to 'control' and 'regulate' this flow (e.g. creating new regulations and even extending its borders beyond the national territory). In the next section, this chapter outlines the main findings of the study with regard to the process of managing the Haitian migratory flow and the negotiating of borders, particularly describing the Haitian migration paths into Brazil and their reasons for entering Brazil via the North Amazon border. Finally, we reflect on the Brazilian migration policy response to Haitian migration.

Findings and outcomes

The process of bordering: remembering the 'forgotten' border

A border can be drawn on a map and then be forgotten. While for the local people, the border challenges constitute everyday struggles, they are not usually portrayed as a major national issue, at least not in the case of the North Amazon Brazilian border with Peru, Bolivia and Colombia. However, a border is much more of a process than a line, because it can become alive and resignified at any time (Balibar 2015). This was the case with the North Amazon frontier between 2010 and 2015. For many years, it was a border that had been forgotten by the media as well as by the authorities, academia and political debates. However, the Haitian migration shed new light on this border, and how it operates within the new global migration flow to Brazil.

Those who live in these localities in Brazil usually lack minimum infrastructure and have a low quality of life. It means living on the periphery, far from the developed areas of the country and the places where the policy decisions are made. However, between 2010 and 2015, the North Amazon border was 'removed' from the periphery and became 'located' at the centre of political and academic debates (Silva 2015). Since 2010, the North Amazon border has made a number of headlines in the main national and international press[5] as well as on television news and documentaries.[6] The headlines have highlighted this border, particularly the large presence and entry of Haitians (Silva 2012; 2015; Handerson 2015b). The increased number of Haitians in the North Amazon border led to attempts to understand how they enter Brazil, and which path or paths they take. Soon it become clear that we could talk about not one path, but several paths.

Haitian migration paths into Brazil

The first Haitian migrant group arrived through the North Amazon border entering Brazil via Tabatinga, a small city in the state of Amazonas, located on the border with Colombia and Peru. The Haitians interviewed in this study reported that their trip to Tabatinga usually begins by bus from Haiti to Santo Domingo in the Dominican Republic. There, they hire a travel agency, which usually charges up to U$ 2,500, to buy the first flight to Panama City (Panamá) and then to Quito (Ecuador). Most of them spend a few days in Quito before travelling by bus to Lima (Peru). After spending a few days in the Peruvian capital, they travel by bus to Iquitos (Peru), near the border with Brazil, where they get a boat to Tabatinga (Brazil, AM). From there, some Haitians plan to travel by bus to French Guiana, but many are stopped by the Immigration Police of the French Overseas Department, or the ones who enter have their asylum claim refused and are deported, or decide to go back to Brazil.

Due to the difficulties with entering French Guiana, a fact which spread by word of mouth via their networks of families and friends, as reported by our interviewees, the Haitians started to redirect their movement flow to Brazil, which affected which border they accessed. First the media, and later, academic studies, posted the Acre border with Peru and Bolivia, particularly the city of Brasiléia, as one of the main entry points to Brazil (Handerson 2015a; Silva 2012; 2015; Zeni and Filippim 2013). The media headline was 'Acre is the route of entry of Haitians into the country' (Antunes 2011). Zerbini, ex-director of CONARE (Brazilian National Refugee Committee), said: 'the choice of Acre came after the so-called "coyotes"[7] noticed Acre had a very low border inspection' (in Antunes 2011). Indeed, some of the interviewees had arrived through this border via the 'coyotes'. Daniel, a thirty-three-year-old living in Brasília since 2013, recalled that despite relatives and friends living abroad advising him not to contact the 'coyotes', travel agencies forced him to purchase this service. He commented:

The travel agency warns that the trip is hard and will not work. I have to travel with coyotes. What would you do? You have to get in touch with a coyote, and I did and I stayed for days in a city in Acre, the name was ... difficult ... Brasiléia. (Daniel, 11 July 2015)

In the case of Brasiléia, the Haitians started using a route through Bolivia and Peru. Through Bolivia, they had to cross the bridge over the Acre River, which is in between the cities of Cobija (Bolivia) and Brasiléia (Brazil). The journey to Cobija was usually made by bus and from Cobija to Brasiléia by taxi. In some cases, the city of Iberia (Bolivia) was reported as being used as another route to get to Brasiléia. For those who continued to travel through Peru, after flying to Lima, they went to Cusco and Puerto Maldonado (Peru) to get to the city of Iñapari (Peru). From there they crossed the 'Friendship Bridge' to the city of Assis Brasil (Brazil), and then continued travelling, usually by taxi, to Brasiléia, which is about one-and-a-half hours. Some Haitians also reported arriving in Iñapari (Peru) but feared they would be deported at the city of Assis Brasil, where there is a Federal Police office, so travelled through Bolivia to the city of Cobija and went directly to Brasiléia.

The boundaries and routes reported were extremely porous and controlled by 'coyotes'. In fact, the coyotes were described as being the taxi drivers, who worked in collaboration with police officers. These routes used by the coyotes were known for drug smuggling into Brazil, but by this time they were being used for people (Silva 2015). In addition, the Haitians interviewed recalled that during their journey between these borders they were assaulted, were blackmailed and suffered physical and psychological violence. Flavio, a twenty-eight-year-old living in Curitiba, reported:

I had money to go to French Guiana, which was my final destination, where I wanted to go, but my money was taken on the way. I was robbed once, but still had some money I hid, but they charged us much more for everything, so I ran out of money to go to French Guiana. (Flavio, 15 August 2015)

While the crossing of borders has become something widely done by people in the global era, which has been facilitated by the network of information and easier and cheaper transport (Castles and Miller 2009), our study reveals that the global dynamic and 'clamour' for travel are clearly not shared by everyone. The Haitians travelling to Brazil undoubtedly show

that for some people arrival at a country requires a long path of negotiation with several borders, and it is not a safe journey. Furthermore, this
also reveals that the border is not a 'neutral' and 'objective' place. Indeed,
some studies have shown that race, gender, ethnicity and religion influence the migrant border experience (Balibar 2015; Juss 2006). Therefore,
it is important to note that, due to the global economic disparities between
countries and the axes of inequality described above, not all people will
travel using the shortest path, the fastest transport or the most used entry
points, such as airports (Silva 2015; Dias 2016). In the case of the Haitians
who came to Brazil, entry into the country via the North Amazon border
was not a natural option, as going through the airports at São Paulo or
Rio de Janeiro, which are the main Brazilian international airports, would
have been the shortest, fastest, cheapest and safest way to enter Brazil. So
what led the Haitians to 'choose' to enter the country through the forgotten North Amazon border?

The reasons for entering Brazil via North Amazon border

As has been previously said, the Haitians travelling to Brazil were running away from the consequences of a terrible natural disaster (the
earthquake of 2010) and the economic hardship of the country, but
according to Brazilian national laws and global agreements, those are
not considered legitimate reasons for fleeing a country and migrating to another as a refugee. The majority of Haitians who migrated to
Brazil could not fulfil the requirements of visa categories such as tourist, labour, student, business. They were, in fact, economic migrants.
Thus, as the nation-state closed down the possibilities, a new door was
opened to overcome these boundaries. Guided by 'coyotes', travel agencies, family members and friends – in other words, by the migration
network – the Haitians arrived in Brazil via the North Amazon border,
because they could travel without any visa, and as soon as they got to
Brazil, they were told to seek asylum.

It became an 'entry tactic' of the Haitians once Brazil ratified the 1951
Refugee Convention, and then could not deny them this request (Silva
2015; Cavalcanti et al. 2015; Handerson 2015b; Tonhati et al. 2016).
Countries that have ratified the Refugee Convention are obliged to pro-
tect refugees that are on their territory, and regarding asylum seekers, the
country cannot deport them until they have been through, in the case of
Brazil, a full, comprehensive analysis of their situation, which is done by
CONARE. Unlike many other countries (such as the UK), Brazil allows

asylum seekers to work while they are waiting for the analysis of their claim. Thus, once in Brazil, the Haitian asylum seekers who held claim forms from the Brazilian Federal Police could obtain a work permit, which allowed them to seek employment and be legally hired.

In this context, the numbers of Haitians entering Brazil via the North Amazon border has continually increased, particularly in the city of Brasiléia (Acre). The complete unpreparedness of the authorities for the arrival of so many people put the North Amazon border, the state of Acre and the Brazilian federal government in the spotlight.

Brasiléia is a small city in Acre which lacks infrastructure (health, housing, jobs), and the daily arrival of a hundred or more Haitians completely changed the city's routine. The Haitians arrived, in most cases, without any money, as they had been exploited on their journey to Brazil. Some of our interviewees recalled being hungry, thirsty and extremely tired on their arrival in Brasiléia. Most of them wanted to continue their trip to São Paulo, Brasília or cities in the south of the country (Curitiba), where some already had contacts and believed they would be able to find a job. However, without the money to continue their trip, and as the Brazilian authorities were not sufficiently prepared to receive so many people (e.g. the Federal Police did not have enough refugee forms), the Haitians had to stay longer in Brasiléia. The city then had to improvise a shelter for them, which soon became overcrowded. The unprecedented situation led the Brazilian government to find 'last minute' solutions.

The political 'settlement' of the border

The number of Haitians crossing the North Amazon border and seeking asylum increased steadily between 2010 and 2015. According to the database on 'asylum seekers' of the Federal Police, 453 Haitians sought asylum in Brazil in 2010, a number that increased to 2,472 in 2011, 3,275 in 2012, 11,763 in 2013 and then 16,924 in 2014. In 2014, there was a total of 34,887 refugee claims. The database shows that the profile of Haitian asylum seekers was 78 per cent men and 19 per cent women. Other important information related to the age distribution; the majority (65 per cent) of Haitians were between 20 and 34 years old, with 30 per cent between 35 and 49 years old. Only 2 per cent of Haitians were under the age of 20, and 3 per cent were over 65 years of age. In addition, the information from this database corroborates the qualitative findings, as it shows that the states of Acre, São Paulo and Amazonas comprised 90 per cent of the total refugee claims made between 2010 and 2014. The one with the highest demand was Acre, with 25,723 requests, followed by São Paulo with 7,158 and Amazonas with 5,121. This finding is relevant to this study, as it reinforces the thesis that entry via the North Amazon border was a 'tactic', in de Certeau's (1984) sense, which implies agency, but does not mean a free choice, as a 'tactic' also involves constraints (Tonhati et al. 2016). Thus, Haitians sought asylum as a way to enter, stay and work in Brazil. It was a 'tactic' by them to move, to somehow take part in a world in *motion*, in the global dynamic.

The high number of Haitian asylum seekers was a consequence of a global mobility totally unanticipated by the Brazilian authorities. In fact, it soon became clear that most of the Haitians would not be granted refugee status, as they did not fit the refugee criteria. They were not 'persons fleeing armed conflict or persecution', they were migrants. Thus, according to UNHCR (2016), they as migrants

> choose to move not because of a direct threat of persecution or death, but mainly to improve their lives by finding work, or in some cases for education, family reunion, or other reasons. Unlike refugees who cannot safely return home, migrants face no such impediment to return. (UNHCR 2016)

Such unexpected factors forced the Brazilian government to create unique measures for this migrant group. In this chapter, we highlight three measures: (1) Resolution 97 (RN); (2) Resolution 102 (RN); and (3) the Humanitarian Visa Application Center.

The first measure was 97 (RN), a normative resolution, created by the National Immigration Council (CNIg) on 13 January 2012. It allowed the Haitians to have a permanent residency visa on humanitarian grounds. The Haitians who sought asylum, but did not qualify for it, would have their cases withdrawn from CONARE and sent to be assessed by the CNIg, which would grant permanent residency visas for humanitarian reasons to Haitians. This regulation was thus intended to resolve the migration status of the large number of Haitians who were already in the country but did not fit into the refugee category, or other visa status. Brazilian law did not allow transferring from a visa or asylum claim to the other in the country; the migrant by law had to leave Brazil and return to their own country and get a visa before travelling to Brazil. However, it was clear to the Brazilian authorities, by that stage, that the Haitians would not be able or willing to return to Haiti, so they were granted humanitarian visas within the country.

This regulation was also intended to control the movement of Haitians through the North Amazon border and put a cap on Haitian migration to Brazil. Regulation 97 (RN) prohibited the entry of Haitians who did not have a visa issued at the Brazilian Embassy in Port-au-Prince. In addition, it established a quota system, limiting visas to a maximum of 1,200 per year. As a result, those who arrived at the border after this measure was introduced were detained at the border, facing deprivation and insecurity, as they could not continue their passage into the country. They could not be deported because, according to the principle of non-return in the 1951 Geneva Convention, the Brazilian government could not take this decision, but they were stopped at the border because they did not have the humanitarian visa.

Therefore, this resolution succeeded with regard to giving visas to the Haitians who were already in the country, but failed in its aim to control the flow of Haitians, as they continued to come to Brazil. The restriction on the number of visas issued by the Brazilian embassy in Port-au-Prince resulted in an increase in the number of people who decided to travel through the North Amazon border, and, at the same time, confined many Haitians at the border as they were no longer accepted into the country, not being considered refugees.

Under a lot of pressure and criticism from different sectors of civil society and the immigrants themselves, the Brazilian government was forced to revoke the quota system on 26 April 2013, via Resolution 102 RN (Normative Resolution). This second measure allowed the Brazilian MRE to issue humanitarian visas to Haitians in council offices outside Haiti as well. Thus, after the 'no restriction' measure (102 RN), according to the Foreign Ministry database, 5,045 humanitarian visas were issued in Port-au-Prince in 2013; 7,020 in 2014; 13,923 in 2015; and 12,975 up to May 2016. In 2013, 1,139 humanitarian visas were issued in Quito, the capital of Ecuador; in 2014 there were 3,138 issued; 3,536 in 2015; and only 2 up to May 2016. The Brazilian Embassy in San Dominguez (Dominican Republic) and in Lima (Peru) issued a small number of visas.

This second measure of 'no restrictions' partially reduced the arrival of Haitians via the North Amazon border. However, the Brazilian Embassy in Port-au-Prince did not have the infrastructure or staff to issue visas to all the Haitians applying for them. The CNIg received reports of several cases of violence outside the Brazilian Embassy, difficulty identifying fake documents, and long queues, with people sleeping overnight in order to be seen (Brasil 2014). The Brazilian government then enacted a third measure. In 2015, the MRE, in partnership with the IOM, launched the Humanitarian Visa Application Center in Port-au-Prince, with the aim of expanding the humanitarian visa granting system (Brasil 2015). According to Shauna Martin, who runs the centre:

> One of the main challenges is completing the visa application form and it is at that moment that the BVAC [Brazil Humanitarian Visa Application Center] enters. [. . .] The agency does not do any kind of set up procedure, this is in charge of NGOs that we have a partnership with . . . Daily, they attended hundreds of people requesting a humanitarian visa. Also occurring were various cases of extortion and fraud. (Shauna Martin, 4 November 2016, in a seminar about Haitian migration in Brazil)

This last measure demonstrates the flexibility of the border beyond national frontiers, and the delegation, albeit partial, of the control of the borders to international organisations. In addition, it also reveals that the desire to control migration is not unique to Northern countries (the US and Europe): we all have our 'South', as Balibar (2015: 1) notes: 'for France, this "South" is Italy, but for the UK it's France. For Germany it's Hungary and beyond, but for Hungary, it's Serbia, Macedonia, Greece, Turkey', and for Brazil it was Haiti. Brazil is a country with extremely porous borders and little control of them, but in order to try and gain control, as the Haitians were Brazil's 'South', the border was transported to that country.

In sum, these three measures, along with the political and financial crisis that hit Brazil strongly at the end of 2015, removed the North Amazon border from the spotlight and it returned to the periphery. It is known that this border is still a migration route for Senegalese, Pakistanis and Ghanaians, but their number is far smaller than for the Haitians (Cavalcanti and Oliveira 2016). Thus, the North Amazon border continues to be porous, but it has once again become forgotten. Thus, as Balibar (2015: 5) says, a border 'is not what a state "decides" it is in terms of power relations and negotiations with other states but what the global context dictates'. Therefore, global changes (political, environmental and economic) can at any time make the dormant North Amazon border erupt again.

Conclusions

The aim of this chapter has been to explore the new complexity of contemporary borders by focusing on a case study of the recent migration flow of Haitians to Brazil, from 2010 to 2015, shedding light on the North Amazon border. It has demonstrated how a long-forgotten border became a place of negotiation, of resilience and, particularly, of media, political and academic attention. The analysis has revealed that a border is a live process, and not just a line drawn on a map. Indeed, a border can influence and be influenced by global changes, mobility and national and international laws and regulations.

The first axis of analysis – the process of bordering: 'remembering' a forgotten border – revealed that a border is not always a place of continuous worries, control and militarisation. In fact, unlike Northern countries, Brazil has a very porous border, 15,179 kilometres of frontiers with ten countries (French Guiana, Suriname, Guyana, Venezuela, Colombia, Peru, Bolivia, Paraguay, Argentina and Uruguay), which has not been subject to political debate. The example of the North Amazon border as an entry point for Haitians reveals the extent to which a border can be activated and deactivated depending on the global (political, economic, environmental) moment. In the case of the Haitians, a natural disaster, along with the poverty of the country and the closing of French Guianan gates, led them to migrate to Brazil. In addition, with the international regulation of the 1951 Refugee Convention, they used a 'back-door' border to seek asylum as a 'tactic' of mobility. The Haitian flow, then, resignified the meaning of this border, and it was through this border that Brazil entered a new stage of its migration history.

The second axis of analysis – the politics of mobility – revealed how national regulations on migration can affect the migration flow. Three main measures were outlined: Regulations 97 RN and 102 RN and the creation of the Humanitarian Visa Application Center, which transformed the Haitians' movement to Brazil. The first measure had no precedent in Brazilian migration history, and was very progressive as it created the humanitarian visa. It resolved the cases of Haitian asylum seekers who were already in the country, but closed the door to new arrivals. Therefore, a second measure was needed to remove migration restrictions. However, the Brazilian Embassy in Port-au-Prince lacked the necessary infrastructure and staff, and could not meet the huge demand for humanitarian visas. Another measure was therefore put in place: the creation of the Humanitarian Visa Application Center, in partnership with the IOM, which could help the Brazilian Embassy with checking documents and filling out forms. All these measures were the national solution to the new demands posed by the global challenge of the Haitian flow to Brazil. This reveals that flows are still monitored and controlled by government institutions, which are capable of 'border producing' and 'reproducing' (Dillon and Lobo-Guerrero 2008).

In sum, the unexpected migration of Haitians to Brazil set their country into global mobility and enlarged the complexity of Brazil's migration history. In addition, it warmed up the debate around the theme in several social spheres (media, academia and politics), and led to discussion about new migration legislation to replace the existing laws dating from dictatorship times. Indeed, while the North Amazon border was the gate for the Haitians, it became a door for Brazil into a new migration era. Brazilian migration has therefore become a much more complex and important research topic, and should be analysed through the lens of global dynamics and its paradoxes.

Notes

1. Quote from the original text. Tania Tonhati has translated this article into Portuguese.
2. IBGE = Instituto Brasileiro de Geografia e Estatística, the 'Brazilian Institute of Geography and Statistics'.
3. Authors' translation
4. Authors' translation
5. *Folha de São Paulo, Estado de São Paulo, O Globo, Agência Notícias do Acre* (AC), *Jornal da Fronteira* (AC).
6. Programmes on TVfolha, TV Senado, TV Governo Federal, Globo (G1), among many others produced by researchers, journalists and the migrants themselves.
7. Colloquial term widely used by migrants referring to the people who smuggling people across borders.

References

Antunes, F. (2011) 'Acre é rota de entrada de haitianos no país.' *Folha de S. Paulo*, <http://www1.folha.uol.com.br/mundo/863927-acre-e-rota-de-entrada-de-haitianos-no-pais.shtml> (last accessed 15 August 2015).

Appadurai, A. (1996) *Modernity at Large: Cultural Dimensions of Globalisation*. Minneapolis: University of Minnesota Press.

Assis, G. (1999) 'Estar aqui . . ., estar lá . . . : uma cartografia da emigração valadarense.' Pp. 125–66 in *Cenas do Brasil Migrante*, edited by R. Reis, and T. Sales. São Paulo: Boitempo.

Assis, G. (2014) 'Gender and migration from invisibility to agency: the routes of Brazilian women from transnational towns to the United States.' *Women's Studies International Forum* 46: 33–44.

Balibar, E. (2015) 'Borderland Europe and the challenge of migration.' openDemocracy, <https://www.opendemocracy.net/can-europe-make-it/etienne-balibar/borderland-europe-and-challenge-of-migration> (last accessed 10 March 2017).

Bauman, Z. (2000) *Liquid Modernity*. Cambridge: Polity.

Beck, U., and E. Beck-Gernsheim (2014) *Distant Love*. Cambridge: Polity.

Beserra, B. (2003) *Brazilian Immigrants in the United States: Cultural Imperialism and Social Class*. El Paso: LFB Scholarly.

Bhabha, H. (1990) *Nation and Narration*. London: Routledge.

Brasil (2014) IX REUNIÃO Ordinária do Conselho Nacional de Imigração – CNIg. Ata da ordem do dia 11 de novembro de 2014. Brasília – DF. Ministério do Trabalho e Emprego, <https://portaldeimigracao.mj.gov.br/pt/atas-de-reunioes> (last accessed 30 December 2019).

Brasil (2015) I REUNIÃO Ordinária do Conselho Nacional de Imigração – CNIg. Ata da ordem do dia 11 de fevereiro de 2015. Brasília – DF. Ministério do Trabalho e Emprego, <https://portaldeimigracao.mj.gov.br/pt/atas-de-reunioes> (last accessed 30 December 2019).

Carvalho, J. A. M. de (1996) 'O saldo dos fluxos migratórios internacionais no Brasil na década de 80: uma tentativa de estimação.' Pp. 227–38 in *Emigração e Imigração Internacionais no Brasil Contemporâneo*, edited by N. Patarra. Campinas: FNUAP.

Castells, M. (1996) *The Information Age: Economy, Society and Culture. Vol. 1: The Rise of the Network Society*. Oxford: Blackwell.

Castles, S., and M. Miller (2009) *The Age of Migration: International Population Movements in the Modern World*, 4th edn. London: Palgrave Macmillan.

Cavalcanti, L., and T. Oliveira (2016) 'A caminho da conclusão meia década de novos fluxos imigratórios no Brasil.' Pp. 142–6 in *A Inserção dos Imigrantes no Mercado de Trabalho Brasileiro*, edited by L. Cavalcanti, A. T. Oliveira and D. Araújo. Observatório das Migrações Internacionais; Ministério do Trabalho/Conselho Nacional de Imigração e Coordenação Geral de Imigração. Brasília, DF: OBMigra.

Cavalcanti, L., S. Almeida, T. Oliveira, T. Tonhati and D. Dutra (2015) 'Os imigrantes haitianos: perfil e características da principal nacionalidade no mercado de trabalho brasileiro.' Pp. 103–23 in *A Inserção dos Imigrantes no Mercado de Trabalho Brasileiro*, edited by L. Cavalcanti, T. Oliveira, T. Tonhati and D. Dutra. Observatório das Migrações Internacionais; Ministério do Trabalho e Previdência Social/ Conselho Nacional de Imigração e Coordenação Geral de Imigração. Brasília, DF: OBMigra.

Cavalcanti, L., T. Tonhati and D. Dutra (2016) *A Imigração Haitiana no Brasil: Características Sociodemográficas e Laborais na Região Sul e no Distrito Federal*. Observatório das Migrações Internacionais; Ministério do Trabalho/Conselho Nacional de Imigração e Coordenação Geral de Imigração; Organização Internacional para Migrações (OIM). Brasília, DF: OBMigra.

De Certeau, M. (1984) *The Practice of Everyday Life*. London: University of California Press.

Dias, G. (2016) 'Viajantes do Caribe: posicionando Brasília nas rotas migratórias haitianas.' Pp. 106–18 in *A Imigração Haitiana no Brasil: Características Sociodemográficas e Laborais na Região Sul e no Distrito Federal*, edited by L. Cavalcanti, T. Tonhati and D. Dutra. Observatório das Migrações Internacionais; Ministério do Trabalho/Conselho Nacional de Imigração e Coordenação Geral de Imigração; Organização Internacional para Migrações (OIM). Brasília, DF: OBMigra.

Dillon, M., and L. Lobo-Guerrero (2008) 'Biopolitics of security in the 21st century: an introduction.' *Review of International Studies* 34: 265–92.

Fernandes, D., and M. Castro (2013) 'Migração e crise: o retorno dos imigrantes brasileiros em Portugal.' *REMHU: Revista Interdisciplinar da Mobilidade Humana* XXI(41): 99–116.

Fernandes, D., and M. Castro (2014) *Migração Haitiana ao Brasil: Diálogo Bilateral.* Brasília: Projeto 'Estudos sobre a Migração Haitiana ao Brasil e Diálogo Bilateral'.

Fernandes, D., and S. Knup (2012) 'Should I stay or should I go? A dúvida da permanência ou retorno: imigrantes brasileiros no estado de Massachusetts.' Pp. 1–17 in *XVIII Encontro Nacional de Estudos Populacionais, Belo Horizonte*, <http://174.121.79.98/~naotembr/anais/files/POSTER[410]ABEP2012.pdf> (last accessed 10 February 2017).

Giddens, A. (1991) *The Consequences of Modernity.* Cambridge: Polity.

Giraldi, R. (2012. 'Saldo do terremoto no Haiti é de 220 mil mortos e 1,5 milhão de des-abrigados.' *Agência Brasil*, <http://agenciabrasil.ebc.com.br/noticia/2011-01-12/saldo-do-terremoto-no-haiti-e-de-220-mil-mortos-e-15-milhao-de-desabrigados> (last accessed 21 March 2017).

Handerson, J. (2015a) 'Diaspora: as dinâmicas da mobilidade haitiana no Brasil, no Suriname e na Guiana Francesa.' PhD thesis, Universidade Federal do Rio de Janeiro Museu Nacional.

Handerson, J. (2015b) 'Diaspora: sentidos sociais e mobilidades haitianas.' *Horizontes Antropológicos* 21(43): 51–78.

Harvey, D. (1999) 'Time-space compression and the postmodern condition.' Pp. 98–119 in *Modernity: Critical Concepts. Vol. IV: After Modernity*, edited by M. Waters. London: Routledge.

Harvey, D. (2006) *Spaces of Global Capitalism: Toward a Theory of Uneven Geographical Development.* London: Verso.

Hirano, F. Y. (2005) *O Caminho para Casa: O Retorno dos Decasséguis.* Rio de Janeiro, <http://www.abep.nepo.unicamp.br/docs/anais/outros/4EncNacSobreMigracao/ST1-2.pdf> (last accessed 1 February 2017).

IBGE (Instituto Brasileiro de Geografia e Estatística) (2010) *Censo Demográfico 2010: Migração e Deslocamento - Resultados da Amostra*, <http://www.ibge.gov.br/home/estatistica/populacao/ censo2000/migracao/censo2000_migracao.pdf> (last accessed 2 March 2015).

Ingold, T. (2008) 'Bindings against boundaries: entanglements of life in an open world.' *Environment and Planning* 40: 1796–1810.

Juss, S. (2006) *International Migration and Global Justice.* Aldershot: Ashgate.

Kearney, M. (1995) 'The local and the global: the anthropology of globalization and transnationalism.' *Annual Review of Anthropology* 24: 547–65.

Knowles, C. (2017) 'Mobilidade.' Pp. 490–5 in *Dicionário Crítico de Migrações*, edited by L. Cavalcanti, T. Tonhati, T. Botega and D. Araujo. Brasília: Universidade de Brasília.

Levy, M. S. F. (1974) 'O papel da migração internacional na evolução da população brasileira (1872 a 1972).' *Revista Saúde Pública* 8 (supl.): 49–90.

Margolis, M. (1994) *Little Brazil: An Ethnography of Brazilian Immigrants in New York City.* Princeton: Princeton University Press.

Margolis, M. (1998) *An Invisible Minority: Brazilians in New York City.* Boston: Ally and Bacon.

Margolis, M. (2013) *Goodbye Brazil: Émigrés from the Land of Soccer and Samba.* Madison: University of Wisconsin Press.

Moraes, I., C. Andrade and B. Mattos (2013) 'A imigração haitiana para o Brasil: causas e desafios.' *Revista Conjuntura Austral* 4(20): 95–114.

Oliveira, A. T. (2013) 'Um panorama da migração internacional a partir do censo demográfico de 2010.' *Revista Internacional de Mobilidade Humana* XXI(40): 195–210.

Oliveira, A. T. (2016) 'A mobilidade especial de ambito internacional no Brasil: uma visão através do sistema de tráfego internacional.' Pp. 34–46 in *A Inserção dos Imigrantes no Mercado de Trabalho Brasileiro*, edited by L. Cavalcanti, A. T. Oliveira and D. Araújo. Observatório das Migrações Internacionais; Ministério do Trabalho/ Conselho Nacional de Imigração e Coordenação Geral de Imigração. Brasília, DF: OBMigra.

Padilla, B. (2006) *Brazilian Migration to Portugal: Social Networks and Ethnic Solidarity.* Lisbon: CIES-ISCTE, <https://repositorio.iscte-iul.pt/bitstream/10071/175/4/ CIES-WP12_Padilla_.pdf> (last accessed 29 August 2014).

Padilla, B. (2009) 'As migrações latino-americanas para a Europa: uma análise retrospectiva para entender a mobilidade actual.' *Revista Migrações: Número Temático Migrações entre Portugal e América Latina*, edited by B. Padilla and M. Xavier, 5: 19–35.

Patarra, N. (2005) 'Migrações internacionais de e para o Brasil contemporâneo: volumes, fluxos, significados e políticas'. *São Paulo em Perspectiva* 19(3): 23–33.

Patarra, N., and R. Baeninger (1995) 'Migrações internacionais recentes: o caso do Brasil.' Pp. 130–42 in *Migración e Integración*, edited by A. Pellegrino. Montevideo: Ediciones Trilce.

Piscitelli, A. (2008) 'Transits: Brazilian women migration in the context of the transnationalization of the sex and marriage markets.' *Horizontes Antropológicos* 15(31): 101–36.

Portes, A. (2001) 'Introduction: the debates and significance of immigrant transnationalism.' *Global Networks* 1(3): 181–93.

Portes, A., L. Guarnizo and P. Landolt (1999) 'The study of transnationalism: pitfalls and promise of an emergent research field.' *Ethnic and Racial Studies* 22(2): 217–37.

Póvoa Neto, H. (2006) 'A imagem da imprensa sobre a emigração brasileira.' *Revista de Estudos Avançados* 20(57): 25–40.

Robertson, S. (2011) 'The new spatial politics of (re) bordering and (re)ordering the state–education–citizen relation.' *International Review of Education* 57(3–4): 277–97, <http://susanleerobertson.com/publications> (last accessed 10 February 2017).

Rumford, C. (2006)' Introduction: theorizing borders, thinking about borders.' *European Journal of Social Theory* 9(2): 155–69.

Sales, T. (1991) 'Novos fluxos migratórios da população brasileira.' *Revista Brasileira de Estudos Populacionais* 8(1/2): 21–32.

Sales, T. (1994) 'Brasil migrante, Brasil clandestino.' *São Paulo em Perspectiva* 8(1): 107–15.

Sales, T. (2000) 'The triennium of disillusionment.' *Brazilian Journal of Population Studies* 2(1): 145–63.

Seyferth, G. (1986) 'Imigração, colonização e identidade étnica.' *Revista de Antropologia* 29(1): 57–73.

Silva, S. (2012) '"Aqui começa o Brasil": haitianos na tríplice fronteira e Manaus.' Pp. 300–21 in *Migrações na Pan-Amazônia: Fluxos, Fronteiras e Processos Socioculturais*, edited by S. Silva. São Paulo: Hucitec Editora,.

Silva, S. (2013) 'Brazil, a new Eldorado for immigrants? The case of Haitians and the Brazilian immigration policy.' *Urbanities* 3: 3–18.

Silva, S. (2015) 'Fronteira Amazônica: passagem obrigatória para haitianos?' *REMHU: Revista Interdisciplinar de Mobilidade Humana* XXIII(44): 119–34.

Sinatti, G. (2008) 'Migraciones, transnacionalismo y locus de investigación multi-localidad y la transición de "sitios" a "campos".' Pp. 93–112 in *Nuevos Retos del transnacionalismo en el Estudio de las Migraciones*, edited by C. Solé, S. Parella and L. Cavalcanti. Madrid: Documentos del Observatorio permanente de la inmigración de España, Gobierno de España 19.

Siqueira, S. (2009) *Sonhos, Sucesso e Frustrações na Emigração de Retorno: Brasil–Estados Unidos*. Belo Horizonte: Argvmentvm.

Smith, P., and E. Guarnizo (1998) 'The locations of transnationalism.' Pp. 3–20 in *Transnationalism from Below*, edited by P. Smith and E. Guarnizo. London: Transaction.

Solé, C., L. Cavalcanti and S. Parella (2011) La Inmigración Brasileña en la Estructura Socioeconómica de España. Madrid: Documentos del Observatório permanente de la inmigración de España, Gobierno de España.

Tonhati, T., L. Cavalcanti, T. Botega and A. T. Oliveira (2016) 'Os imigrantes haitianos no Brasil: a empregabilidade dos haitianos no mercado de trabalho brasileiro.' Pp. 38–60 in *A Imigração Haitiana no Brasil: Características Sociodemográficas e Laborais na Região Sul e no Distrito Federal*, edited by L. Cavalcanti, T. Tonhati and D. Dutra. Observatório das Migrações Internacionais; Ministério do Trabalho/ Conselho Nacional de Imigração e Coordenação Geral de Imigração; Organização Internacional para Migrações (OIM). Brasília, DF: OBMigra..

Tsuda, T. (2003) *Strangers in the Ethnic Homeland: Japanese Brazilian Return Migration in Transnational Perspective*. New York: Columbia University Press.

UNHCR (2016) 'UNHCR viewpoint: 'Refugee' or 'migrant' – which is right?' UNHCR, <http://www.unhcr.org/news/latest/2016/7/55dfoe556/unhcr-viewpoint-refugee-migrant-right.html> (last accessed 3 February 2017).

Urry, J. (1999) *Sociology Beyond Societies: Mobilities for the Twenty-First Century*. London: Routledge.

Urry, J. (2003) 'Social networks, travel and talk.' *British Journal of Sociology* 54(2): 155–75.

Vertovec, S. (1999) 'Conceiving and researching transnationalism.' *Ethnic and Racial Studies* 22(2): 447–62.

Vertovec, S. (2009) *Transnationalism*. London: Routledge.

Zeni, K., and E. Filippim (2013) 'Imigração haitiana para o Brasil: acolhimento e políticas públicas.' *Pretexto* 15(2): 11–27.

8

Macedonian Refugees from the Greek Civil War: From Separation to a Transnational Community

Anna Kurpiel

STARTING IN 1948, POLAND accommodated a large number of ref-ugees from the Greek Civil War – both ethnic Greeks and ethnic Macedonians. Even though the general pattern of migration as well as the institutional care provided by Poland was similar for both groups of migrants, I argue that Macedonian migration to Poland was a differ-ent phenomenon from the Greek one. There are two main characteris-tics. First of all the Macedonians in Poland were a 'minority within the minority' and this condition influenced their trajectories as a separate group. Second, the Macedonian migration to Poland is deeply rooted in the political situation of Europe after World War II, which had an impact on actual Macedonian possibilities (i.e. connected to repatria-tion or war compensation) as well as the politics of remembrance, which stay closely related to identity. The chapter develops the charac-teristics of Macedonians migration and focuses on the processes shap-ing the identity of migrants, including how facing old and new borders translates into new conceptions of both the self and others. The text follows chronological order, discussing issues of 'separation' via 'assim-ilation' to a 'new space of identification'. The three problem fields con-nected with Macedonian identity are the question of the Macedonian homeland(s); integration within the refugees' group and with Poles; and self-organisation, politics and the politics of remembrance. I base my analysis on biographical interviews with Macedonian refugees (who were mostly children at that time), which I conducted in Poland, Mace-donia and Canada, as well as on selected documents from Polish and Macedonian archives.[1]

It was the autumn of 1948 when the first train with refugees from the Greek Civil War crossed the Polish–Czechoslovakian border. The first refugees were children, a total of 1,048. The following years brought even more transports to Poland: 800 children arrived in April 1949, and another 200 in August 1949. Then the refugees started coming by the sea: both adults and youths. In July, September and October 1949, ships with refugees came to Polish ports in Świnoujście, Dziwnów and Gdańsk. In 1950, the total number of refugees in Poland was 10,722. By 1955, as a result of family reunification, the number increased to 15,215 (Słabig 2008: 314).

Just after arrival, most of the refugees were transported to small resorts in the Lower Silesian Mountains,[2] except the wounded and sick, for whom a hospital on Wolin Island was created (Barcikowski 1989). The Polish Ministry of Education established the so-called State Educational Centre (Pol. *Państwowy Ośrodek Wychowawczy*) for refugees – a combination of children's home, school and hospital. Adults were provided with work, both in factories and in agriculture (state agricultural farms). Everything was very well organised.[3] The so-called 'Greek Action' was coordinated and financially supported by the Ministry of Education, the Ministry of Health, the Ministry of Social Policy and the Employee Holiday Fund. However, the most surprising fact for the Polish Government and the people involved in the 'Greek Action' was that the group of refugees from Greece was not homogeneous. 'Refugees from Greece' were supposed to be only of Greek origin. In fact, ethnic Greeks constituted only half of the migrants. The other half were Macedonians, a group of Slavic origin, speaking the Macedonian language, similar to Polish.[4].

Who are 'those' Macedonians?

Aegean Macedonians are a Slavic minority group living in northern Greece. Their ancestors were inhabitants of Macedonia – the part of the Balkan Peninsula which historically stayed under the rule of the Ottoman Empire for the longest period. The perfect location of Macedonia – in the middle of the peninsula, on the crossroads of important trade roads and, even more importantly, with access to the sea, Thessaloniki being an essential port – made the region a bone of contention between neighbouring nations (Barker 1999; Stawowy-Kawka 2000). Liberating the territory from Turkish dominance resulted in its partition after the Balkan Wars (1912–13). One part, called Vardar Macedonia, together with the second most important Macedonian city of Skopje, was incorporated into Serbia (it later became a part of Yugoslavia, and today it constitutes an independent Macedonian state); the region known as Pirin Macedonia was taken by Bulgarians; Aegean Macedonia with Thessaloniki became a northern province of Greece.

Centuries of Ottoman dominance with its politics of forced resettle-ments shaped Macedonia as a multi-ethnic region. It was inhabited mainly by Slavs (both Christian and Muslim), but also by Turks, Albanians and Vlachs. In the middle of the nineteenth century, when nation-building processes were very intense in the Balkans, Macedonian inhabitants, especially Slavs, started to see themselves as a separate ethnic group, with national ambitions. The problem of Macedonian self-identity and its rec-ognition by other nations is called the 'Macedonian question'. Tchavar Marinov defines the Macedonian question as 'a debate on the history and identity of Macedonian Slavs' (Marinov 2010: 15).

Macedonian ethno-national identity and identification with the inhab-ited land were considered an obstacle by neighbouring countries to realis-ing their dreams of Greater Serbia, Greater Bulgaria and Greater Greece (Gr. *Megali Idea*). Thus, in every part of partitioned Macedonia, new gov-ernments started politics of assimilation of the Macedonian population, which were particularly bloody in Greece. The Macedonian language was forbidden, and Slavic names, surnames and place names were translated into the Greek language. Even singing Macedonian national songs resulted in imprisonment. This Hellenisation policy against the Slavic minority was enforced during the dictatorship of Ioannis Metaxas (1936–41).

The Greek Communists gave hope to the Aegean Macedonians. They not only officially recognised Macedonians as a minority in 1935 but also propagated the image of the Communist state free of radical right-wing nationalistic attitudes, ruling according to the principle of internationalism. This is why lots of Macedonians supported Greek partisans during World War II, and a few years later during the Greek Civil War (1946–9).[5] The Communist support for Macedonians and from Macedonians entailed Yugoslav support for the Communist Party of Greece (KKE).

Displacement

The Greek Civil War resulted in the defeat of the Democratic Army of Greece and, as a consequence, in mass forced migrations of parti-sans and their families. Macedonians, together with Greeks, had to leave their homeland. Aegean Macedonia, the main battlefield during the war, was almost depopulated. However, the displacement was not only the consequence of the defeat. The first big wave of migration took place in 1948, when the Communist Party was still hoping to win. In the spring of 1948, around 15,000 children between the ages of 3 and

14 crossed the montane border with Yugoslavia (Danforth and Van Boeschoten 2011). They were led by young women called *Majka* (Eng. 'mother') and a few partisans. In Yugoslavia, children were put into merchandise trains and sent to selected cities in the Federation (mostly in the Socialist Republics of Serbia and Croatia) as well as to Romania, Czechoslovakia, Hungary, Poland and the GDR.[6]

The children's emigration (called 'exodus' by Macedonians[7]) was the result of an action plan called 'Rescue our children!' led by the Greek Communists. The Greek Communist Party turned to other Communist parties of the then Eastern Bloc for help. The official reason was to keep the children safe, so the action was called 'temporary evacuation', and it was presented to the parents of the displaced children under this name. However, the more likely explanation is that it was a strategic move. After the deportation of children, almost all the civilian populations of the region, including women, were mobilised. Moreover, right-wing Greeks, as well as Western Europe, have their own explanation. They accused Greek Communists of kidnapping the children – *'paidomazoma'*. According to this version, children were taken from their parents to be brought up as 'janissaries of Communism'.

The answer lies at the crossroads of those hypotheses. In 1948, Communist Greeks were still hoping to win despite their worsening situation. That is why childless parents were more than needful. Just after the children's deportation, all the people including women and the elderly were engaged in helping the military effort, for instance by digging trenches. On the other hand, the idea of 'janissaries of Communism' is also probable. The Greek Communists not only raised and educated children in the spirit of loyalty to the Party, Stalin and General Markos Vafiadis (the leader of the Democratic Army of Greece), but also in 1948 sent the older children back to the front (mainly as cannon fodder).[8] Poland - the place of my research interest presented below – was the only country that didn't allow this cruel practice (Nakovski 2008).

Separation

Separation is one of the most significant concepts for Macedonian war migration as well as the Macedonian nation as a whole. It includes both individual and collective levels and hence influences individual and collective identity as well as individual and collective memory.

The first significant level was a separation of the Macedonians from their 'private' homeland,, to use the terminology of Stanisław Ossowski (1984). The collective level of this first initial separation was connected to the politics of post-war Communist parties as well as the distribution of political forces in Europe. During the Greek Civil War, Aegean Macedonia was decisively cut off from its 'official sister', Vardar Macedonia, which became a part of Yugoslavia as an autonomous republic. It was a consequence of the Tito–Stalin split in 1948, resulting in Yugoslavia's expulsion from the Cominform (Communist Information Bureau). The semi-open Greek–Yugoslavian border, which until 1948 enabled transborder contacts between Macedonians living in Yugoslavia and in Greece (even intermarriages), was closed for good. This not only meant an end of cross-border relations, but for Yugoslav Macedonia it was and still is an unforgettable loss of an essential part of the fatherland. For Macedonians who managed to stay in the region, it meant a short step to complete Hellenisation and separation from all Slavic influence. For Macedonian refugees, finally, it meant return was impossible.

All the refugees of the Greek Civil War were hoping for repatriation, but until the end of the 1970s, this was impossible due to the politics of the right-wing Greek government. After the political change, however, the Greeks could come back to their homeland. Then Prime Minister Andreas Papandreu[9] opened the border for returnees, but exclusively for those of Greek origins. Macedonians could come back only if they declared their Greek ethnicity, and this was not acceptable for the majority of them (especially taking into consideration the Macedonian struggle against politics of Hellenisation and their wish to be recognised as an independent ethnic and national group).

The second level of separation was related to family and social bonds. Children were separated from their parents (by being evacuated), as well as from their siblings, cousins or friends. One of the stories that recurs in many biographical narrations is about train carriages with family members or friends being detached in individual stations and different countries.

Later we went by train to Czechoslovakia. And when we were in Hungary, two carriages stayed in Hungary. Two carriages in Poland. And so on. And some brothers and sisters which were not in the same carriage were separated. They separated the children. (Jane Bandevski, Macedonia)

The highly controversial image of carriage separation is probably one of the myths empowering the image of the tragic fate of Macedonian children. It could also be a result of the still unrevealed answer to the question of how the children were divided into states and cities and who was responsible for their separation. However, the separation of siblings was a fact even for placements within one state. Child refugees were classified by age for different children's homes connected with schools. Younger children stayed in different buildings within their age groups, older kids in different ones again, and the oldest teenagers in the third category of the State Educational Centre (Wojecki 1989). Siblings could visit or see each other only on Sundays, in the special meeting territory called, according to Doca Gogarowska, 'donkey meadow' (Pol. *ośla łączka*).[10]

The same situation occurred with children and their parents. If the family had a chance of a reunion within one state (an action led by the Red Cross), it was only a partial reunification. Children were obliged to stay at the State Educational Centre, whereas parents had to work to earn their living. As a result, members of one family were living in different cities. They could spend time with each other only for a limited period during the summer holidays (Wojecki 1989: 40). Even more dramatic situations occurred when family members migrated to different countries and for some reason reunion was not possible. In some cases, their first meeting after the war took place many years after the separation. For some of them, it was a very emotional and joyful moment. For others, however, the meeting after years of separation was a confirmation of family breakdown. Parents and children didn't recognise each other not only physically but also culturally. The distinction between widely understood 'Balkan culture' and Polish acculturation was insurmountable.[11]

The third and the last form of separation was the separation of the refugees from Polish society, mainly during the first years of their stay in Poland. The choice of settling the refugees in Lower Silesia and Pomerania already meant separation from Polish society. Those regions, called in propaganda 'Recovered Territories', were annexed to Poland after World War II. As a result of border change, the whole population of the western territories of Poland was exchanged. The old inhabitants, mainly Germans, were expelled to Germany and new ones from all over Europe settled in. In 1949, Lower Silesia was called the 'Polish Wild West'. It was just the beginning of a long process of creation of a new society. Everyone was a stranger. That is why it was easy to hide 15,000 war refugees in this area, full of uncoordinated migrant groups. What is more, the arrival of Greek and Macedonian children was officially kept secret. Teachers and other staff working with refugee children had to sign a special document about the confidential character of their job. No cameras were allowed in the territory of the Educational Centre.[12]

Adult refugees were also kept separate from society, although more ideologically and psychologically than physically. The main slogan of the Communist Party of Greece at that time was 'With gun in hand, ready to fight': of course for 'free Greece' or 'Communist Greece'. The defeat was not accepted. All the refugees were kept in the constant belief that soon the war would start again, and they would come back home. Everyone was hoping for a swift return. This is why the refugees did not start the assimilation process in the very first years of their stay in Poland. Zgorzelec, a town where the majority of them were placed, was called the 'Greek Republic' not only because of the sizeable number of the refugees from Greece but due to its character as an almost entirely self-dependent and self-governed society in exile. Even marriages were solemnised in front of a Communist Party representative, not in a Polish office (Wojecki 1989: 69).

The last two types of separation (inside the family and from Polish society) were not limited exclusively to Macedonians. Nevertheless, the 'Macedonian question' is a key factor even in those cases. The problem of family separation is even more complicated in the case of Macedonians, taking into consideration the impossibility of their return and the challenge of many homelands (I will develop this issue in the last part of this chapter). The problem of separation from Polish society meant for Macedonians complete dependency on Greek comrades, who often continued the policy of Hellenisation of their Slavic companions.[13] And finally, in the mid-1950s, when the period of separation was over, the inclusion of the Macedonians in Polish society was more complicated than that of their Greek fellows, since it raised the fundamental question of which culture they should be assimilated to: Greek or Polish?

Assimilation

The primary condition of Macedonian refugees in Poland – being a 'minority within the minority' – made them dependent upon both Greeks and Poles. Poles organised the whole life of the refugees from Greece in exile: from the children's education to the adults' working places. The refugees were also constantly observed by the Polish security service. However, inside the new Polish reality the 'old' one – the Greek Communist Party (KKE), later transformed into the separate organisation of the refugees from Greece – was still in existence. All refugees were dependent on the KKE and its leaders. Finally, inside the group of all refugees from Greece there was the smallest bubble – that of Macedonians, who didn't have their own structures or leaders. The question of a separate Macedonian identity was not questioned in Poland as much as in Greece. However, as I will explain below, there was always a 'however', from both – Polish and Greek – sides.

In reality, the assimilation of Macedonian refugees included both the behavioural and structural dimensions (Gordon 1961) as well as both dominant groups: Poles and Greeks. Both dominant groups recognised Macedonians as a separate ethnicity and at the same time promoted their own political and cultural superiority. Each national group hid its assimilationist aspirations under a different ideological veil.

For the Greeks, the official cover for their policy of domination over Macedonians was 'unity and brotherhood inside the Party'. According to this slogan, Greeks and Macedonians were to keep close together within one Communist Party of Greece for a wished-for better future of an 'independent Greece' where Communist internationalism would replace nationalism. For that (official) reason Macedonians were not allowed to create their own independent organisation.[14] Despite their strong efforts to create such organisations, they were gathered within the main organisation of Greek refugees in exile: the 'Nikos Beloyannis Association of the Refugees from Greece in Poland'. Greeks dominated the organisation's leadership as well as most of its activities. In official Greek propaganda, every Macedonian step towards independence or affirmation of their own national or ethnic identity was interpreted as an attack on the unity of all refugees. All institutions in exile were under ethnic Greek dominance.

The situation was even more complicated during the Stalin–Tito split (until the mid-1950s.). Then everything Macedonian was associated with Yugoslav Macedonia (and so with Tito), and thus denounced. Even the Macedonian language was forbidden - as too connected to Tito - and replaced by a 'Slavomacedonian' language, based on the Bulgarian alphabet. Macedonian names and surnames stayed in Greek translation.

In the Polish case, mainly cultural, but also - for obvious reasons – institutional assimilation was hidden under care for the refugees' education. As Wacław Kopczyński, the man responsible for children's education wrote in his report:

We do not want to Polonize and at the same time to uproot Macedonians, but we have to Polonize the children to educate them, to prepare them in the Polish economic and social environment as the future builders of Macedonia. There is no other way. (Nakovski 2008: 98)

The primary language for children gathered at the State Educational Centre was Polish. It was the language of education: almost all classes were held in Polish (with the exception of Greek and Macedonian language courses) because the teachers were Poles. What is more, soon the Polish language started being used as a primary language among young Greeks and Macedonians. At the beginning, this was only in interethnic communication; later on, it was in everyday use even among children of the same ethnicity. Macedonian children were also assimilated to Polish culture by classes in Polish literature and history. In every house of the State Education Centre, there was a library from which children could borrow books - and they did (at least in their memories), thus learning about Polish literature and history.

Both Macedonian and Greeks adult refugees were not provided with Polish language courses, although they had to work with Poles and to manage living alone in Polish society. In this respect, however, Macedonian refugees were in a much better situation because the Macedonian language is very similar to Polish. A lot of basic words are the same as well as the pronunciation. From the beginning of their stay in Poland, Macedonian children and adults felt understood when they asked for basic needs. This fact was gladly underlined in almost every interview.

The Macedonian language and Polish are very similar languages. And when you talk slowly - you can understand everything. And when fast - then it starts to be problematic.

But slowly - the same! 'Hand' is 'hand'. 'Water' - 'water. 'Nose' - 'nose'. 'Teeth' - 'teeth'. Same! There are the same words! A bit transformed, but generally the same. I mean - the Slavic nations had a common language. A common, an old Slavic language. (Mihail Lazaru, Macedonia)

The fact that both Macedonians and Poles are Slavs made Macedonian refugees feel more 'at home' in Poland than in other countries, namely Romania or Hungary. They felt a cultural closeness with Poles within the (spiritual) unity of all Slavic nations.[15] Concurrently, Poland after the war was more developed economically and culturally than northern

Greece. Many refugees saw electricity, trains, toilets, big factories, well-equipped houses and so on for the first time in their lives (especially well-developed was the region of Lower Silesia, which was German before the war). That is why, in the assimilationist competition game which was implicitly played between Poles and Greeks, Macedonians often stayed on the Polish side, especially children who were acculturated in the Polish State Educational Centres. What is more, I argue that among other narrative structures visible in Macedonian biographical narratives, two interpretative topoi (Welzer et al. 2009) are very present: those of a 'good Pole' and a 'bad Greek'.

The topos of a 'bad Greek' has its roots in the period of World War II and later in the Civil War. It referred originally to Greek nationalists or 'monarcho-fascists', in Communist nomenclature. However, as time passed it developed and started to be associated as well with Greek officials, Greek teachers or Greek educators in Poland. One of the reasons for this process could be the fact that Greek teachers were far more restrictive than Poles, especially in the Educational Centre in Zgorzelec. Corporal punishment or shutting children in a dark basement were two of the methods reported by a Polish teacher[16] that led even to the suicide of one pupil.[17] Three Macedonian children were expelled from the Educational Centre for using pro-Macedonian slogans that were not in line with official Greek propaganda.[18] Macedonian children felt discriminated against because they had to learn both Greek and Macedonian, whereas their Greek peers had to learn only Greek.

Later, in the second half of the 1950s and the 1960s, when children had better contact with their parents (some of them had already finished primary school), the idea of 'a bad Greek' could come directly from their relatives, who often discussed political issues in front of children. The adult Greek and Macedonians were basically keeping together; however, their relationship was not free from political and ideological conflicts. Children even witnessed fights between the two groups; for instance, one of my interviewees recalled her uncle who 'was always fighting with the Greeks'.[19]

On the other hand, the topos of 'a bad Greek' was not associated with children of Greek origins. Even though children stayed with their own national group – Macedonians with Macedonians, Greeks with Greeks – intergroup friendship was also very popular. This fact is often mentioned in narrations: national differences were not a problem among children in everyday life in Poland. As one interviewee said 'We were all children from an orphanage, and that was the most important.'[20]

However, in the Macedonian narratives, those remembered as 'the good ones' were Poles. This image includes teachers and educators of the State Educational Centre as well as Poles in general, the whole nation, politicians included. In the narrations of the then Macedonian children, there is an image of a very warm and thoughtful Polish teacher, who for them took the place of their parents. Wacław Kopczyński was the most popular among them. One of the interviewees noted with great emotion his visit to Skopje in the 1970s:

> [At the beginning of the ceremony] Mr Kopczyński got up and greeted us: my beloved children! Well, I do not know who was able to refrain from crying! We all started to cry! (Sofia Lazaru, Macedonia)

In the narration of the then Macedonian children, Polish teachers cared for them and their future, often being the only ones to listen to them and give some advice.[21] However, at the political and institutional level too, Poles seemed to 'care' about Macedonians in exile. The most important fact for Macedonians is that Poles recognised them as a separate nation, and in some situations helped them in the battle for independence. Thanks to Polish teachers, Macedonian children's names and surnames were retranslated from Greek into Macedonian. Poles launched courses in the Macedonian language as well as a college of education for Macedonians.[22]

What is more, thanks to Poles, the artificially created 'Slavomacedonian' language was replaced by real Macedonian. School books for Macedonian language, literature and history were written and published in Poland and then sent to other countries of Macedonian war migration (Kurpiel 2015: 130–5). Poles also mediated disputes between Greeks and Macedonians, often staying on the side of the Macedonians – especially when it came to children's education. All of these examples, together with acculturation practices that positively approved of Polish culture, consolidated the image of 'a good Pole' who is well educated and cares for others, especially for Macedonians dependent on Greeks.

A new field of identification

The question of a Macedonian fatherland is very complicated in the case of Aegean Macedonians who, as refugees from the Greek Civil War, migrated to Poland. There are three basic possibilities.

The first fatherland – 'little' or 'private' homeland – is Aegean Macedonia. This is the land of childhood, first memories and experiences. In every narration, it is valorised very positively. Aegean Macedonia is presented as a land of natural beauty: mountains, lakes, waterfalls, fields and pastures. Despite wars and traumatic events connected to it, the little homeland is remembered with great nostalgia, as a place of family and social life, of poor but carefree childhood. However, this is also a place to which return is impossible.

The second fatherland – the ideological one – is the Republic of North Macedonia and, before 1993, the Socialist Republic of Macedonia within the Yugoslav Federation. After Stalin's death and thereby the improvement of Soviet–Yugoslavian relations, the Socialist Republic of Macedonia started to be present in the life of Macedonians in exile. Soon it was promoted as a primary fatherland - 'dear fatherland' (Mac. *skapa tatkovina*) – especially for those who wanted to discourage relating to Greek comrades. Simultaneously Yugoslavia opened its borders to those Macedonians who wanted to settle in the Socialist Republic of Macedonia. The government promised accommodation, workplaces and organisation of travel.

In consequence, the majority of Macedonians from Poland left for Yugoslavia in a few migration waves, starting in the mid-1950s. Many of them already had some members of their family there. However, what attracted them most to the Yugoslavian republic was the freedom of expressing and manifesting Macedonian identity. Macedonian was the official language of the Socialist Republic of Macedonia. Inhabitants could call themselves 'Macedonians'. Children could learn about the Macedonian nation. Such liberty was previously unknown to Aegean Macedonians.

However, the return (it was more an 'ideological return') to the fatherland was not as easy as expected. Aegean Macedonians faced many problems, from lack of housing to a hostile social environment. The complicated relations between Macedonians living in Yugoslavia and the 'Aegeans' who started to settle in the country after the Greek Civil War are very well described by Miladiana Monova (2002), who proves that integration between the arriving and local Macedonians did not proceed quickly and without problems. Although ethnically both groups were identical, the diversity of life trajectories and the distinctness of the contexts of their socialisation – on the one hand Yugoslav (Serbian) and on the other hand Greek – introduced elements that divided and hindered common dialogue. Aegean Macedonian settlers in Yugoslav Macedonia were accused of taking jobs and homes from 'native' Macedonians. This problem is well known from the sociology of migration and the relation between a dominant and a minority group. Aegean Macedonians who migrated to Yugoslavia were treated as 'others'.[23]

The migration from Poland to Yugoslav Macedonia was primarily the decision of adults, who could not or did not want to stay in Poland and adapt to the new country. Although few adult Macedonians entered into close relations with Poles, the majority of them were looking for further migration. Despite the cultural 'unity of Slavs', Poland was perceived as an unfamiliar country by adult refugees. Besides social and cultural factors which were important elements for the feeling of alienation, the natural environment played a crucial role. First of all, people lacked food products traditionally used in Macedonian cuisine such as paprika, sweetcorn or fresh mint. Second, the weather is much worse in Poland than in sunny Greece. One of the interviewees mentioned his father's words explaining further migration to the Balkans: 'And the climate in Poland does not suit me, and I often go to the doctor.'[24]

On the other hand, the majority of children and young people very quickly assimilated in Poland. After leaving the State Education Centre, in which they stayed until the end of primary school, they went to secondary schools and integrated with Polish teens. They were already well acculturated, speaking perfect Polish. What is more, due to the limited contact with their parents and other Macedonian adults, young refugees were partly uprooted. It was a peer group which replaced their family ties. That is why, when the adult refugees wanted to migrate to Macedonia, many of the children did not follow their parents. They finished schools, started jobs and married in Poland. They have Polish citizenship, and even though they have a significant sentiment towards Macedonia, the majority of them did not transmit any element of Macedonian culture to their children, language included. Moreover, even for those child refugees who migrated to Macedonia together with their parents, Poland stayed as a vital place of self-identification. They speak about Poland with immense nostalgia, often calling it 'the second homeland':

> Poland was our second homeland. It was - I mean - we were brought up there, we were educated, we were eating there, drinking - everything. It was our home when we were in Poland. (Gigo Čačkirovski, Canada)

Even though Macedonians who stayed in Poland are assimilated and integrated into Polish society, they still preserve their Macedonian identity. However, there is no space in Poland to express it. For many years of forced close friendship with their Greek fellows, Macedonians could not organise themselves legally. The situation has changed with the political transformation, so the first legal Macedonian organisation, the Association of Macedonians in Poland, was registered in 1989. Unfortunately, it existed only for several years.

There are at least three reasons why the organisation of Macedonians in Poland, which was anticipated for many years, failed. The most evident one is that it was created too late. By the end of the 1980s, the majority of Macedonians had already left Poland (for Yugoslavia, the US, Canada or Australia), and those who stayed were well integrated into Polish society. Another reason is that the profile of the association was too radical. The head of the organisation concentrated on the battle against Greece and the right to reparation or political rights of Macedonians living in Greece, whereas the 'Polish' Macedonians were more interested in the Polish reality, common gatherings, celebrations and so on. Finally, the third possibility, raised by one interviewee and close to my hypothesis, is the lack of power among Macedonians, who always stayed in a position of dependency vis-à-vis Greeks or Poles. After 1989 they found themselves in the new political and social reality of freedom. However, it was a freedom close to the post-colonial one. Macedonians who stayed in Poland were not capable of self-organising suitably, whereas the Greeks succeeded – there are several Greek associations (in Wrocław, Szczecin, and Warsaw).[25]

This situation leads to another issue: lack of recognition of Macedonians by Polish society. Ethnic Greeks dominate all places of remembrance. There is a 'Greek Boulevard', a monument and a commemorative plaque in Zgorzelec – all about the 'Greek refugees' who came to Poland after the war. There is a Festival of Greek Music (Pol. *Festiwal Piosenki Greckiej*), and a few Greek restaurants. Finally, all the articles in the mass media focus only on Greeks. Despite the promising beginning of Macedonian–Polish relations (based on pan-Slavic unity but also real, everyday life contacts), Poles forgot about the Macedonians.

In the case of Macedonian refugees it seems three fatherlands are still not enough. Moreover, for some, each choice is a bad choice. That is why the fourth possibility appeared: the transnational community of Macedonian refugees, which started to be a basis of self- and group identification. After the migration to Yugoslavia, many Macedonians could not integrate into the Vardar Macedonian communities and decided to migrate further – mainly to the United States, Canada and Australia. In each country, they established powerful communities, which became a leading force for Macedonians in exile. Diasporas in Canada and Australia are the most active. They organise many events (including the gathering of so-called 'child refugees' in Skopje), publish books and memoirs and support their fellows in Europe financially (Danforth 1995).

Within the transnational community of all Aegean Macedonians in exile, there is, I argue, a strong community of 'Polish Macedonians', the refugees who stayed for several years in Poland, assimilated and acculturated to the Polish society. The centre of the transnational community of Macedonians who were in Poland is Toronto. They keep together within the group as well as with the Polish minority in the city. However, they also preserve an intense relationship with other Macedonians who stayed in Poland or in Yugoslavia. The most popular channels of communication are Facebook and Skype. Thanks to the internet they stay in contact with Polish culture – music, films and books – as well as with the politics. When they meet with other 'Polish Macedonians' they often speak Polish and use their Polish nicknames. They feel a great nostalgia when they recollect their life in Poland. As one of the Macedonians living in Canada concluded his life story:

> I came [to Canada] as a Canadian. Macedonian, but Canadian. Because my father was a Canadian citizen. I had to go to the Ministry of Foreign Affairs [in Poland] so that they would give me the right to leave Poland. And the Minister told me: you came here as a child. They educated you, they spent a lot of money on you to teach you to help Poland one day. But you are leaving, he says, to Canada. Good luck to you, he says, good luck. I have only one requirement from you - do not forget Poland. For sixty years - twenty, thirty, fifty times a day I remember, I hark back to Poland.
>
> (Christo Lazaru, Canada)

Conclusions and discussion

Macedonian refugees from the Greek Civil War are a unique group of migrants. Their characteristic is based on their condition as a minority inside a minority, with four spaces of self-identification: own homeland, ideological fatherland, 'second fatherland' in exile and a transnational community of Macedonians, which can be seen as an imagined community (Anderson 1994). Their life trajectories are reflected in their names and surnames. Almost all of them have a Greek, a Macedonian and a Polish name, which they use according to the situation.[26]

What is more, the Aegean Macedonians came the difficult way in geographical, social and symbolic ways: from separation and social disconnection to a wide open community. Borders, both geographical and symbolic, could be the core concepts of their migrant fate. The process of bordering and rebordering is strongly connected to the process of their identification and self-identification: as Macedonians in Greece, Macedonians in Poland and abroad, but also as Aegean Macedonians in Yugoslavia, or Aegean Macedonians in transnational communities. Politically and geographically, the borders that divided the territory of so-called Great Macedonia after the Treaty of Bucharest initially shaped the Macedonian identity as that of Aegeans dependent on Greeks, Hellenised, and later expelled as part of the defeated Communist forces after the Greek Civil War. Those borders were not the only essential elements of Macedonian fate. The creation of Yugoslav Macedonia, and later an independent Macedonian state, influenced not only the identity but also the memory of Macedonian migrants. The remembrance of the war and expulsion is created from the present-day perspective that is connected with a new nation-state: the Republic of North Macedonia with all its internal and external politics.[27]

The process of bordering and rebordering could also be interpreted in the context of social groups and their boundaries. The forced migration destabilised and rebuilt Macedonian social structures, family ties and everyday life practices. The process of acculturation to Polish culture, connected with the separation of children from society, could be seen as a process of rebordering their social and ethnic boundaries. For child refugees, the family was replaced by a mixed Graeco-Macedonian peer group and Polish teachers. It meant not only a new level of social ties but also a new field of cultural identification, and hence reformulation of personal identity. Every step of their – often chained – migration, to Poland, Yugoslavia, Canada/US/Australia, meant rebordering their social group boundaries and reshaping their identity, which is formulated in opposition to others.

The case of (Aegean) Macedonian refugees shows that the classical anthropological concept of territorialising people and their identities is rightly criticised by many scientists, especially those connected with migrant studies (Bloch 2011). People are not grounded in one territory, but their identity is shaped through the whole process of migration, that is, facing new borders, boundaries and others. In the new concepts of migration, the condition of being a migrant is not necessarily abnormal and the migration doesn't need to end in one place. The status of being uprooted could be interpreted not as a deviation, but as a new, legitimised identity. It happened to Macedonian refugees who finally did not 'return' to the lost homeland, but found a new, entirely virtual, space of their identification – the borderless transnational community.

Notes

1. The majority of the interviews I conducted for my PhD thesis, published in 2015 as a book (Kurpiel 2015); the rest I carried out in Canada in 2014. In Poland, the topic of refugees from the Greek Civil War appeared only in the context of ethnic Greeks (Wojecki 1989; Barcikowski 1989; Biernacka 1973). Only a few works about Macedonian refugees, written mainly by European historians and anthropologists, were published (Baerentzen 1987; Van Boeschoten 2003; Brown 2003; Danforth and Van Boeschoten 2011; Marinov 2010; Monova 2002).
2. Mainly in Lądek Zdrój, Szczawno-Zdrój and Międzygórze. Later, in 1950, the majority were settled in Zgorzelec, a town on the Polish-German border. Then, after a few years, almost all of the children were placed in Pomerania, in the State Education Centre in Police. At the same time, the main Greek institutions in exile were moved from Zgorzelec to Wrocław.
3. As underlined in a recently published book by a descendant of the Greek refugees (Sturis 2017).
4. In 1950 in Poland there were 5,344 Greeks and 5,378 Macedonians. In 1955, there were 7,410 Macedonians, 7,357 Greek and 448 Aromanians.
5. To be honest, I have to add that in the latter example Macedonian support for the Greek Democratic Army was not always gained peacefully.
6. The most commonly accepted number for children refugees from the Greek Civil War is 26,000. However, Van Boeschoten and Danforth (2011) argue that there were not more than 20,000 children who left Greece without parents in the organised departures during the war. According to Stefan Troebst, almost 12,000 refugees got to the USSR (including an unspecified number of children); the same number went to Czechoslovakia (including 3,500 children), 9,100 to Romania (including 4,256 children), a little over 7,000 to Hungary (including 3,000 children), and 3,000 to Bulgaria (including 672 children). The East Germans accepted only children and teenagers to the number of 1,288, while the number of refugees in Yugoslavia and Albania is difficult to determine: it is estimated almost 2,000 children were accepted in Yugoslavia (Troebst 2004: 717–36).
7. The biblical connotation while speaking about the Greek Civil War and particularly about the children's migration is very popular. The other frequently used word is 'Golgotha'.
8. The idea of kidnapping children was popular not only among the Ottomans. Right-wing Greeks were also 'kidnapping' children and sending them to the so-called Schools of Queen Frederica on the Greek islands (Baerentzen 1987).

9. During his first period in power, from 1981 to 1989.
10. Doca Gogarowska, Poland.
11. Among the narrations about meeting with parents, three are the most frequent: food differences (paprika vs potatoes), family relations (parents' authority vs children's independence and the wish to decide for themselves) and attitude towards women (in the Balkans, dependent on men; in Poland, independent and respected).
12. State Archive in Szczecin: APSz 560/38, k. 33 – Protocol No. 12 on the meeting of the Board of Team Leaders and representatives of Greek pedagogical staff held on 13 January 1949; APSz 560/53 - Inspection report in the children's sanatoriums of Rabka-Zdrój, Sanatorium 'Limba' and Smrek', 13 February 1950.
13. One example of the practice of Hellenisation is writing the names of Macedonians in Greek translation.
14. There were a few attempts to create an independent Macedonian organisation in Poland, but Greek officials suppressed all of them. The two best-known underground organisations were created at the beginning of the 1960s by local Macedonian activists: Egejska Zora (in Legnica) and Makedonska Zaednica (in Szczecin). Their activity was orientated towards promoting an independent Macedonian identity. Both existed for only two years, before being were discovered and dissolved by the Greeks (Kurpiel 2015: 70–3).
15. The idea of the unity of all Slavs had been developed by nineteenth-century intellectuals and was well known in the Balkan Peninsula (Moroz-Grzelak 2011).
16. AAN KC PZPR 237/XXII – 418, k. 42 – Report of the Chief Executive of the SEC for the first quarter of 1951.
17. Por. AAN KC PZPR 237 XXII – 420 – Report on the election meeting of the PPLP Basic Party Organization at SEC in Zgorzelec, which took place on 20 April 1951.
18. AAN KCPZPR 237/XXII – 418 – Report of the Chief Executive of the SEC for the first quarter of 1951, Zgorzelec, 5 April 1951, p. 41.
19. Tronda Pejović, Macedonia.
20. Nicola Naskow, Poland.
21. Donka Koch, Poland, recalled the head of school who advised her to continue her studies when she had doubts about her future plans.
22. Report of the Chief Executive of the State Educational Centre, Master Wacław Kopczyński, regarding the admission of children from Aegean Macedonia (Nakovski 2008: 100).
23. Many Macedonians decided to settle in Yugoslavia just before the earthquake that destroyed Skopje in 1963. It made integration with Vardar Macedonians even more complicated. Skopje inhabitants who lost everything during the earthquake didn't have any empathy for those who had just settled in the town. Lack of housing raised the question of whether everyone should be equal in the distribution of goods or whether those who were 'first' in the city should be 'first' in line for a new apartment.
24. Juzef Ivanowski, Macedonia.
25. The Greeks' situation was better because they organised themselves on the basis of the already existing Nikos Beloyannis Association. Moreover, the number of Greeks living in Poland at that time was much higher than the number of Macedonians.

26. Some of them, however, chose one of the names. For instance, Juzef Ivanowski, after migrating from Poland to Yugoslavia, decided to keep his Polish name but with Macedonian transliteration.

27. Especially with the anti-Greek discourse that was a core element of (the then Republic of) Macedonia, at the time I conducted my research (2008–13).

References

Anderson, Benedict (1994) *Imagined Communities: Reflections on the Origin and Spread of Nationalism*. London: Verso.

Baerentzen, Lars (1987) 'The *"paidomazoma"* and the queen's camps.' Pp. 127–57 in *Studies on the History of the Greek Civil War 1945–1949*, edited by L. Baerentzen, J. O. Iatrides and O. L. Smith. Copenhagen: Museum Tusculanum Press.

Barcikowski, Władysław (1989) *Szpital grecki na Wyspie Wolin*. Szczecin: Krajowa Agencja Wydawnicza.

Barker, Elisabeth (1999) 'The origin of the Macedonian dispute.' Pp. 3–14 in *The New Macedonian Question*, edited by J. Pettifer. Basingstoke: Palgrave Macmillan.

Biernacka, Maria (1973) 'Osady uchodźców greckich w Bieszczadach.' *Etnografia Polska* 1: 83–93.

Bloch, Natalia (2011). *Urodzeni uchodźcy: Tożsamość pokolenia młodych Tybetańczyków w Indiach*. Wrocław: Wydawnictwo Uniwersytetu Wrocławskiego.

Brown, Keith (2003) *Macedonia's Child-Grandfathers: The Transnational Politics of Memory, Exile and Return 1948–1998*. Washington, DC: University of Washington

Danforth, Loring M. (1995) *The Macedonian Conflict: Ethnic Nationalism in a Transnational World*. Princeton: Princeton University Press.

Danforth, Loring M., and Riki Van Boeschoten (2011) *Children of the Greek Civil War: Refugees and the Politics of Memory*. Chicago: University of Chicago Press.

Gordon, Milton M. (1961) 'Assimilation in America: theory and reality.' *Daedalus* 90(2): 263–85.

Kurpiel, A. (2015) *Cztery nazwiska, dwa imiona: Macedońscy uchodźcy wojenni na Dolnym Śląsku*. Poznań: Wydawnictwo Nauka i Innowacje.

Marinov, Tchavar (2010) *La question macédonienne de 1944 á nos jours: Communisme et nationalisme dans le Balkans*. Paris: L'Harmattan.

Monova, Miladina (2002) 'De la logique de retour à la logique d'établissement: le cas des réfugies de la Guerre Civile Greque en République de Macédoine.' *Études Balkaniques: L'outres dans le Sud-Est Européen* 9: 75–92.

Moroz-Grzelak, Lilla (2011) *Bracia słowianie: Wizje wspólnoty a rzeczywistość*. Warsaw: Slawistyczny Ośrodek Wydawniczy.

Nakovski, Petre (ed.) (2008) Macedońscy uchodźcy w Polsce: *Dokumenty 1948–1975*. Vol. 1. Skopje: Naczelna Dyrekcja Archiwów Państwowych – Archiwum Państwowe Republiki Macedonii.

Ossowski, Stanisław (1984) *O ojczyźnie i narodzie*. Warsaw: Państwowe Wydawnictwo Naukowe.

Słabig, Arkadiusz (2008) *Aparat bezpieczeństwa wobec mniejszości narodowych na Pomorzu Zachodnim w latach 1945–1989*. Szczecin: Instytut Pamięci Narodowej.

Stawowy-Kawka, Irena (2000) *Historia Macedonii*. Wrocław: Zakład Narodowy im. Ossolińskich.

Sturis, D. (2017) *Nowe życie: jak Polacy pomagali uchodźcom z Grecji*. Warsaw: Grupa Wydawnicza Foksal.

Troebst, Stefan (2004) 'Die "Griechenlandkinder-Aktion" 1949/50: die SEd und die Aufnahme minderjähriger Bürgerkiegsflüchtlinge aus Griechenland in der SBZ/DDR.' *Zeitschrift für Geschichtswissenschaft* 8: 717–36.

Van Boeschoten, Riki (2003). '"Unity and brotherhood"? Macedonian political refugees in Eastern Europe.' *History and Culture of South Eastern Europe: An Annual Journal* 5: 189–202.

Welzer, H., S. Moller and K. Tschuggnall (2009) 'Dziadek nie był nazistą: Narodowy socjalizm i Holokaust w pamięci rodzinnej.' Pp. 351–410 in *Pamięć zbiorowa i kulturowa. Współczesna perspektywa niemiecka*, edited by M. Saryusz-Wolska. Cracow: Towarzystwo Autorów i Wydawców Prac Naukowych Universitas.

Wojecki, Mieczysław (1989) *Uchodźcy polityczni z Grecji w Polsce 1948-1975*. Jelenia Góra: Urząd Wojewódzki.

Index

EU representative:
Easy Access System Europe
Mustamäe tee 50, 10621 Tallinn, Estonia
Gpsr.requests@easproject.com

www.ingramcontent.com/pod-product-compliance
Lightning Source LLC
Chambersburg PA
CBHW070844300326
41935CB00039B/1426